ADOBE® AFTER EFFECTS® CS4

Ae

CLASSROOM IN A BOOK®

The official training workbook from Adobe Systems

Adobe

Adobe Press books are published by Peachpit, a division of Pearson Education located in Berkeley, California. For the latest on Adobe Press books, go to www.adobepress.com. To report errors, please send a note to errata@peachpit.com. For information on getting permission for reprints and excerpts, contact permissions@peachpit.com.

Printed and bound in the United States of America
ISBN-13:   978-0-321-57383-4
ISBN-10:   0-321-57383-8

9 8 7 6 5 4 3 2

Writer: Brie Gyncild
Design Director: Andrew Faulkner, afstudio design
Designers: Keely Reyes, Elaine Gruenke, afstudio design
Production: Lisa Fridsma
Technical Reviewer: Todd Kopriva

We offer our sincere thanks to the following people for their support and help with this project: Lisa Fridsma, Jill Merlin, Stephen Schleicher and Christine Yarrow. We couldn't have done it without you.

WHAT'S ON THE DISC

Here is an overview of the contents of the Classroom in a Book disc

Lesson files ... and so much more

The *Adobe After Effects CS4 Classroom in a Book* disc includes the lesson files that you'll need to complete the exercises in this book, as well as other content to help you learn more about Adobe After Effects CS4 and use it with greater efficiency and ease. The diagram below represents the contents of the disc, which should help you locate the files you need.

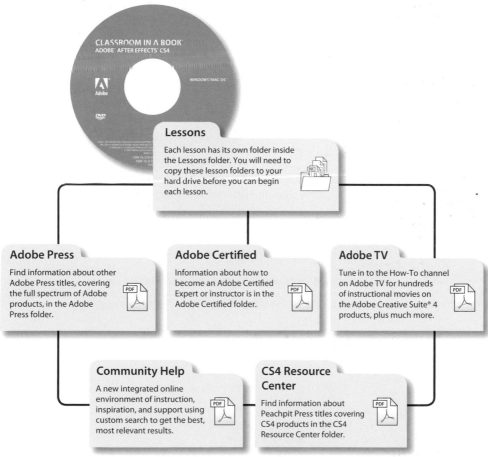

Lessons

Each lesson has its own folder inside the Lessons folder. You will need to copy these lesson folders to your hard drive before you can begin each lesson.

Adobe Press

Find information about other Adobe Press titles, covering the full spectrum of Adobe products, in the Adobe Press folder.

Adobe Certified

Information about how to become an Adobe Certified Expert or instructor is in the Adobe Certified folder.

Adobe TV

Tune in to the How-To channel on Adobe TV for hundreds of instructional movies on the Adobe Creative Suite® 4 products, plus much more.

Community Help

A new integrated online environment of instruction, inspiration, and support using custom search to get the best, most relevant results.

CS4 Resource Center

Find information about Peachpit Press titles covering CS4 products in the CS4 Resource Center folder.

CONTENTS

7 WORKING WITH MASKS

8 DISTORTING OBJECTS WITH THE PUPPET TOOLS

9 KEYING

10 PERFORMING COLOR CORRECTION

11 BUILDING 3D OBJECTS

12 USING 3D FEATURES

GETTING STARTED

Adobe® After Effects® CS4 provides a comprehensive set of 2D and 3D tools for compositing, animation, and effects that motion-graphics professionals, visual effects artists, web designers, and film and video professionals need. After Effects is widely used for digital post-production of film, video, DVD, and the web. You can composite layers in various ways, apply and combine sophisticated visual and audio effects, and animate both objects and effects.

About Classroom in a Book

Adobe After Effects CS4 Classroom in a Book is part of the official training series for Adobe graphics and publishing software developed by experts at Adobe Systems. The lessons are designed to let you learn at your own pace. If you're new to Adobe After Effects, you'll learn the fundamental concepts and features you'll need to master the program. And, if you've been using Adobe After Effects for a while, you'll find that Classroom in a Book teaches many advanced features, including tips and techniques for using the latest version.

Although each lesson provides step-by-step instructions for creating a specific project, there's room for exploration and experimentation. You can follow the book from start to finish, or do only the lessons that match your interests and needs. Each lesson concludes with a review section summarizing what you've covered.

Prerequisites

Before beginning to use *Adobe After Effects CS4 Classroom in a Book*, make sure that your system is set up correctly and that you've installed the required software and hardware. You should have a working knowledge of your computer and operating system. You should know how to use the mouse and standard menus and commands, and also how to open, save, and close files. If you need to review these techniques, see the printed or online documentation included with your Microsoft® Windows® or Apple® Mac® OS software.

Installing After Effects

You must purchase the Adobe After Effects CS4 software separately. For system requirements and complete instructions on installing the software, see the Adobe After Effects ReadMe.html file on the application DVD. You must also have Apple QuickTime 7.1.5 or later installed on your system.

Install After Effects from the Adobe After Effects CS4 application DVD onto your hard disk; you cannot run the program from the DVD. Follow the onscreen instructions.

Make sure that your serial number is accessible before installing the application; you can find the serial number on the registration card or on the back of the DVD case.

Optimizing performance

Creating movies is memory-intensive work for a desktop computer. After Effects CS4 requires a minimum of 2GB of RAM. The more RAM that is available to After Effects, the faster the application will work for you.

OpenGL support

OpenGL is a set of standards for delivering high-performance 2D and 3D graphics for a wide variety of applications. Although After Effects can function without it, OpenGL accelerates various types of rendering, including rendering to the screen for previews.

To use OpenGL in After Effects, you'll need an OpenGL card that supports OpenGL 2.0 and has Shader support and support for NPOT (Non Power of Two) textures. When you first start After Effects, it will attempt to determine if your OpenGL card meets the requirements, and it will enable or disable OpenGL as appropriate.

To view information about your OpenGL card, as well as enable or disable OpenGL in After Effects, choose Edit > Preferences > Previews (Windows) or After Effects > Preferences > Previews (Mac OS). Select the Enable OpenGL option to enable OpenGL; click the OpenGL Info button to learn more about your card.

To learn more about OpenGL support in After Effects, see After Effects Help.

Color management

After Effects CS4 supports color management workflows. We encourage you to take advantage of the color management features in After Effects, especially for professional projects. For an introduction to color management, see the appendix, "Color Management in After Effects CS4."

Restoring default preferences

The preferences file controls the way the After Effects user interface appears on your screen. The instructions in this book assume that you see the default interface when they describe the appearance of tools, options, windows, panels, and so forth. Because of this, it's a good idea to restore the default preferences, especially if you are new to After Effects.

Each time you quit After Effects, the panel positions and certain command settings are recorded in the preferences file. If you want to restore the panels to their original default settings, you can delete the current After Effects preferences file. (After Effects creates a new preferences file if one doesn't already exist the next time you start the program.)

Restoring the default preferences can be especially helpful if someone has already customized After Effects on your computer. If your copy of After Effects hasn't been used yet, this file won't exist, so this procedure is unnecessary.

Important: If you want to save the current settings, you can rename the preferences file instead of deleting it. When you are ready to restore those settings, change the name back and make sure that the file is located in the correct preferences folder.

Note: (Windows only) If you do not see the Prefs file, be sure that the Show Hidden Files And Folders option is selected for Hidden Files on the View tab of the Folder Options dialog box.

1 Locate the After Effects preferences folder on your computer:

- For Windows XP: .../Documents and Settings/*<user name>*/Application Data/Adobe/After Effects/9.0.

- For Windows Vista: .../Program Files/Common Files/Adobe/Keyfiles/ AfterEffects.

- For Mac OS: .../*<user name>*/Library/Preferences.

2 Delete or rename the Adobe After Effects 9.0 Prefs file.

3 Start Adobe After Effects.

▶ **Tip:** You can also press Ctrl+Alt+Shift (Windows) or Option+Command+Shift (Mac OS) while starting After Effects to restore default preferences settings.

Copying the lesson files

The lessons in *Adobe After Effects CS4 Classroom in a Book* use specific source files, such as image files created in Adobe Photoshop® and Adobe Illustrator®, audio files, and prepared QuickTime movies. To complete the lessons in this book, you must copy these files from the *Adobe After Effects CS4 Classroom in a Book* DVD (inside the back cover of this book) to your hard disk.

1 On your hard disk, create a new folder in a convenient location and name it **AECS4_CIB**, following the standard procedure for your operating system:

- Windows: In Explorer, select the folder or drive in which you want to create the new folder, and choose File > New > Folder. Then type the new name.
- Mac OS: In the Finder, choose File > New Folder. Type the new name and drag the folder to the location you want to use.

Now, you can copy the source files onto your hard disk.

2 Copy the Lessons folder (which contains folders named Lesson01, Lesson02, and so on) from the *Adobe After Effects CS4 Classroom in a Book* DVD onto your hard disk by dragging it to your new AECS4_CIB folder.

When you begin each lesson, you will navigate to the folder with that lesson number, where you will find all of the assets, sample movies, and other project files you need to complete the lesson.

If you have limited storage space on your computer, you can copy each lesson folder individually as you need it, and delete it afterward if desired. Some lessons build on preceding lessons; in those cases, a starting project file is provided for you for the second lesson or project. You do not have to save any finished project if you don't want to, or if you have limited hard disk space.

About copying the sample movies and projects

You will create and render one or more QuickTime movies in some lessons in this book. The files in the Sample_Movie folders are examples that you can use to see the end results of each lesson and to compare them with your own results. These files tend to be large, so you may not want to devote the storage space or time to copying all the sample movies before you begin. Instead, find the appropriate Sample_Movie folder on the book's DVD and copy the file it contains onto your hard disk as you begin work on a lesson. (You cannot play movies from the DVD.) After you finish viewing the movie, you can delete it from your hard drive.

The files in the End_Project_File folders are samples of the completed project for each lesson. Use these files for reference if you want to compare your work in progress with the project files used to generate the sample movies. These end project files vary in size from relatively small to a couple of megabytes, so you can either copy them all now if you have ample storage space, or copy just the end project file for each lesson as needed, and then delete it when you finish that lesson.

How to use these lessons

Each lesson in this book provides step-by-step instructions for creating one or more specific elements of a real world project. Some lessons build on projects created in preceding lessons; some stand alone. All of these lessons build on each other in terms of concepts and skills, so the best way to learn from this book is to proceed through the lessons in sequential order. In this book, some techniques and processes are explained and described in detail only the first few times you perform them.

Many aspects of the After Effects application can be controlled by multiple techniques, such as a menu command, a button, dragging, and a keyboard shortcut. Only one or two of the methods are described in any given procedure so that you can learn different ways of working even when the task is one you've done before.

The organization of the lessons is also design-oriented rather than feature-oriented. That means, for example, that you'll work with layers and effects on real-world design projects over several lessons, rather than in just one lesson

Additional resources

Adobe After Effects CS4 Classroom in a Book is not meant to replace documentation that comes with the program. This book explains only the commands and options actually used in the lessons, so there's much more to learn about After Effects. Classroom in a Book aims to give you confidence and skills so that you can start creating your own projects. For more comprehensive information about program features, see:

- Adobe After Effects CS4 Community Help, which you can view by choosing Help > After Effects Help. Community Help is an integrated online environment of instruction, inspiration, and support. It includes custom search of expert-selected, relevant content on and off Adobe.com. Community Help combines content from Adobe Help, Support, Design Center, Developer Connection, and Forums—along with great online community content so that users can easily find the best and most up-to-date resources. Access tutorials, technical support, online product help, videos, articles, tips and techniques, blogs, examples, and much more.

- Adobe After Effects CS4 Product Support Center, where you can find and browse support and learning content on Adobe.com. Visit www.adobe.com/support/aftereffects/.

- Adobe TV, where you will find programming on Adobe products, including a channel for professional photographers and a How To channel that contains hundreds of movies on After Effects CS4 and other products across the Adobe Creative Suite 4 lineup. Visit http://tv.adobe.com/.

Also check out these useful links:

- The After Effects CS4 product home page at www.adobe.com/products/aftereffects/.
- After Effects user forums at www.adobe.com/support/forums/ for peer-to-peer discussions of Adobe products.
- Adobe Exchange at www.adobe.com/cfusion/exchange/ for extensions, functions, code, and more.

Adobe certification

The Adobe Certified program is designed to help Adobe customers and trainers improve and promote their product-proficiency skills. There are three levels of certification:

- Adobe Certified Expert (ACE)
- Adobe Certified Instructor (ACI)
- Adobe Authorized Training Center (AATC)

The Adobe Certified Expert program is a way for expert users to upgrade their credentials. You can use Adobe certification as a catalyst for getting a raise, finding a job, or promoting your expertise.

If you are an ACE-level instructor, the Adobe Certified Instructor program takes your skills to the next level and gives you access to a wide range of Adobe resources.

Adobe Authorized Training Centers offer instructor-led courses and training on Adobe products, employing only Adobe Certified Instructors. A directory of AATCs is available at http://partners.adobe.com.

For information on the Adobe Certified program, visit www.adobe.com/support/certification/main.html.

1 GETTING TO KNOW THE WORKFLOW

Lesson overview

In this lesson you'll learn how to do the following:

- Create a project and import footage.

- Create compositions and arrange layers.

- Navigate the Adobe After Effects interface.

- Use the Project, Composition, and Timeline panels.

- Apply basic keyframes and effects.

- Preview your work using standard and RAM previews.

- Customize the workspace.

- Adjust preferences related to the workspace.

- Find additional resources for using After Effects.

 A basic After Effects workflow follows six steps: importing and organizing footage, creating compositions and arranging layers, adding effects, animating elements, previewing your work, and rendering and outputting the final composition so that it can be viewed by others. In this lesson, you will create a simple animated video using this workflow, and along the way, you'll learn your way around the After Effects interface. This lesson will take about an hour to complete.

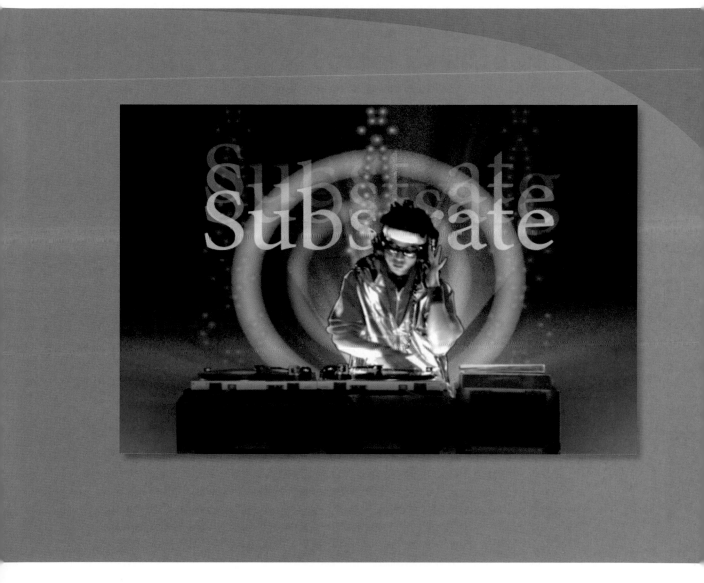

Whether you use After Effects to animate a simple DVD title sequence or to create complex special effects, you generally follow the same basic workflow. The After Effects interface facilitates your work and adapts to each stage of production.

Getting started

First, you'll preview the final movie to see what you'll create in this lesson.

1   Make sure the following files are in the AECS4_CIB/Lessons/Lesson01 folder on your hard disk, or copy them from the *Adobe After Effects CS4 Classroom in a Book* DVD now.

   • In the Assets folder: bgwtext.psd, DJ.mov, gc_adobe_dj.mp3, kaleidoscope_waveforms.mov, pulsating_radial_waves.mov

   • In the Sample_Movie folder: Lesson01.mov

2   Open and play the Lesson01.mov sample movie to see what you will create in this lesson. When you are done, quit QuickTime Player. You may delete this sample movie from your hard disk if you have limited storage space.

Creating a project and importing footage

When you begin each lesson of this book, it's a good idea to restore the default preferences for After Effects. (See "Restoring default preferences" on page 3.) You can do this with a simple keyboard shortcut.

1   Press Ctrl+Alt+Shift (Windows) or Option+Command+Shift (Mac OS) while starting After Effects to restore default preferences settings. When prompted, click OK to delete your preferences file.

2   Click Close to close the Welcome window.

After Effects opens to display an empty, untitled project.

An After Effects project is a single file that stores references to all the footage you use in that project. It also contains *compositions*, which are the individual containers used to combine footage, apply effects, and, ultimately, drive the output.

About the After Effects workspace

After Effects offers a flexible, customizable workspace. The main window of the program is called the *application window*. Panels are organized in this window in an arrangement called a *workspace*. The default workspace contains groups of panels as well as panels that stand alone, as shown in the following figure.

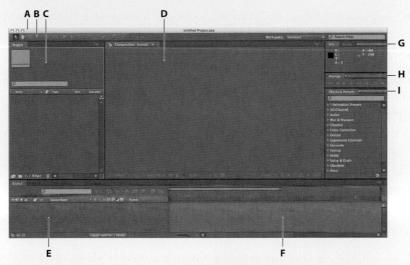

A. Application window *B.* Tools panel *C.* Project panel *D.* Composition panel
E. Timeline panel *F.* Time graph *G.* Grouped panels (Info and Audio) *H.* Preview panel
I. Effects & Presets panel

You customize a workspace by dragging the panels into the configuration that best suits your working style. You can drag panels to new locations, move panels into or out of a group, place panels alongside each other, and undock a panel so that it floats in a new window above the application window. As you rearrange panels, the other panels resize automatically to fit the window.

When you drag a panel by its tab to relocate it, the area where you can drop it—called a *drop zone*—becomes highlighted. The drop zone determines where and how the panel is inserted into the workspace. Dragging a panel to a drop zone results in one of two behaviors: docking or grouping.

If you drop a panel along the edge of another panel, group, or window, it will *dock* next to the existing group, resizing all groups to accommodate the new panel.

If you drop a panel in the middle of another panel or group, or along the tab area of a panel, it will be added to the existing group and be placed at the top of the stack. Grouping a panel does not resize other groups.

You can also open a panel in a floating window. To do so, select the panel and then choose Undock Panel or Undock Frame from the panel menu. Or, drag the panel or group outside the application window.

▶ **Tip:** To quickly maximize a panel, position the pointer over it and press the ` (accent grave) key (the unshifted character under the tilde, ~, on standard US keyboards). Press the key again to return the panel to its original size.

▶ **Tip:** You can also double-click in the lower area of the Project panel to open the Import File dialog box, choose File > Import > Multiple Files to select files located in different folders, or drag and drop files from Explorer or the Finder. You can use Adobe Bridge to search for, manage, preview, and import footage.

When you begin a project, often the first thing you'll do is add footage to it.

3 Choose File > Import > File.

4 Navigate to the Assets folder in your AECS4_CIB/Lessons/Lesson01 folder. Shift-click to select the DJ.mov, gc_adobe_dj.mp3, kaleidoscope_waveforms. mov, and pulsating_radial_waves.mov files (all the files except bgwtext.psd). Then click Open.

A footage item is the basic unit in an After Effects project. You can import many types of footage items, including moving-image files, still-image files, still-image sequences, audio files, layered files from Adobe Photoshop and Adobe Illustrator, other After Effects projects, and projects created in Adobe Premiere Pro. You can import footage items at any time.

As you import assets, After Effects reports its progress in the Info panel.

Because one of the footage items for this project is a multilayer Photoshop file, you'll import it separately as a composition.

5 Double-click in the lower area of the Project panel to open the Import File dialog box.

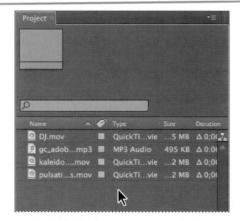

6 Navigate to the Lesson01/Assets folder again, and select the bgwtext.psd file. Choose Composition from the Import As menu, and then click Open.

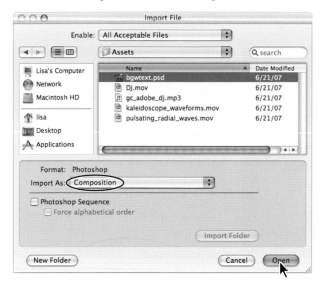

After Effects opens an additional dialog box with options for the file you're importing.

7 In the Bgwtext.psd dialog box, choose Composition from the Import Kind menu to import the layered Photoshop file as a composition. Select Editable Layer Styles in the Layer Options area, and then click OK. The footage items appear in the Project panel.

8 In the Project panel, deselect all footage items and then click to select any of them. Notice that a thumbnail preview appears at the top of the Project panel. You can also see the file type and size, as well as other information about each item, in the Project panel columns.

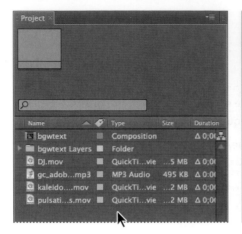 

When you import files, After Effects doesn't copy the video and audio data itself into your project. Instead, each footage item in the Project panel contains a reference link to the source files. When After Effects needs to retrieve image or audio data, it reads it from the source file. This keeps the project file small, and it allows you to update source files in another application without modifying the project.

To save time and minimize the size and complexity of a project, import a footage item once and then use it multiple times in a composition. In some cases, you may need to import a source file more than once, such as if you want to use it at two different frame rates.

After you've imported footage, it's a good time to save the project.

9 Choose File > Save. In the Save As dialog box, navigate to the AECS4_CIB/ Lessons/Lesson01/Finished_Project folder. Name the project **Lesson01_ Finished.aep**, and then click Save.

Creating a composition and arranging layers

The next step of the workflow is to create a composition. You create all animation, layering, and effects in a composition. An After Effects composition has both spatial dimensions and a temporal dimension (time).

Compositions include one or more layers, arranged in the Composition panel and in the Timeline panel. Any item that you add to a composition—such as a still image, moving-image file, audio file, light layer, camera layer, or even another composition—becomes a new layer. Simple projects may include only one composition, while elaborate projects may include several compositions to organize large amounts of footage or intricate effects sequences.

To create a composition, you will drag the footage items into the Timeline panel, and After Effects will create layers for them.

1   In the Project panel, Ctrl-click (Windows) or Command-click (Mac OS) to select the bgwtext composition as well as the DJ, gc_adobe_dj, kaleidoscope_ waveforms, and pulsating_radial_waves footage items.

2   Drag the selected footage items into the Timeline panel. The New Composition From Selection dialog box appears.

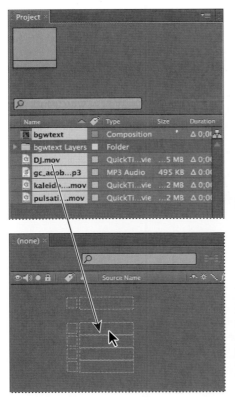

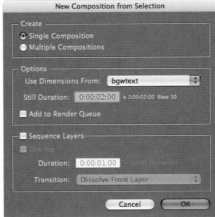

After Effects bases the dimensions of the new composition on the selected footage. In this example, all of the footage is sized identically, so you can accept the default settings.

3 Click OK to create the new composition. The footage items appear as layers in the Timeline panel, and After Effects displays the composition, named Bgwtext 2, in the Composition panel.

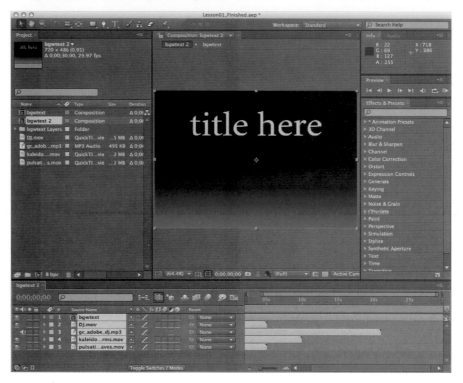

When you add a footage item to a composition, the footage becomes the source for a new layer. A composition can have any number of layers, and you can also include a composition as a layer in another composition, which is called *nesting*.

About layers

Layers are the components you use to build a composition. Any item that you add to a composition—such as a still image, moving-image file, audio file, light layer, camera layer, or even another composition—becomes a new layer. Without layers, a composition consists only of an empty frame.

Using layers, you can work with specific footage items in a composition without affecting any other footage. For example, you can move, rotate, and draw masks for one layer without disturbing any other layers in the composition, or you can use the same footage in more than one layer and use it differently in each instance. In general, the layer order in the Timeline panel corresponds to the stacking order in the Composition panel.

In this composition, there are five footage items and therefore five layers in the Timeline panel. Depending on the order in which the elements were selected when you imported them, your layer stack may differ from the one shown in the preceding figure. The layers need to be in a specific order as you add effects and animations, however, so you'll rearrange them now.

4 Click in an empty area of the Timeline panel to deselect the layers, and then drag Bgwtext to the bottom of the layer stack if it is not already there. Drag the other four layers so that they're in the order shown in the figure.

● **Note:** You may need to click a blank area of the Timeline panel or press F2 to deselect layers before you can select an individual layer.

From this point forward in the workflow, you should be thinking about layers, not footage items. You'll change the column title accordingly.

5 Click the Source Name column title in the Timeline panel to change it to Layer Name.

6 Choose File > Save to save your project so far.

Adding effects and modifying layer properties

Note: This exercise is just the tip of the iceberg. You will learn more about effects and animation presets in Lesson 2, "Creating a Basic Animation Using Effects and Presets," and throughout the rest of this book.

Now that your composition is set up, you can start having fun—applying effects, making transformations, and adding animation. You can add any combination of effects and modify any of a layer's properties, such as size, placement, and opacity. Using effects, you can alter a layer's appearance or sound, and even generate visual elements from scratch. The easiest way to start is to apply any of the hundreds of effects included with After Effects.

Preparing the layers

You'll apply the effects to duplicates of selected layers—the DJ layer and the kalei-doscope_waveforms layer. Working with duplicates lets you apply an effect to one layer and then use it in conjunction with the unmodified original.

1   Select the first layer, DJ.mov, in the Timeline panel, and then choose Edit > Duplicate. A new layer with the same name appears at the top of the stack, so the first two layers are now both named DJ.mov.

2 Select the second layer and rename it to avoid confusion: Press Enter (Windows) or Return (Mac OS) to make the name editable, and type **DJ_with_effects**. Then press Enter or Return again to accept the new name.

3 Select the kaleidoscope_waveforms layer and make two duplicates. Then, rename the duplicates **kaleidoscope_left** and **kaleidoscope_right**.

4 Drag if necessary to rearrange the layers in the Timeline panel so that they're in the order shown.

▶ **Tip:** Use the keyboard shortcut Ctrl+D (Windows) or Command+D (Mac OS) to duplicate the layers quickly.

Adding a Radial Blur effect

The Radial Blur effect creates blurs around a specific point in a layer, simulating the effects of a zooming or rotating camera. You'll add a Radial Blur effect to the DJ.

1 Select the DJ_with_effects layer in the Timeline panel. Notice that layer handles appear around the layer in the Composition panel.

● **Note:** If you double-click a layer in the Timeline panel, it appears in the Layer panel. To return to the Composition panel, click the Composition tab.

2 In the Effects & Presets panel at the right side of the application window, type **radial blur** in the search box.

After Effects searches for effects and presets that contain the letters you type, and displays the results interactively. Before you have finished typing, the Radial Blur effect, located in the Blur & Sharpen category, appears in the panel.

3 Drag the Radial Blur effect onto the DJ_with_effects layer in the Timeline panel. After Effects applies the effect and automatically opens the Effect Controls panel in the upper-left area of the workspace.

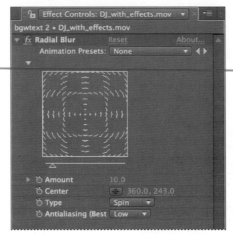

Now you'll customize the settings.

4 In the Effect Controls panel, choose Zoom from the Type menu.

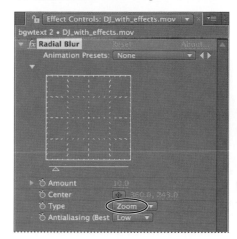

5 In the Composition panel, move the center point of the blur lower by dragging the center cross-hair (⊕) down until it's below the turntables. As you drag the cross-hair, the Center value updates in the Effect Controls panel. The left and right values are x and y coordinates, respectively. Center the blur at approximately 375, 450.

▶ **Tip:** You can also type the x and y values directly into the coordinate fields in the Effect Controls panel, or you can position the pointer over the fields to see the double-arrow icon (↔) and then drag right or left to increase or decrease the values, respectively. Dragging to change values is called *scrubbing*.

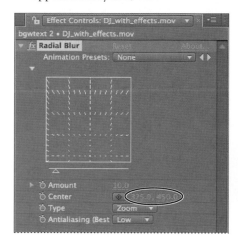

6 Finally, increase the Amount to **200**.

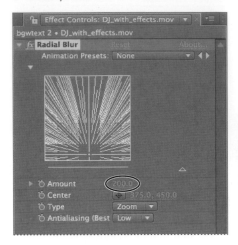 

Adding an exposure effect

To punch up the brightness of this layer, you will apply the Exposure color-correction effect. This effect lets you make tonal adjustments to footage. It simulates the result of modifying the exposure setting (in f-stops) of the camera that captured the image.

1 Locate the Exposure effect in the Effects & Presets panel by doing one of the following:

- Type **Exposure** in the search box.

- Click the triangle next to Color Correction to expand the list of color-correction effects in alphabetical order.

2 Drag the Exposure effect in the Color Correction category onto the DJ_with_ effects layer name in the Timeline panel. After Effects adds the Exposure settings to the Effect Controls panel under the Radial Blur effect.

▶ **Tip:** Make sure to select the Exposure effect in the Color Correction category, not the Exposure animation preset in the Lights And Optical category.

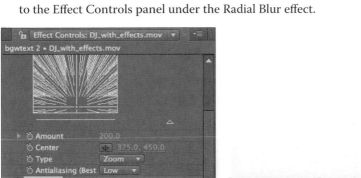

3 In the Effect Controls panel, click the triangle next to the Radial Blur effect to collapse those settings so that you can see the Exposure settings more easily.

4 For Master Exposure, enter **1.60**. This will make everything brighter in the layer to simulate an overexposed image.

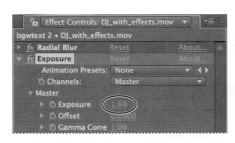

Transforming layer properties

The DJ looks smashing, so you can turn your attention to the kaleidoscope wave-forms that are part of the background. You'll reposition the copies you created earlier to create an edgy effect.

1 Select the kaleidoscope_left layer (layer 5) in the Timeline panel.

2 Click the triangle to the left of the layer number to expand the layer, and then expand the layer's Transform properties: Anchor Point, Position, Scale, Rotation, and Opacity.

▶ **Tip:** With any layer selected in the Timeline panel, you can display any single Transform property by pressing a keyboard shortcut:
P displays Position
A displays Anchor Point
S displays Scale
R displays Rotation
T displays Opacity.

3 If you can't see the properties, scroll down the Timeline panel using the scroll bar at the right side of the panel. Better yet, select the kaleidoscope_left layer name again and press **P**. This keyboard shortcut displays only the Position property, which is the only property you want to change for this exercise.

You'll move this layer to the left about 200 pixels.

4 Change the x coordinate for the Position property to **160**. Leave the y coordinate at 243.

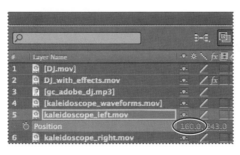 

5 Select the kaleidoscope_right layer (layer 6), and press **P** to display its Position property. You will move this layer to the right.

6 Change the x coordinate for the kaleidoscope_right Position property to **560**. Leave the y coordinate at 243. Now you can see the three waveforms—left, center, and right—in the Composition panel, hanging like a beaded light curtain.

To contrast the left and right waveforms with the center waveform, you will reduce their opacity.

7 Select the kaleidoscope_left layer in the Timeline panel and press **T** to reveal its Opacity property. Set it to **30%**.

8 Select the kaleidoscope_right layer in the Timeline panel, press **T** to reveal its Opacity property, and set it to **30%**.

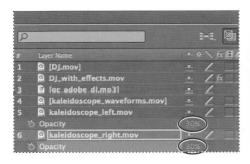

▶ **Tip:** To change the Opacity property for multiple layers at once, select the layers, press **T**, and change the property for one of the selected layers.

9 Choose File > Save to save your work so far.

Animating the composition

So far, you've started a project, created a composition, imported footage, and applied some effects. It all looks great, but how about some movement? You've applied only static effects.

In After Effects, you can change any combination of a layer's properties over time using conventional keyframing, expressions, or keyframe assistants. You'll explore many of these methods throughout the lessons of this book. For this exercise, you will animate the Position property of a text layer using keyframes, and then use an animation preset so that the letters appear to rain down on the screen.

About the Timeline panel

Use the Timeline panel to animate layer properties and set In and Out points for a layer. (In and Out points are the points at which a layer begins and ends in the composition.) Many of the Timeline panel controls are organized in columns of related functions. By default, the Timeline panel contains a number of columns and controls, as shown in the following figure:

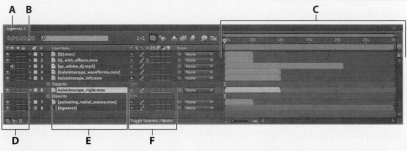

A. Composition name *B. Current time* *C. Time graph/Graph Editor area* *D. Audio/Video Switches column* *E. Source Name/Layer Name column* *F. Layer switches*

About the time graph

The time graph portion of the Timeline panel (the right side) contains a time ruler, markers to indicate specific times, and duration bars for the layers in your composition.

● **Note:** When you click the Graph Editor button (▦) in the Timeline panel, the layer bars in the time ruler are replaced with the Graph Editor. You'll learn more about the Graph Editor in Lesson 6, "Animating Layers."

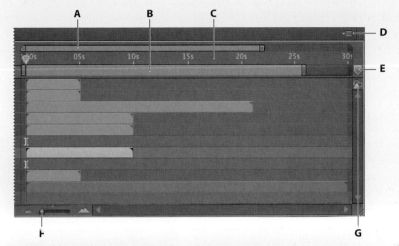

*A. Time navigator start and end brackets **B.** Work area start and end brackets
C. Time ruler **D.** Timeline panel menu **E.** Time zoom slider **F.** Composition button
G. Composition marker bin*

Before delving too deep into animation, it helps to understand at least some of these controls. The duration of a composition, a layer, or a footage item is represented visually in the time ruler. On the time ruler, the current-time indicator indicates the frame you are viewing or editing, and the frame appears in the Composition panel.

The work area start and end brackets indicate the part of the composition that will be rendered for previews or final output. When you work on a composition, you may want to render only part of a composition. Do this by specifying a part of the composition time ruler as a work area.

A composition's current time appears in the upper-left corner of the Timeline panel. To move to a different time, drag the current-time indicator in the time ruler or click the current-time field in the Timeline panel or Composition panel, type a new time, and click OK.

For more information about the Timeline panel, see After Effects Help.

Preparing the text composition

For this exercise, you'll work with a separate composition—the one you imported from a layered Photoshop file.

1 Click the Project tab to display the Project panel, and then double-click the bgwtext composition to open it as a composition in its own Timeline panel.

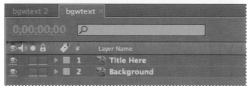

This composition is the layered Photoshop file you imported. Two layers, Background and Title Here, appear in the Timeline panel. The Title Here layer contains placeholder text that was created in Photoshop.

● **Note:** You can quickly navigate within a composition network using the Composition Mini-Flowchart. To display the flowchart, tap the Shift key when a Composition, Timeline, or Layer panel is active.

At the top of the Composition panel is the Composition Navigator bar, which displays the relationship between the main composition (Bgwtext 2) and the current composition (Bgwtext), which is nested within the main composition.

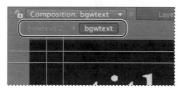

You can nest multiple compositions within each other; the Composition Navigator bar displays the entire composition path. Arrows between the composition names indicate the direction in which pixel information flows.

Before you can replace the text, you need to make the layer editable.

2 Select the Title Here layer (layer 1) in the Timeline panel and then choose Layer > Convert to Editable Text.

A T icon appears next to the layer name in the Timeline panel, indicating that it is now an editable text layer. The layer is also selected in the Composition panel, ready for you to edit.

Animating text with Position keyframes

You'll start by replacing the placeholder text with real text. Then, you'll animate it.

1 Select the Horizontal Type tool (T) in the Tools panel, and drag over the placeholder text in the Composition panel to select it. Then, type **Substrate**.

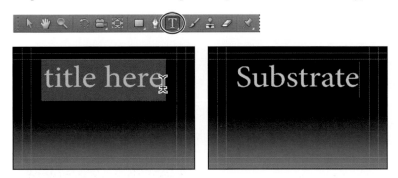

2 Select the Title Here layer in the Timeline panel again, and press **P** to display its Position property.

3 Make sure you're at the first frame of the animation by doing one of the following:

- Drag the current-time indicator all the way to the left of the time ruler, to 0:00.

- Press the Home key on your keyboard.

About timecode and duration

The primary concept related to time is *duration*, or length. Each footage item, layer, and composition in a project has its own duration, which is reflected in the beginning and ending times displayed in the time rulers in the Composition, Layer, and Timeline panels.

The way you view and specify time in After Effects depends on the display style, or unit of measure, that you use to describe time. By default, After Effects displays time in Society of Motion Picture and Television Engineers (SMPTE) timecode: hours, minutes, seconds, and frames. Note that the figures are separated by semicolons in the After Effects interface, representing drop-frame timecode (which adjusts for the real-time frame rate), but this book uses a colon to represent non-drop-frame timecode.

To learn when and how to change to another system of time display, such as frames or feet and frames of film, see After Effects Help.

4   Using the Selection tool (↖), drag the text layer down and off the bottom of the Composition panel, out of the viewing area. Press Shift after you start dragging to constrain the operation to the vertical axis.

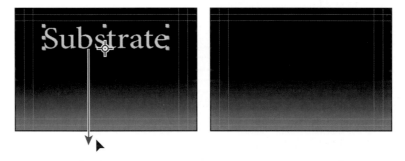

5   In the Timeline panel, click the stopwatch icon (●) for the layer's Position property to create a Position keyframe. An orange diamond appears in the Position bar for the layer in the time graph, indicating the new keyframe.

Keyframes are used to create and control animation, effects, audio properties, and many other kinds of changes that occur over time. A keyframe marks the point in time where you specify a value, such as spatial position, opacity, or audio volume. Values between keyframes are *interpolated*. When you use keyframes to create a change over time, you must use at least two keyframes—one for the state at the beginning of the change, and one for the state at the end of the change.

6   Go to 3:00 by doing one of the following:

- Drag the current-time indicator to the right in the time ruler so that it's positioned at 3:00.

- Click the Current Time field in the Timeline panel or Composition panel, type **300** (for 3 seconds) in the Go To Time dialog box, and click OK.

Now you can drag the Substrate title to its final position, but since you dragged it off the screen in step 4, you'll need to zoom out to grab it.

7   With the Title Here layer still selected in the Timeline panel, select the Zoom tool (🔍) and Alt-click (Windows) or Option-click (Mac OS) to zoom out so that you can see the text layer on the pasteboard of the Composition panel.

8   Switch back to the Selection tool (▶) and drag the text layer up in the Composition panel, to the top quarter of the viewing area. Press Shift to constrain the drag operation to the vertical axis. Your final Position values should be approximately 359, 135.

▶ **Tip:** Instead of zooming and dragging, you could also type the values into the text layer's Position fields in the Timeline panel.

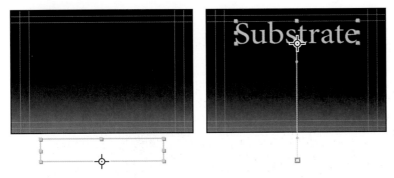

After Effects automatically creates a second keyframe at this position.

9 To zoom back in to the composition, choose Fit Up To 100% from the Magnification Ratio pop-up menu in the lower-left corner of the Composition panel.

The blue lines at the top, bottom, and sides of the Composition panel indicate title-safe and action-safe zones. Television sets enlarge a video image and allow some portion of its outer edges to be cut off by the edge of the screen. This is known as *overscan*. The amount of overscan is not consistent between television sets, so you should keep important parts of a video image, such as action or titles, within margins called *safe zones*. Keep your text inside the inner blue guides to ensure that it is in the title-safe zone, and keep important scene elements inside the outer blue guides to ensure that they are in the action-safe zone.

Even though this is a simple animation, you'll learn good animation practices right away by adding ease-in controls using the Easy Ease feature. Easing into (and out of) animations keeps the motion from appearing to be too sudden or robotic.

10 Right-click (Windows) or Control-click (Mac OS) the Position keyframe at 3:00 and choose Keyframe Assistant > Easy Ease In. As the text approaches its final position, it will ease to a smooth stop. The keyframe icon changes to an arrow.

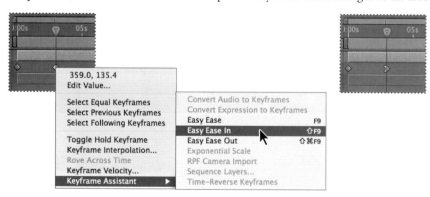

Adding an animation preset

So far, the text is moving onto the screen. After it arrives, you don't want it to just sit there. Applying an animation preset will bring it to life.

1   With the Title Here layer still selected in the Timeline panel, go to 2:10, the point at which the text is almost at its final position. Remember, you can go to the time by dragging the current-time indicator or by clicking the Current Time field in the Timeline panel or Composition panel.

2   Click the Effects & Presets tab, and then type **raining** in the search box to quickly locate the Raining Characters animation presets.

3   Drag the Raining Characters Out effect onto the word *Substrate* in the Composition panel to apply it to the text layer.

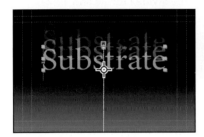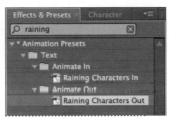

The Effect Controls panel opens so that you can customize the Echo effect, which is a component of the animation preset. The default settings are fine for this project.

4   Choose File > Save to save your work so far.

Previewing your work

You're probably eager to see the results of your work. After Effects provides several methods for previewing compositions, including standard preview, RAM preview, and manual preview. (For a list of manual preview controls, see After Effects Help.) All three methods are accessible through the Preview panel, which appears on the right side of the application window in the Standard workspace.

Using standard preview

Standard preview (commonly called a *spacebar preview*) plays the composition from the current-time indicator to the end of the composition. Standard previews usually play more slowly than real time. They are useful when your composition is simple or in its early stages and doesn't require additional memory for displaying complex animations, effects, 3D layers, cameras, and lights. You'll use it now to preview the text animation.

1 In the Bgwtext Timeline panel, make sure that the Video switch (👁) is selected for the layers that you want to preview—the Title Here and Background layers, in this case.

2 Press the Home key to go to the beginning of the time ruler.

3 Do one of the following:

- Click the Play/Pause button (▶) in the Preview panel.

- Press the spacebar.

4 To stop the standard preview, do one of the following:

- Click the Play/Pause button in the Preview panel.

- Press the spacebar.

Using RAM preview

RAM preview allocates enough RAM to play the preview (with audio) as fast as the system allows, up to the frame rate of the composition. Use RAM preview to play footage in the Timeline, Layer, or Footage panel. The number of frames played depends on the amount of RAM available to the application.

In the Timeline panel, RAM preview plays either the span of time you specify as the work area, or from the beginning of the time ruler. In the Layer and Footage panels, RAM preview plays only untrimmed footage. Before you preview, check which frames are designated as the work area.

You'll preview the entire composition—the animated text plus graphic effects—using a RAM preview.

1 Click the Bgwtext 2 tab in the Timeline panel to bring it forward.

2 Make sure that the Video switch (👁) is turned on for all of the layers in the composition, and press F2 to deselect all layers.

3 Drag the work area brackets to the time span you want to preview: the work area start bracket should be at 0:00, and the work area end bracket should be at 10:00.

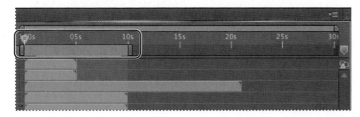

4 Drag the current-time indicator to the beginning of the time ruler, or press the Home key.

5 Click the RAM Preview button (⏵) in the Preview panel or choose Composition > Preview > RAM Preview.

A green progress bar indicates which frames are cached to RAM. When all of the frames in the work area are cached, the RAM preview plays back in real time.

▶ **Tip:** You can interrupt the caching process at any time by pressing the spacebar, and the RAM preview will play back only the frames that have been cached to that point.

6 To stop the RAM preview, press the spacebar.

The more detail and precision you want to see, the more RAM is required for RAM preview. You can control the amount of detail shown in either the standard or RAM preview by changing the resolution, magnification, and preview quality of your composition. You can also limit the number of layers previewed by turning off the Video switch for certain layers, or limit the number of frames previewed by adjusting the composition's work area.

7 Choose File > Save to save your project.

About OpenGL previews

OpenGL provides high-quality previews that require less rendering time than other playback modes. It provides fast screen previewing of a composition without degrading resolution, which makes it a desirable preview option for many situations. When OpenGL does not support a feature, it simply creates a preview without using that feature. For example, if your layers contain shadows and your OpenGL hardware does not support shadows, the preview will not contain shadows. You can view information about your OpenGL card, if you have one, as well as enable or disable OpenGL, by choosing Edit > Preferences > Previews (Windows) or After Effects > Preferences > Previews (Mac OS). See After Effects Help for more information about using OpenGL.

Optimizing performance in After Effects

How you configure After Effects and your computer determines how quickly After Effects renders projects. Complex compositions can require a large amount of memory to render, and the rendered movies can take a large amount of disk space to store. Refer to "Improve Performance" in After Effects Help for tips that can help you configure your system, After Effects preferences, and your projects for better performance.

Rendering and exporting your composition

When you're finished with your masterpiece—as you are now—you can render and export it at the quality settings you choose and create movies in the formats that you specify. You will learn more about exporting compositions in subsequent lessons, especially in Lesson 14, "Rendering and Outputting." If you'd like to skip ahead to Lesson 14 and render and export this project, you're welcome to do so. Otherwise, you can just save it, and continue getting acquainted with the After Effects workspace.

Customizing the workspace

In the course of this project, you may have resized or repositioned some panels, or opened new ones. As you modify the workspace, After Effects saves those modifications, so the next time you open the project, the most recent version of the workspace is used. However, you can choose to restore the original workspace at any time by choosing Window > Workspace > Reset "Standard."

Alternatively, if you find yourself frequently using panels that aren't part of the Standard workspace, or if you like to resize or group panels for different types of projects, you can save time by customizing the workspace to suit your needs. You can save any workspace configuration, or use any of the preset workspaces that come with After Effects. These predefined workspaces are suitable for different types of workflows, such as animation or effects work.

Using predefined workspaces

Take a minute to explore the predefined workspaces in After Effects.

1 If you closed the Lesson01_Finished.aep project, open it—or any other project—to explore the workspaces.

2 Choose Window > Workspace > Animation. After Effects opens the following panels at the right side of the application window: Info and Audio (grouped), Preview, Smoother, Wiggler, Motion Sketch, and Effects & Presets.

You can also change workspaces using the Workspace menu at the top of the window.

3 Choose Paint from the Workspace menu at the top of the application window, next to the Search Help box. The Paint and Brushes panels open. The Composition panel is replaced by the Layer panel, for easy access to the tools and controls you need to paint in your compositions.

Saving a custom workspace

You can save any workspace, at any time, as a custom workspace. Once saved, new and edited workspaces appear in the Window > Workspace submenu and in the Workspace menu at the top of the application window. If a project with a custom workspace is opened on a system other than the one on which it was created, After Effects looks for a workspace with a matching name. If After Effects finds a match (and the monitor configuration matches), it uses that workspace; if it can't find a match (or the monitor configuration doesn't match), it opens the project using the current local workspace.

1   Close the Paint and Brushes panels by clicking the small *x* next to the panel names.

2   Choose Window > Effects & Presets to open that panel, and then drag it into a group with the Preview panel.

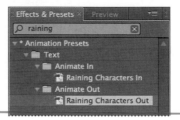

3   Choose Window > Workspace > New Workspace. Enter a name for the workspace and click OK to save it, or click Cancel if you don't want to save it.

Controlling the brightness of the user interface

You can brighten or darken the After Effects user interface. Changing the brightness preference affects panels, windows, and dialog boxes.

1   Choose Edit > Preferences > Appearance (Windows) or After Effects > Preferences > Appearance (Mac OS).

2 Drag the Brightness slider to the left or right and notice how the screen changes.

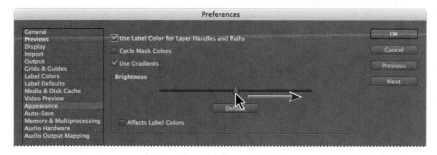

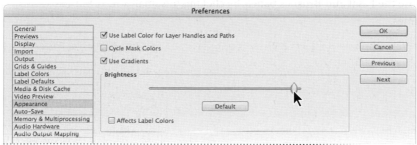

3 Click OK to save the new brightness setting or Cancel to leave your preferences unchanged. You can click Default to restore the default brightness setting.

Finding resources for using After Effects

For complete and up-to-date information about using After Effects panels, tools, and other application features, visit the Adobe website. To search for information in After Effects Help and support documents, as well as other websites relevant to After Effects users, simply enter a search term in the Search Help box in the upper-right corner of the application window. You can narrow the results to view only Adobe Help and support documents, as well.

If you plan to work in After Effects when you're not connected to the Internet, download the most current PDF version of After Effects Help from www.adobe.com/go/documentation.

For additional resources, such as tips and techniques and the latest product information, check out the Adobe Community Help page at community.adobe.com/help/main.

● **Note:** If After Effects detects that you are not connected to the Internet when you start the application, choosing Help > After Effects Help opens the Help HTML pages installed with After Effects. For more up-to-date information, view the Help files online or download the current PDF for reference.

Checking for updates

Adobe periodically provides updates to software. You can easily obtain these updates through Adobe Updater, as long as you have an active Internet connection.

1 In After Effects, choose Help > Updates. The Adobe Updater automatically checks for updates available for your Adobe software.

Note: To set your preferences for future updates, click Preferences. Select how often you want Adobe Updater to check for updates, for which applications, and whether to download them automatically. Click OK to accept the new settings.

2 In the Adobe Updater dialog box, select the updates you want to install, and then click Download And Install Updates to install them.

Congratulations. You've finished Lesson 1. Now that you're acquainted with the After Effects workspace, you can continue to Lesson 2 to learn how to create and animate compositions using effects and preset animations, or you can proceed to another lesson in this book.

Review questions

1 What are the basic components of the After Effects workflow?

2 What is a composition?

3 Describe three ways to preview your work in After Effects.

4 How can you customize the After Effects workspace?

Review answers

1 Most After Effects workflows include these steps: import and organize footage, create compositions and arrange layers, add effects, animate elements, preview your work, and export the final composition.

2 A composition is where you create all animation, layering, and effects. An After Effects composition has both spatial dimensions and time. Compositions include one or more layers—video, audio, still images—arranged in the Composition panel and in the Timeline panel. Simple projects may include only one composition, while elaborate projects may include several compositions to organize large amounts of footage or intricate effects sequences.

3 You can manually preview your work in After Effects by moving the current-time indicator, or you can view either a standard or RAM preview. A standard preview plays your composition from the current-time indicator to the end of the composition, usually more slowly than real time. A RAM preview allocates enough RAM to play the preview (with audio) as fast as the system allows, up to the frame rate of the composition.

4 You can customize the After Effects workspace by dragging the panels into the configuration that best suits your working style. You can drag panels to new locations, move panels into or out of groups, place panels alongside each other, and undock a panel so that it floats above the application window. As you rearrange panels, the other panels resize automatically to fit the application window. You can save custom workspaces by choosing Window > Workspace > New Workspace.

2 CREATING A BASIC ANIMATION USING EFFECTS AND PRESETS

Lesson overview

In this lesson you'll learn how to do the following:

- Use Adobe Bridge to preview and import footage items.

- Work with the layers of an imported Adobe Illustrator file.

- Apply drop shadow and emboss effects.

- Apply a text animation preset.

- Adjust the time range of a text animation preset.

- Precompose layers.

- Apply a dissolve transition effect.

- Adjust the transparency of a layer.

- Render an animation for broadcast use.

- Export an animation in SWF format for the web.

In this lesson, you will continue to learn the basics of the Adobe After Effects project workflow. You'll learn new ways to accomplish basic tasks as you create a simple newscast identification graphic for a fictional TV station, Channel 5. You will animate the newscast ID so that it fades to become a watermark that can appear in the lower-right corner of the screen during other TV programs. Then, you'll export the ID for use in broadcast output and as an SWF file for the web. This lesson will take about an hour to complete.

After Effects lets you hit the ground running with a variety of effects and animation presets. You can use them to create great-looking animations quickly and easily.

Getting started

1   Make sure the following files are in the AECS4_CIB/Lessons/Lesson02 folder on your hard disk, or copy them from the *Adobe After Effects CS4 Classroom in a Book* DVD now.

   •   In the Assets folder: 5logo.ai, ggbridge.jpg

   •   In the Sample_Movie folder: Lesson02.mov

2   Open and play the Lesson02.mov sample movie to see what you will create in this lesson. When you are done, quit QuickTime Player. You may delete this sample movie from your hard disk if you have limited storage space.

When you begin the lesson, restore the default application settings for After Effects. See "Restoring default preferences" on page 3.

3   Press Ctrl+Alt+Shift (Windows) or Command+Option+Shift (Mac OS) while starting After Effects. When asked whether you want to delete your preferences file, click OK.

4   Click Close to close the Welcome window.

After Effects opens to display a blank, untitled project.

5   Choose File > Save As.

6   In the Save As dialog box, navigate to the AECS4_CIB/Lessons/Lesson02/ Finished_Project folder.

7   Name the project **Lesson02_Finished.aep**, and then click Save.

Importing footage using Adobe Bridge

In Lesson 1, you chose File > Import > File to import footage. However, After Effects also offers another, more powerful and flexible way to import footage for a composition: using Adobe Bridge. You can use Adobe Bridge to organize, browse, and locate the assets you need to create content for print, the web, television, DVD, film, and mobile devices. Adobe Bridge keeps native Adobe files (such as PSD and PDF files) as well as non-Adobe application files available for easy access. You can drag assets into your layouts, projects, and compositions as needed; preview assets; and even add metadata (file information) to assets to make files easier to locate.

In this exercise, you will jump to Adobe Bridge to import the still-image file that will serve as the background of your composition.

▶ **Tip:** To open Adobe Bridge directly, choose Adobe Bridge from the Start menu (Windows) or double-click the Adobe Bridge icon in the Applications /Adobe Bridge folder (Mac OS).

1   Choose File > Browse In Bridge. If you receive a message about adding an extension to Adobe Bridge, click OK.

Adobe Bridge opens, displaying a collection of panels, menus, and buttons.

2 Click the Folders tab in the upper-left corner of Adobe Bridge.

3 In the Folders panel, navigate to the AECS4_CIB/Lessons/Lesson02/Assets folder. Click the arrows to open nested folders. You can also double-click folder thumbnail icons in the Content panel.

● **Note:** We're using the Essentials workspace, which is the default workspace in Bridge.

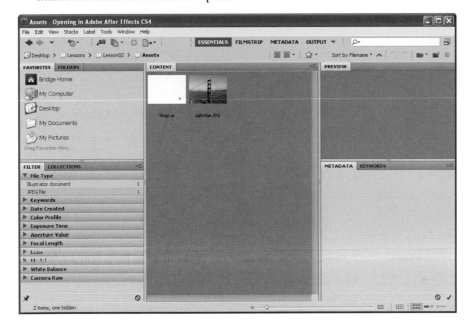

The Content panel updates interactively. For example, when you select the Assets folder in the Folders panel, thumbnail previews of the folder's contents appear in the Content panel. Adobe Bridge displays previews of image files such as those in PSD, TIFF, and JPEG formats, as well as Illustrator vector files, multipage Adobe PDF files, QuickTime movie files, and more.

4 Drag the thumbnail slider at the bottom of the Adobe Bridge window to enlarge the thumbnail previews.

▶ **Tip:** You can emphasize different information in Adobe Bridge by changing the workspace. To change the workspace, choose Window > Workspace > and then select a workspace. See Adobe Bridge Help to learn more about customizing Adobe Bridge.

5 Select the ggbridge.jpg file in the Content panel, and notice that it appears in the Preview panel, as well. Information about the file, including its creation date, bit depth, and file size, appears in the Metadata panel.

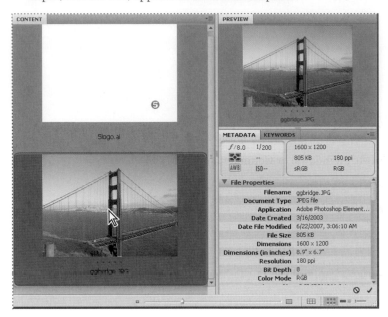

6 Double-click the ggbridge.jpg thumbnail in the Content panel to place the file in your After Effects project. Alternatively, you can drag the thumbnail into the Project panel in After Effects.

Adobe Bridge returns you to After Effects when you place the file. You can close Adobe Bridge if you'd like. You won't be using it again during this lesson.

Creating the composition

Following the After Effects workflow you learned in Lesson 1, the next step to building the TV news ID is to create a new composition. In Lesson 1, you created the composition based on footage items that were selected in the Project panel. You can also create an empty composition, and then add your footage items to it.

1   Create a new composition by doing one of the following:

- Click the Create A New Composition button (▦) at the bottom of the Project panel.

- Choose Composition > New Composition.

- Press Ctrl+N (Windows) or Command+N (Mac OS).

2   In the Composition Settings dialog box, do the following:

- Name the composition **Channel_5_News**.

- Choose NTSC D1 from the Preset pop-up menu. NTSC D1 is the resolution for standard-definition television in the United States and some other countries. This preset automatically sets the width, height, pixel aspect ratio, and frame rate for the composition to NT3C standards.

- In the Duration field, type **300** to specify 3 seconds.

- Click OK.

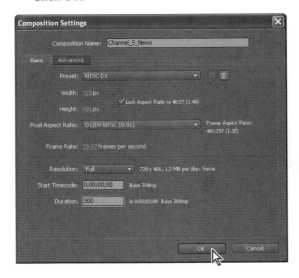

After Effects displays an empty composition named Channel_5_News in the Composition panel and in the Timeline panel. Now, you'll add the background.

3 Drag the ggbridge.jpg footage item from the Project panel to the Timeline panel to add it to the Channel_5_News composition.

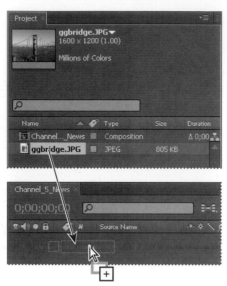

▶ **Tip:** The keyboard shortcut for fitting a layer to a composition is Ctrl+Alt+F (Windows) or Command+Option+F (Mac OS).

4 With the ggbridge layer selected in the Timeline panel, choose Layer > Transform > Fit To Comp to scale the background image to the dimensions of the composition.

Importing the foreground element

Your background is in place. The foreground object is a layered vector graphic that was created in Illustrator.

1 Choose File > Import > File.

2 In the Import File dialog box, navigate to the 5logo.ai file in the AECS4_CIB/ Lessons/Lesson02/Assets folder. (The file appears as 5logo if you've hidden file extensions in Windows.)

3 Select Composition from the Import As menu, and then click Open.

The Illustrator file is added to the Project panel as a composition named 5logo. A folder named 5logo Layers also appears. This folder contains the three individual layers of the Illustrator file. Click the triangle to open the folder and see its contents if you'd like.

4 Drag the 5logo composition file from the Project panel into the Timeline panel above the ggbridge layer.

You should now see both the background image and the logo in the Composition panel and in the Timeline panel.

Working with imported Illustrator layers

The Channel 5 logo graphic was created in Illustrator; your job in After Effects is to add text and animate it for the station's newscast. To work with the layers of the Illustrator file independently of the background footage, you'll open the 5logo composition in its own Timeline and Composition panels.

1 Double-click the 5logo composition in the Project panel. The composition opens in its own Timeline and Composition panels.

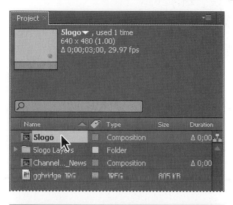

2 Select the Horizontal Type tool (T) in the Tools panel and click in the Composition panel to the left of the Channel 5 logo.

3 Type **NEWS**, all capitals, and then select all of the text you just entered.

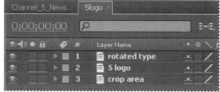

4 In the Character panel, select a sans serif typeface such as Myriad Pro and change the Font Size to **30** pixels. Leave all other options in the Character panel at their defaults.

● **Note:** If the Character panel isn't open, choose Window > Character.

5 In the Paragraph panel, click the Right Align Text button (≣). Leave all other options in the Paragraph panel at their defaults. You'll learn more about working with text in Lesson 3, "Animating Text."

● **Note:** If the Paragraph panel isn't open, choose Window > Paragraph.

6 Select the Selection tool (▶), and then drag the text in the Composition panel to position it as it appears in the following figure. Notice that when you switch to the Selection tool, the generic Text 1 layer name in the Timeline panel changes to NEWS, the text you typed.

▶ **Tip:** Choose View > Show Grid to make the nonprinting grid visible to help you position objects. Choose View > Show Grid again to hide the grid when you're done.

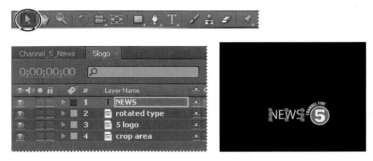

Applying effects to a layer

Now you will return to the main composition, Channel_5_News, and apply an effect to the 5logo layer. This will apply the effect to all of the layers nested in the 5logo composition.

Applying and controlling effects

You can apply or remove an effect at any time. Once you've applied effects to a layer, you can temporarily turn off one or all the effects in the layer to concentrate on another aspect of your composition. Effects that are turned off do not appear in the Composition panel and typically are not included when the layer is previewed or rendered.

By default, when you apply an effect to a layer, the effect is active for the duration of the layer. However, you can make an effect start and stop at specific times, or make the effect more or less intense over time. You'mjll learn more about creating animation using keyframes or expressions in Lesson 5, "Animating a Multimedia Presentation," and Lesson 6, "Animating Layers."

You can apply and edit effects on adjustment layers just as you do with other layers. However, when you apply an effect to an adjustment layer, the effect is applied to all layers below it in the Timeline panel.

Effects can also be saved, browsed, and applied as animation presets.

1 Click the Channel_5_News tab in the Timeline panel, and select the 5logo layer. The effect you create next will be applied only to the logo elements, and not to the background image of the bridge.

2 Choose Effect > Perspective > Drop Shadow. A soft-edged shadow appears behind the nested layers of the 5logo layer—the logo graphic, the rotated type, and the word *news*—in the Composition panel.

You can customize the effect using the Effect Controls panel, which appears in front of the Project panel when you apply an effect.

3   In the Effect Controls panel, reduce the drop shadow's Distance to **3** and increase its Softness to **4**. You can set these values by clicking the field and typing the number, or by dragging the orange, underlined value.

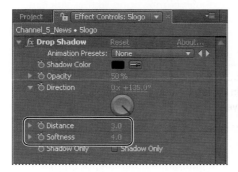 

The drop shadow is nice, but the logo will stand out even more if you apply an emboss effect. You can use either the Effect menu or the Effects & Presets panel to locate and apply effects.

4   Click the Effects & Presets tab to bring that panel forward. Then, click the triangle next to Stylize to expand the category.

5   With the 5logo layer selected in the Timeline panel, drag the Color Emboss effect into the Composition panel. The Color Emboss effect sharpens the edges of objects in the layer without suppressing the original colors. The Effect Controls panel displays the Color Emboss effect below the Drop Shadow effect.

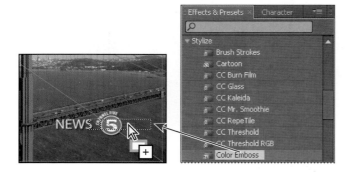

6   Choose File > Save to save your work.

Applying an animation preset

You've positioned the news logo and applied some effects to it. It's time to add some animation. You will learn several ways to animate text in Lesson 3. For now, you'll use a simple animation preset that will fade the word *news* onto the screen next to the Channel 5 logo. You'll need to work in the 5logo composition so that you can apply the animation to only the NEWS text layer.

1   Click the 5logo tab in the Timeline panel, and select the NEWS layer.

2   Move the current-time indicator to 1:10, which is when you want the text to start fading in.

3   In the Effects & Presets panel, navigate to Animation Presets > Text > Blurs.

4   Drag the Bullet Train animation preset onto the NEWS layer in the Timeline panel or over the word *news* in the Composition panel. Don't worry about the text disappearing. You're looking at the first frame of the animation, which happens to be blank.

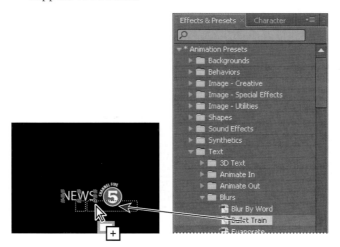

5 Click in a blank area of the Timeline panel to deselect the NEWS layer, and then drag the current-time indicator to 2:10 to manually preview the text animation. The text appears, letter by letter, until the word *news* is fully onscreen at 2:10.

Precomposing layers for a new animation

The news ID is coming along nicely, and you're probably eager to preview the complete animation. Before you do, however, you'll add a dissolve to all of the logo elements except the word *news*. To do this, you need to precompose the other three layers of the 5logo composition: rotated type, 5 logo, and crop area.

Precomposing is a way to nest layers within a composition. Precomposing moves the layers to a new composition. This new composition takes the place of the selected layers. When you want to change the order in which layer components are rendered, precomposing is a quick way to create intermediate levels of nesting in an existing hierarchy.

1 Shift-click to select the rotated type, 5 logo, and crop area layers in the 5logo Timeline panel.

2 Choose Layer > Pre-compose.

3 In the Pre-compose dialog box, name the new composition **Dissolve_logo**. The Move All Attributes Into The New Composition option is selected by default. Then, click OK.

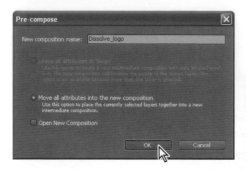

The three layers are replaced in the 5logo Timeline panel with a single layer, Dissolve_logo. This new, precomposed layer contains the three layers that you selected in step 1. You can apply the dissolve effect to it without affecting the NEWS text layer and its Bullet Train animation.

4 Make sure the Dissolve_logo layer is selected in the Timeline panel and press the Home key to go to 0:00.

▶ **Tip:** To locate the Dissolve – Vapor preset quickly, type **vap** in the search box in the Effects & Presets panel.

5 In the Effects & Presets panel, open the Animation Presets > Transitions – Dissolves category, and then drag the Dissolve – Vapor animation preset onto the Dissolve_logo layer in the Timeline panel or in the Composition panel.

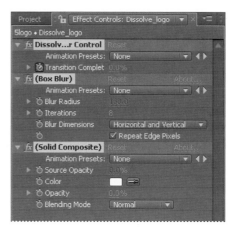

The Dissolve – Vapor animation preset includes three components—a master dissolve, a box blur, and a solid composite, all of which appear in the Effect Controls panel. The default settings are fine for this project.

6 Choose File > Save.

Previewing the effects

It's time to preview all of the effects together.

1   Click the Channel_5_News tab in the Timeline panel to switch to the main composition. Press the Home key to make sure you're at the beginning of the time ruler.

2   Make sure the Video switch (👁) is selected for both layers of the Channel_5_News Timeline panel.

3   Click the Play button (▶) in the Preview panel or press the spacebar to watch the preview. Press the spacebar to stop playback at any time.

Adding transparency

Many TV stations display logos semi-transparently in the corner of the frame to emphasize the brand. You'll reduce the opacity of the ID so that it can be used this way.

1   Still in the Channel_5_News Timeline panel, go to 2:24.

2   Select the 5logo layer and press **T** to display its Opacity property. By default, the Opacity is 100%—fully opaque. Click the stopwatch icon (⏱) to set an Opacity keyframe at this location.

3   Press the End key to go to the end of the time ruler (2:29), and change the Opacity to **40%**. After Effects adds a keyframe.

Now, the logo appears, the word *news* flies in, and it all fades to 40% opacity.

4 Watch a preview of your composition by clicking the Play button in the Preview panel, by pressing the spacebar, or by pressing 0 on your numeric keypad. Press the spacebar to stop playback when you're done.

5 Choose File > Save to save your project.

Rendering the composition

You're ready to prepare your Channel 5 news ID for output. When you create output, the layers of a composition and each layer's masks, effects, and properties are rendered frame by frame into one or more output files or, in the case of a sequence, into a series of consecutive files.

Making a movie from your final composition can take a few minutes or many hours, depending on the composition's frame size, quality, complexity, and compression method. When you place your composition in the render queue, it becomes a render item that uses the render settings assigned to it. While After Effects renders the item, you are unable to work in the program.

● **Note:** For more about output formats and rendering, see Lesson 14, "Rendering and Outputting."

After Effects provides a variety of formats and compression types for rendering output; the format you choose depends on the medium from which you'll play your final output or on the requirements of your hardware, such as a video-editing system. You will prepare this animation for two formats so that it can be used for broadcast purposes as well as on a website.

Exporting broadcast-quality output

You'll start by rendering and exporting the composition so that it can be broadcast on television.

1 Do one of the following to add the composition to the render queue:

- Select the Channel_5_News composition in the Project panel, and then choose Composition > Add to Render Queue. The Render Queue panel opens automatically.

- Choose Window > Render Queue to open the Render Queue panel, and then drag the Channel_5_News composition from the Project panel onto the Render Queue panel.

2 Choose Maximize Frame from the Render Queue panel menu so that the panel fills the application window.

▶ **Tip:** The keyboard shortcut for the Maximize Frame command is the accent grave (`) character, which shares a key with the tilde (~) character.

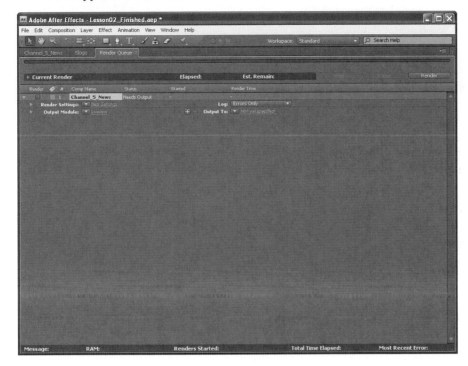

3 Click the triangle to expand the Render Settings options. By default, After Effects renders compositions at the Best Quality and Full Resolution. The default settings are fine for this project.

4 Click the triangle to expand the Output Module options. By default, After Effects uses lossless compression to encode the rendered composition into a movie file, which is fine for this project. However, you need to identify where to save the file.

5 Click the underlined words *Not Yet Specified* next to the Output To pop-up menu.

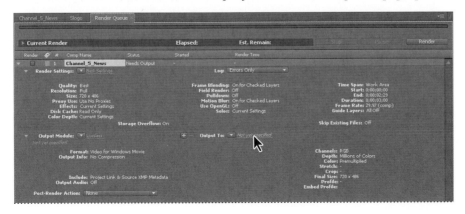

6 In the Output Movie To dialog box, accept the default movie name (Channel_5_News), select the AECS4_CIB/Lessons/Lesson02/Finished_Project folder for the location, and then click Save.

7 Back in the Render Queue panel, click the Render button.

After Effects displays a progress bar in the Render Queue panel as it encodes the file, and issues an audio alert when all items in the Render Queue have been rendered and encoded.

8 When the movie is complete, choose Restore Frame Size from the Render Queue panel menu to restore your workspace.

Exporting a composition for the web

The production manager at Channel 5 wants to use this news ID on the station's website, as well. For that purpose, you need to render and export the composition in SWF format. The SWF format is a widely used vector graphics and animation format for the web. It is a compact, binary format that can contain audio and vector objects. Web browsers with the Flash Player plug-in can play SWF files.

Before exporting to SWF, you need to adjust the composition a bit for online display.

1 Select the Channel_5_News composition in the Project panel, and then choose Composition > Composition Settings.

2 In the Basic tab of the Composition Settings dialog box, choose Web Video, 320 x 240 from the Preset menu, and then click OK.

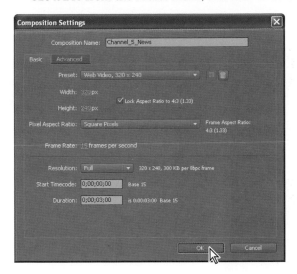

After Effects applies the new web-appropriate resolution—320 x 240 pixels   to the composition. As a result, both the background and 5logo layers are about twice as big as the composition, which is now smaller, has a different aspect ratio, and has a different frame rate (15 fps). So you need to reposition and resize the layers for the new output medium, including centering the logo in the composition.

3 Open the Channel_5_News Timeline panel, select the ggbridge layer, and press Ctrl+Alt+F (Windows) or Command+Option+F (Mac OS) to fit the layer to the composition size.

4 Go to 2:12, which is when the logo starts to fade in at the new frame rate.

5 Select the 5logo layer in the Timeline panel, and then press **P** to reveal its Position property.

6 Change the Position values to **-4.4, -26.1** to center the logo in the composition.

Now, you're ready to render and export the composition to SWF format.

Note: SWF files can be played directly by Flash Player. The Flash Video (FLV) command in the Export submenu saves video content so that it can be published online, but it must be embedded in a SWF file to be played by Flash Player.

7 With the Channel_5_News composition selected in the Project panel, choose File > Export > Adobe Flash Player (SWF).

8 In the Save File As dialog box, accept the default filename (Channel_5_News. swf), select the AECS4_CIB/Lessons/Lesson02/Finished_Project folder for the location, and then click Save.

9 In the SWF Settings dialog box, select Medium from the JPEG Quality menu. This setting preserves image quality nicely but also reduces the file size somewhat. Leave all other settings at their defaults, and then click OK.

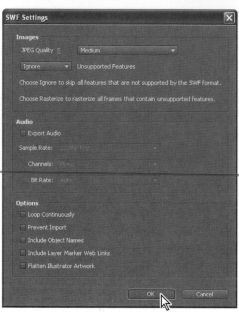

After Effects displays a progress bar as it renders the file and exports it to SWF format. It also saves a report in HTML to the same folder as the SWF file.

10 Choose File > Save to save the final file.

11 In Explorer (Windows) or the Finder (Mac OS), navigate to the AECS4_CIB/ Lessons/Lesson02/Finished_Project folder.

12 Double-click the HTML file to open it in your default web browser, and preview the SWF file by clicking the link on the page. This Flash animation could be used as part of a splash screen on the TV station's website, or as part of an ad, for example.

Congratulations. You've created a broadcast news show ID and watermark.

Note: After Effects exports text layers to SWF as vector graphics. Some layer types and layer switches are not supported, such as 3D Layers, 3D Cameras, and 3D Lights. Nested layers are rasterized. For more on SWF export, see After Effects Help.

Review questions

1 How do you use Adobe Bridge to preview and import files?

2 What is *precomposing*?

3 How do you customize an effect?

4 How do you modify the transparency of a layer in a composition?

Review answers

1 Choose File > Browse In Bridge to jump from After Effects to Adobe Bridge, where you can search for and preview image assets. When you locate the asset you want to use in an After Effects project, double-click it or drag it to the Project panel.

2 *Precomposing* is a way to nest layers within a composition. Precomposing moves the layers to a new composition, which takes the place of the selected layers. When you want to change the order in which layer components are rendered, precomposing is a quick way to create intermediate levels of nesting in an existing hierarchy.

3 After you apply an effect to a layer in a composition, you can customize its properties in the Effect Controls panel. This panel opens automatically when you apply the effect, or you can open it at any time by selecting the layer with the effect and choosing Window > Effect Controls.

4 To modify the transparency of a layer, reduce its opacity. Select the layer in the Timeline panel, press **T** to reveal its Opacity property, and enter a value lower than 100%.

3 ANIMATING TEXT

Lesson overview

In this lesson, you'll learn to do the following:

- Create and animate text layers.
- Stylize text using the Character and Paragraph panels.
- Animate text using animation presets.
- Preview animation presets in Adobe Bridge.
- Customize an animation preset.
- Animate text using keyframes.
- Animate layers using parenting.
- Edit and animate imported Adobe Photoshop text.
- Use a text animator group to animate selected characters on a layer.
- Apply a text animation to a graphic object.
- Import SWF files.
- Export a project for further work in Adobe Flash.

 Adobe After Effects offers many ways to animate text. You can animate text layers by manually creating keyframes in the Timeline panel, using animation presets, or using expressions. You can even animate individual characters or words in a text layer. In this lesson, you'll employ several different animation techniques, including some that are unique to text, while you design the opening title credits for an animated documentary called *The Pond*. This lesson will take approximately 2 hours to complete.

The Pond

an animated documentary

directed by

Your type doesn't need to sit still while your audience is reading it. In this lesson, you'll learn several ways to animate type in After Effects, including time-saving methods unique to text layers.

Getting started

As in other projects, you'll begin by previewing the movie you're creating, and then opening After Effects.

1 Make sure the following files are in the AECS4_CIB/Lessons/Lesson03 folder on your hard disk, or copy them from the *Adobe After Effects CS4 Classroom in a Book* DVD now:

   • In the Assets folder: credits.psd, dragonfly.ai, Lotus.swf, pondbackground.mov

   • In the Sample_Movie folder: Lesson03.mov

2 Open and play the Lesson03.mov sample movie to see the title credits you will create in this lesson. When you are done, quit QuickTime Player. You may delete this sample movie from your hard disk if you have limited storage space.

As you start the application, restore the default settings for After Effects. See "Restoring default preferences" on page 3.

3 Press Ctrl+Alt+Shift (Windows) or Command+Option+Shift (Mac OS) while starting After Effects. When asked whether you want to delete your preferences file, click OK.

4 Click Close to close the Welcome window.

After Effects opens to display a blank, untitled project.

5 Choose File > Save As, and navigate to the AECS4_CIB/Lessons/Lesson03/ Finished_Project folder.

6 Name the project **Lesson03_Finished.aep**, and then click Save.

Importing the footage

You need to import two footage items to begin this lesson.

1 Double-click an empty area of the Project panel to open the Import File dialog box.

2 Navigate to the AECS4_CIB/Lessons/Lesson03/Assets folder on your hard disk, Ctrl-click (Windows) or Command-click (Mac OS) to select the Lotus.swf and pondbackground.mov files, and then click Open.

After Effects can import several file formats including Adobe Photoshop, Adobe Illustrator, and SWF files, as well as QuickTime and AVI movies. This makes After Effects an incredibly powerful application for compositing and motion graphics work.

Creating the composition

Now, you'll create the composition.

1 Press Ctrl+N (Windows) or Command+N (Mac OS) to open the Composition Settings dialog box.

2 In the Composition Settings dialog box, name the composition **Pond_Title_Sequence**, select NTSC DV from the Preset menu, and set the Duration to **10:00**, which is the length of the pond background movie. Then, click OK.

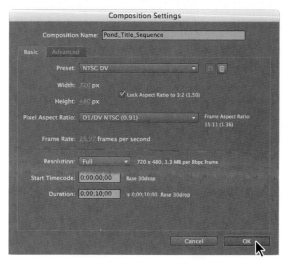

3 Drag the pondbackground.mov and Lotus.swf footage items from the Project panel to the Timeline panel. Arrange the layers so that Lotus.swf is above pondbackground.mov in the layer stack.

Now, position and scale the Lotus.swf layer in the composition.

4 With the Lotus layer selected in the Timeline panel, press the **S** key to reveal its Scale property.

5 Change the Scale amount to **30%** for both the horizontal and vertical values. Because the two values are linked (), changing one value automatically changes both.

6 Press the **P** key to reveal the Position property, and change its values to **170, 520**. The lotus moves to the lower-left corner of the composition, so that only a small amount of the flower is on the screen.

7 Press **P** to hide the Position property, and then choose File > Save.

You're ready to add the title text to the composition.

About text layers

In After Effects, you can add text to layers with flexibility and precision. You can create and edit text directly on the screen in the Composition panel and quickly change the font, style, size, and color of the text. You can add horizontal or vertical text anywhere in a composition. The Tools, Character, and Paragraph panels contain a wide range of text controls. You can apply changes to individual characters and set formatting options for entire paragraphs, including alignment, justification, and word-wrapping. In addition to all of these style features, After Effects provides tools for easily animating specific characters and properties, such as text opacity and hue.

After Effects uses two types of text: point text and paragraph text. Use *point text* to enter a single word or a line of characters; use *paragraph text* to enter and format text as one or more paragraphs.

In many ways, text layers are just like any other layer in After Effects. You can apply effects and expressions to text layers, animate them, designate them as 3D layers, and edit the 3D text while viewing it in multiple views. As with layers imported from Illustrator, text layers are continuously rasterized, so when you scale the layer or resize the text, it retains crisp, resolution-independent edges. The main differences between text layers and other layers are that you cannot open a text layer in its own Layer panel, and that you can animate the text in a text layer using special text animator properties and selectors.

Creating and formatting point text

When you enter point text, each line of text is independent—the length of a line increases or decreases as you edit the text, but it doesn't wrap to the next line. The text you enter appears in a new text layer. The small line through the I-beam marks the position of the text baseline.

1 In the Tools panel, select the Horizontal Type tool (T).

2 Click anywhere in the Composition panel and type **The Pond**. Then, press Enter on the numeric keypad to exit text-editing mode and to select the text layer in the Composition panel. Or, select the layer name to exit text-editing mode.

● **Note:** If you press Enter or Return on the regular keyboard instead of on the numeric keypad, you'll begin a new paragraph.

Using the Character panel

The Character panel provides options for formatting characters. If text is highlighted, changes you make in the Character panel affect only the highlighted text. If no text is highlighted, changes you make in the Character panel affect the selected text layers and the text layers' selected Source Text keyframes, if any exist. If no text is highlighted and no text layers are selected, the changes you make in the Character panel become the new defaults for the next text entry.

1 Choose Window > Workspace > Text to display only those panels you need while working with text.

▶ **Tip:** To open the panels individually, choose Window > Character or Window > Paragraph. To open both panels, select the Horizontal Type tool and then click the Toggle The Character And Paragraph Panels button in the Tools panel.

Tip: To select a font quickly, begin typing its name in the Font Family box. The Font Family menu jumps to the first font on your system that matches the letters you've typed, and the text in the Composition panel takes on the newly selected font.

2 In the Character panel, choose Myriad Pro from the Font Family menu. If you don't have Myriad Pro, then choose another heavy sans serif typeface, such as Verdana.

3 Choose Bold from the Font Style menu. If Bold isn't available, click the Faux Bold button (𝕋) in the lower-left corner of the panel.

4 Set the Font Size to **72** pixels.

5 Leave all other options at their default settings.

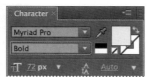

Using the Paragraph panel

Use the Paragraph panel to set options that apply to entire paragraphs, such as alignment, indentation, and leading. For point text, each line is a separate paragraph. You can use the Paragraph panel to set formatting options for a single paragraph, multiple paragraphs, or all paragraphs in a text layer. You just need to make one adjustment in the Paragraph panel for this composition's title text.

1 In the Paragraph panel, click the Center Text button (≣). This aligns horizontal text to the center of the layer, not to the center of the composition.

2 Leave all other options at their default settings.

Positioning the type

To precisely position layers, such as the text layer you're working on now, you can display rulers, guides, and grids (both regular and proportional) in the Composition panel. These visual reference tools don't appear in the final rendered movie.

1 Select the The Pond text layer in the Timeline panel.

2 Choose Layer > Transform > Fit To Comp Width. This scales the layer to fit it to the width of the composition.

Now, you can position the text layer using a grid.

3 Choose View > Show Grid and then View > Snap to Grid.

4 Using the Selection tool (), drag the text vertically in the Composition panel until the base of the letters sits on the horizontal grid line in the center of the composition. Press Shift after you start dragging to constrain the movement and help you position the text.

5 When the layer is in position, choose View > Show Grid again to hide the grid.

This project isn't destined for broadcast TV, so it's okay that the title and the lotus flower extend beyond the title-safe and action-safe areas of the composition at the beginning of the animation.

6 Choose Window > Workspace > Standard to return to the Standard workspace, and then choose File > Save to save your project.

Using a text animation preset

Now you're ready to animate the title. The easiest way to do that is to use one of the many animation presets that come with After Effects. After applying an animation preset, you can customize it and save it to use again in other projects.

1 Press the Home key to make sure the current-time indicator is at the beginning of the time ruler. After Effects applies animation presets from the current time.

2 Select the The Pond text layer.

Browsing animation presets

You already applied an animation preset in Lesson 2, "Creating a Basic Animation Using Effects and Presets." But what if you're not sure which animation preset you want to use? To help you choose the right animation preset for your projects, you can preview them in Adobe Bridge.

1 Choose Animation > Browse Presets. Adobe Bridge opens and displays the contents of the After Effects Presets folder.

2 In the Content panel, double-click the Text folder, and then the Blurs folder.

3 Click to select the first preset, Blur By Word. Adobe Bridge plays a sample of the animation in the Preview panel.

4 Select a few other presets and watch them in the Preview panel.

5 Preview the Evaporate preset and then double-click its thumbnail preview. Alternatively, you can right-click (Windows) or Control-click (Mac OS) the thumbnail and choose Place In After Effects. After Effects applies the preset to the selected layer, which is the The Pond layer.

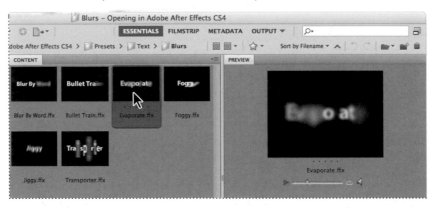

● **Note:** Leave Adobe Bridge open in the background. You'll use it again later in the lesson.

Nothing appears to change in the composition. This is because at 0:00, the first frame of the animation, the letters haven't evaporated yet.

Previewing a range of frames

Now, preview the animation. Although the composition is 10 seconds long, you only need to preview the first few seconds, which is where the text animation occurs.

1 In the Timeline panel, move the current-time indicator to 3:00, and press **N** to set the end bracket of the work area.

2 Press **0** on the numeric keypad or click the RAM Preview button (▶) in the Preview panel to watch a RAM preview of the animation. The letters appear to evaporate into the background. It looks great—but you want the letters to fade in and remain onscreen, not disappear into the murky depths of the pond. So you will customize the preset to suit your needs.

3 Press the spacebar to stop the preview, and then press the Home key to move the current-time indicator is back at 0:00.

Customizing an animation preset

After you apply an animation preset to a layer, all of its properties and keyframes are listed in the Timeline panel.

1 Select the The Pond text layer in the Timeline panel and press **U**. The U key, sometimes referred to as the *überkey*, is a valuable keyboard shortcut that reveals all the animated properties of a layer.

2 Click the Offset property name to select both of its keyframes. The Offset property specifies how much to offset the start and end of the selection.

▶ **Tip:** If you press **U** twice (**UU**), After Effects displays all modified properties for the layer, instead of only the animated properties. Press the **U** key again to hide all the layer's properties.

3 Choose Animation > Keyframe Assistant > Time-Reverse Keyframes. This command switches the order of the two Offset keyframes so that the letters are invisible at the beginning of the composition, and then emerge into view.

4 Drag the current-time indicator from 0:00 to 3:00 to manually preview the edited animation. The letters now fade into rather than disappear from the composition.

5 Press **U** to hide the layer's properties.

6 Press the End key to move the current-time indicator to the end of the time ruler, and then press **N** to set the end bracket of the work area.

7 Choose File > Save to save your project.

Animating with scale keyframes

The text layer was scaled to more than 200% when you applied the Fit To Comp command to it earlier in this lesson. Now, you'll animate the layer's scale so that the type gradually shrinks down to its original size.

1 In the Timeline panel, move the current-time indicator to 3:00.

2 Select the The Pond text layer, and press the **S** key to reveal its Scale property.

3 Click the stopwatch icon (image) to add a Scale keyframe at the current time, 3:00.

4 Move the current-time indicator to 5:00.

5 Reduce the layer's Scale values to **100, 100%**. After Effects adds a new Scale keyframe at the current time.

Previewing the scale animation

Now, preview the change.

1   Move the current-time indicator to 5:10, and press **N** to set the end of the work area. The scale animation ends shortly before 5:10.

2   Watch a RAM preview of the animation from 0:00 to 5:10. The movie title fades in and then scales to a smaller size.

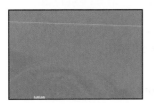 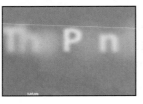 

▶ **Tip:** You can experiment with scale text animation presets, included with After Effects. They're located in the Presets/Text/ Scale folder in the After Effects CS4 folder on your hard drive..

3   Press the spacebar to stop the playback after you've viewed the animation.

Adding Easy Ease

The beginning and end of the scale animation are rather abrupt. In nature, nothing comes to an absolute stop. Instead, objects ease into and out of starting and stopping points.

1   Right-click (Windows) or Control-click (Mac OS) the Scale keyframe at 3:00, and choose Keyframe Assistant > Easy Ease Out. The keyframe becomes a left-pointing icon.

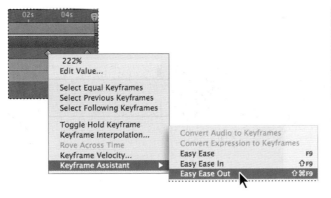

2 Right-click (Windows) or Control-click (Mac OS) the Scale keyframe at 5:00, and choose Keyframe Assistant > Easy Ease In. The keyframe becomes a right-pointing icon.

3 Watch another RAM preview. Press the spacebar to stop it when you're done.

4 Choose File > Save.

Animating using parenting

The next task is to make it appear as if the virtual camera is zooming away from the composition. The text scale animation you just applied gets you halfway there, but you need to animate the scale of the lotus flower, as well. You could manually animate the Lotus layer, but it's easier to take advantage of parenting relationships in After Effects.

1 Press the Home key to go to the beginning of the time ruler.

2 In the Timeline panel, click the Parent pop-up menu for the Lotus layer, and choose 1. The Pond. This sets the The Pond text layer as the parent of the Lotus layer, which in turn becomes the child layer.

As the child layer, the Lotus layer inherits the Scale keyframes of its parent layer (The Pond). Not only is this a quick way to animate the lotus flower, but it also ensures that the lotus flower scales at the same rate and by the same amount as the text layer.

3 Move the current-time indicator from 3:00 to 5:00 to manually preview the scaling. Both the text and the lotus flower scale down in size, making it seem like the camera is zooming away from the scene.

4 Press the Home key to return to 0:00, and drag the work area end bracket to the end of the time ruler.

5 Select the The Pond layer in the Timeline panel and press **S** to hide its Scale property. Then, choose File > Save.

About parent and child layers

Parenting assigns one layer's transformations to another layer, called a *child layer*. Creating a parenting relationship between layers synchronizes the changes in the parent layer with the corresponding transformation values of the child layers, except opacity. For example, if a parent layer moves 5 pixels to the right of its starting position, then the child layer also moves 5 pixels to the right of its starting position. A layer can have only one parent, but a layer can be a parent to any number of 2D or 3D layers within the same composition. Parenting layers is useful for creating complex animations such as linking the movements of a marionette, or depicting the orbits of planets in the solar system.

For more on parent and child layers, see After Effects Help.

Animating imported Photoshop text

If all text animations involved just two short words, such as *The Pond*, life would be easy. But in the real world, you must often work with longer blocks of text, and they can be tedious to enter manually. Fortunately, After Effects lets you import text from Photoshop or Illustrator. You can preserve text layers and edit and animate them in After Effects.

You'll import text from a layered Photoshop file for this title sequence and continue to animate it.

Importing text

Some of the remaining text for this composition is in a layered Photoshop file, which you'll import now.

1   Double-click an empty area in the Project panel to open the Import File dialog box.

2   Select the credits.psd file in the AECS4_CIB/Lessons/Lesson03/Assets folder. Choose Composition – Cropped Layers from the Import As menu, and then click Open.

3   In the Credits.psd dialog box, select Editable Layer Styles, and click OK.

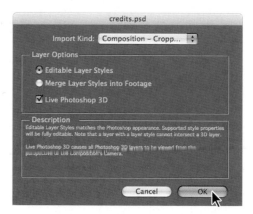

After Effects can import Photoshop layer styles, retaining the appearance of the layers you're importing. The imported file is added as a composition to the Project panel; its layers are added in a separate folder.

4   Drag the credits composition from the Project panel into the Timeline panel, placing it at the top of the layer stack.

Because you imported the credits.psd file as a composition with layers intact, you can work on it in its own Timeline panel, editing and animating its layers independently.

Editing imported text

The text you imported isn't currently editable in After Effects. You'll change that so that you can control the type and apply animations. And if you have a sharp eye, you've noticed some typos in the imported text. So, first you'll clean up the type.

1   Double-click the credits composition in the Project panel to open it in its own Timeline panel.

2   Shift-click to select both of the layers in the Credits Timeline panel, and choose Layer > Convert To Editable Text. (Click OK if you see a warning about missing fonts.) Now the text layers can be edited, and you can fix the typos.

3 Deselect both layers, and then double-click layer 2 in the Timeline panel to select the text and automatically switch to the Horizontal Type tool (T).

4 Type an *e* between the *t* and *d* in the word *animated*. Then, change the *k* to a *c* in *documentary*.

● **Note:** The layer name does not change in the Timeline panel when you correct the spelling in the layer. This is because the original layer name was created in Photoshop. To change a layer's name, select it in the Timeline panel, press Enter (Windows) or Return (Mac OS), type the new name, and press Enter or Return again.

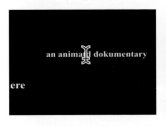

5 Switch to the Selection tool (▶) to exit text-editing mode.

6 Shift-click to select both layers in the Timeline panel.

7 If the Character panel isn't open, choose Window > Character to open it.

8 Choose the same typeface you used for the words *The Pond*. (We used Myriad Pro.) Leave all other settings as they are.

Animating the subtitle

You want the letters of the subtitle, *an animated documentary*, to fade onscreen from left to right under the movie title. The easiest way to do this is to use another text animation preset.

1 Go to 5:00 in the timeline. At that point, the title and lotus have finished scaling to their final size.

2 Select the subtitle layer (layer 2) in the Timeline panel.

3 Press Ctrl+Alt+Shift+O (Windows) or Command+Option+Shift+O (Mac OS) to jump to Adobe Bridge.

4 Navigate to the Presets/Text/Animate In folder.

5 Select the Fade Up Characters animation preset and watch it in the Preview panel. This will work nicely.

6 Double-click the Fade Up Characters preset to apply it to the subtitle layer in After Effects.

7 With the subtitle layer selected in the Timeline panel, press **UU** to see the properties modified by the animation preset. You should see two keyframes for Range Selector 1 Start: one at 5:00, and one at 7:00. You still have a lot of animation to do in this composition, so you will speed up the effect by 1 second.

8 Go to 6:00, and then drag the second Range Selector 1 Start keyframe to 6:00.

9 Drag the current-time indicator across the time ruler between 5:00 and 6:00 to see the letters fade in.

10 When you're done, select the subtitle layer and press **U** to hide the modified properties. Then, choose File > Save to save your work.

Animating text using a path animation preset

You've seen how versatile and convenient text animation presets can be. You'll use another type of text animation preset to animate the words *directed by* along a motion path. After Effects includes several animation presets that animate text along a prebuilt path. These presets also provide placeholder text with formatting when you apply them, so in this exercise, you will enter and format your text *after* you apply the animation preset.

1 Select the Pond_Title_Sequence tab in the Timeline panel.

2 Deselect all layers, and then go to 5:00.

3 Press Ctrl+Alt+Shift+O (Windows) or Command+Option+Shift+O (Mac OS) to jump to Adobe Bridge.

4 Navigate to the Presets/Text/Paths folder.

5 Double-click the Pipes animation preset. Adobe Bridge returns you to After Effects, where the preset automatically creates a new layer, pipes, with a predefined path that zigzags across the composition. The text on the path is obscured by the movie title. You'll fix that soon.

Customizing the preset path

Now, you need to change the placeholder word *pipes* to *directed by*.

1 In the Timeline panel, go to 6:05, when the word *pipes* is visible—and horizontal—onscreen.

2 Double-click the pipes layer in the Timeline panel. After Effects switches to the Horizontal Type tool (T) and selects the word *pipes* in the Composition panel.

3 Type **directed by** to replace the word *pipes*. Press Enter on the numeric keypad or select the layer name when you're done. After Effects updates the Timeline panel with the new layer name.

4 In the Character panel, do the following:

- Set the Font Family to Minion Pro or another serif typeface.

- Set the Font Style to Regular.

- Set the Font Size to **20** pixels.

- Leave all other settings at their defaults.

 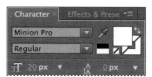

5 Drag the current-time indicator across the time ruler between 5:00 and 8:00 to see how the words *directed by* move onscreen—and then off the screen. You'll fix the text so that it stays onscreen, but now is a good time to adjust the position of the path in the composition so that it doesn't interfere with the movie title.

6 Using the Selection tool (⬉), double-click the yellow motion path in the Composition panel.

7 Drag the path down until the words *The Pond* are centered in the top curve and the lotus flower is centered in the lower curve. You may find it easiest to use the arrow keys.

8 Press Enter (Windows) or Return (Mac OS) to accept the change.

Later in the lesson, you'll attach a dragonfly graphic to the path so it appears to be pulling the text. But first, you'll finish animating the credits.

9 Select the directed by layer in the Timeline panel and hide its properties. Then, choose File > Save to save your work.

Animating type tracking

Next, you'll animate the appearance of the director's name in the composition using a text animation tracking preset. By animating tracking, you can make words appear to expand outward as they appear onscreen from a central point.

Customizing placeholder text

Currently, the director's name is simply a layer with placeholder text—*Your Name Here*. Before you animate it, change it to your own name.

1 Switch to the Credits timeline in the Timeline panel, and select the Your Name Here layer.

● **Note:** It doesn't matter where the current-time indicator is located when you edit the text of this layer. Currently, the text is onscreen for the duration of the composition. That will change once you animate it.

2 Select the Horizontal Type tool (T), and then replace *Your Name Here* in the Composition panel with your own name. Use a first, middle, and last name so that you have a nice long string of text to animate. Click the layer name when you're done.

Applying a tracking preset

Now you will animate the director's name with a tracking preset so that it starts to appear onscreen shortly after the words *directed by* reach the center of the composition.

1 Go to 7:10.

2 Select the Your Name Here layer in the Timeline panel.

3 Jump to Adobe Bridge and go to the Presets/Text/Tracking folder. Double-click the Increase Tracking preset to apply it to the Your Name Here layer in After Effects.

4 Drag the current-time indicator across the time ruler between 7:10 and 9:10 to manually preview the tracking animation.

Customizing the tracking animation preset

The text expands, but you need the letters to be so close initially that they're on top of each other, and then to expand to a reasonable, readable distance apart. The animation should also occur faster. You'll adjust the Tracking Amount to fix both problems.

1 Select the Your Name Here layer in the Timeline panel and press **UU** to reveal the properties that were modified.

2 Go to 7:10.

3 Under Animator 1, change the Tracking Amount to **-5** so that the letters are squeezed together.

4 Click the Go To Next Keyframe arrow for the Tracking Amount property, and then change the value to 0.

5 Drag the current-time indicator across the time ruler between 7:10 and 9:10. The letters expand as they appear onscreen and stop animating at the last keyframe.

Animating text opacity

You'll take the animation of the director's name a little further by having it fade onscreen as the letters expand. To do this, you'll animate the layer's Opacity property.

1 Select the Your Name Here layer in the Credits timeline.

2 Press **T** to reveal only its Opacity property.

3 Go to 7:10 and set the Opacity to **0%**. Then, click the stopwatch icon (🕑) to set an Opacity keyframe.

4 Go to 7:20 and set the Opacity to **100%**. After Effects adds a second keyframe. Now, the letters of the director's name should fade in as they expand onscreen.

5 Drag the current-time indicator across the time ruler between 7:10 and 8:10 to see the letters of the director's name fade in as they spread out.

6 Right-click (Windows) or Control-click (Mac OS) the ending Opacity keyframe and choose Keyframe Assistant > Easy Ease In.

7 Choose File > Save.

Using a text animator group

Text animator groups let you animate individual letters within a block of text in a layer. You'll use a text animator group to animate only the characters in your middle name without affecting the tracking and opacity animation of the other names in the layer.

About text animator groups

A text animator group includes one or more *selectors* and one or more *animator properties*. A selector is like a mask—it specifies which characters or section of a text layer you want an animator property to affect. Using a selector, you can define a percentage of the text, specific characters in the text, or a specific range of text.

Using a combination of animator properties and selectors, you can create complex text animations that would otherwise require painstaking keyframing. Most text animations require you to animate only the selector values—not the property values. Consequently, text animators use a small number of keyframes even for complex animations.

For more about text animator groups, see After Effects Help.

1 In the Timeline panel, go to 8:10.

2 Hide the Opacity property for the Your Name Here layer. Then, expand the layer to see its Text property group name.

3 Next to the Text property name, click the Animate pop-up menu and choose Skew. A property group named Animator 2 appears in the layer's Text properties.

4 Select Animator 2, press Enter (Windows) or Return (Mac OS), and rename it **Skew Animator**. Then, press Enter or Return again to accept the new name.

Now, you're ready to define the range of letters that you want to skew.

5 Expand the Skew Animator's Range Selector 1 properties. Each animator group includes a default range selector. Range selectors constrain the animation to particular letters in the text layer. You can add additional selectors to an animator group, or apply multiple animator properties to the same range selector.

6 While watching the Composition panel, drag the Skew Animator's Range Selector 1 Start value up (to the right) until the left selector indicator (▶) is just before the first letter of your middle name (the letter *B* in *Bender*, in this example).

7 Drag the Skew Animator's Range Selector 1 End value down (to the left) until its indicator (◀) is just after the last letter of your middle name (the *r* in *Bender*, in this example) in the Composition panel.

Now, any properties that you animate with the Skew Animator will only affect the middle name that you selected (*Bender*, here).

Skewing the range of text

Now, make that middle name shake and shimmy by setting Skew keyframes.

1 Drag the Skew Animator's Skew value left and right, and notice that only the middle name sways. The other names in the line of text remain steady.

2 Set the Skew Animator's Skew value to **0**.

3 Go to 8:05 and click the stopwatch icon (⏱) for Skew to add a keyframe to the property.

4 Go to 8:08 and set the Skew value to **50**. After Effects adds a keyframe.

5 Go to 8:15 and change the Skew value to **-50**. After Effects adds another keyframe.

6 Go to 8:20 and change the Skew value to **0** to set the final keyframe.

7 Click the Skew property name to select all of the Skew keyframes. Then, choose Animation > Keyframe Assistant > Easy Ease. This adds an Easy Ease to all keyframes.

8 Drag the current-time indicator across the time ruler from 7:10 to 8:20 to see how the director's name fades in and expands onscreen, and the middle name rocks side to side while the other names are unaffected.

9 Hide the properties for the Your Name Here layer in the Timeline panel.

10 Select the Pond_Title_Sequence tab to open its timeline.

11 Press End, and then **N**, to set the end bracket for the work area at the end of the composition.

12 Press Home to go to the beginning of the time ruler, and then play a RAM preview of the entire composition.

13 Press the spacebar to stop playback, and then choose File > Save to save your work.

▶ **Tip:** To quickly remove all text animators from a text layer, select the layer in the Timeline panel and choose Animation > Remove All Text Animators. To remove only one animator, select its name in the Timeline panel and press Delete.

Cleaning up the path animation

Currently, the words *directed by* fade in and out as they wind along the Pipes path preset. You'll modify the text properties so that the words are opaque for the entire animation and come to a rest just above your name.

1 With the directed by layer selected in the Timeline panel, press **U** to display the animated properties for the layer.

2 Click the stopwatch icon (⏱) for the Range Selector 1 Offset property to delete all of its keyframes.

3 Depending on where the current-time indicator is located in the time ruler, the resulting value for Range Selector 1 Offset may or may not be set to 0%. Set it to **0%** if it is not. Now, *directed by* will be visible throughout the composition.

Next, you'll modify the First Margin property to make the text stop animating above your name.

4 Select the last keyframe for the First Margin property in the Timeline panel and delete it. Because the middle keyframe (now the last keyframe) is set to Easy Ease, the words *directed by* come gently to rest above the lotus flower.

5 Go to 6:14 and change the First Margin value to **685**.

You also need to adjust the path shape so that it starts and ends off the screen.

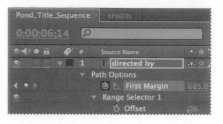

6 Using the Selection tool (⬉) in the Composition panel, Shift-drag the control point at the top of the S-shaped curve to the right and off the screen. Drag it far enough off that the dragonfly will not be visible.

7 Click the control point at the end of the S-shaped curve and Shift-drag the control point off to the left side of the screen, so that the dragonfly will not be visible.

 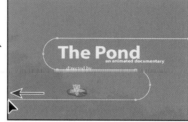

● **Note:** Depending on how far you move the beginning and ending control points of the path, you may need to change the First Margin value again to reposition the text.

8 Preview the animation from about 5:00 to 6:20 to see the corrected path.

9 If the text does not stop directly above the lotus flower, adjust the final keyframe for the First Margin value again.

10 Hide the properties for the directed by layer in the Timeline panel, and then choose File > Save.

Animating a nontext layer along a motion path

To cap off this project, you'll use a mask from a text layer to animate a nontext layer. Specifically, you'll use the mask shape for the *directed by* path to create a motion path for a dragonfly graphic so that it appears to be pulling the text. First, you'll import the dragonfly graphic and add it to your composition.

1 Double-click an empty area in the Project panel to open the Import File dialog box.

2 In the AECS4_CIB/Lessons/Lesson03/Assets folder, select the dragonfly.ai file, choose Composition – Cropped Layers from the Import As menu, and then click Open.

3 Drag the dragonfly composition from the Project panel to the top of the layer stack in the Pond_Title_Sequence Timeline panel.

Copying the mask shape

Now you're ready to copy the mask shape from the path of the directed by layer to the Dragonfly layer.

1 Go to 5:00.

2 Select the directed by layer in the Timeline panel and press **M** to display its Mask Path property.

3 Click the Mask Path property name to select it, and then choose Edit > Copy.

4 Select the dragonfly layer, and then press **P** to display its Position property.

5 Click the Position property name to select it, and then choose Edit > Paste.

After Effects copies the Position keyframes from the directed by layer to the dragonfly layer.

Orienting the object

Unfortunately, the dragonfly is flying backward, but that's easy to fix.

1 With the dragonfly layer selected in the Timeline panel, choose Layer > Transform > Auto-Orient.

2 In the Auto-Orientation dialog box, select Orient Along Path, and then click OK.

Now, the dragonfly is facing forward as it flies.

3 Select the dragonfly layer in the Timeline panel and press **P** to hide its Position property.

Coordinating the text and object timing

Next, you need to coordinate the timing of the dragonfly's motion with the words *directed by* so that the words correctly trail behind the dragonfly.

1 Select the directed by layer and press **U** to display its Path Options in the Timeline panel.

2 Go to 5:18 and change the First Margin value to **373**. After Effects adds a keyframe, and the text moves behind the dragonfly.

3 Go to 5:25 and change the First Margin value to **559**.

4 Go to 4:24 and drag the first First Margin keyframe to that position.

5 Manually preview the corrected path animation by dragging the current-time indicator across the time ruler from about 4:20 to 7:10. The words follow the dragonfly and come to rest above your name, while the dragonfly continues to fly along the path and off the screen.

6 Hide the properties for the directed by layer, and then press the Home key to go to the beginning of the time ruler.

Adding motion blur

Motion blur is the blur that occurs as an object moves. You'll apply motion blur to finesse the composition and make the movement look more natural.

1 In the Timeline panel, enable motion blur for all of the layers *except* the pondbackground and credits layers.

Now, apply motion blur to the layers in the credits composition.

2 Switch to the Credits Timeline panel and enable motion blur for both layers.

3 Switch back to the Pond_Title_Sequence Timeline panel and now select the Motion Blur switch for the credits layer. Then, click the Enable Motion Blur button () at the top of the Timeline panel so that you can see the motion blur in the Composition panel.

4 View a RAM preview of the entire, completed animation.

5 Choose File > Save.

Exporting to Adobe Flash CS4 Professional

If you're preparing a project for a web page, you may want to continue working with it in Adobe Flash CS4 Professional. You can export an After Effects composition as an XFL file for use in Flash. The XFL format retains the composition's layers and keyframe data for its Transform properties (Position, Opacity, Scale, and Rotation).

You'll export your project to XFL format so that you could work with it in Flash to integrate it with other animations or continue to polish it for the web.

1 Select the Pond_Title_Sequence composition in the Project panel.

2 Choose File > Export > Adobe Flash Professional (XFL).

3 In the Adobe Flash Professional (XFL) Settings dialog box, select Rasterize To, and then select FLV from the Format pop-up menu. Then, click OK.

With this setting, After Effects will render elements that it can't export natively as FLV components.

Note: If After Effects can't export an element of a composition as unrendered data, it either ignores the element or renders it into a PNG or FLV item, depending on whether you choose to ignore unsupported features.

4 In the Export As Adobe Flash Professional (XFL) dialog box, click Save.

After Effects exports the project. This process may take a while, depending on the size of the project. After Effects displays a progress bar as it exports the composition.

5 If you have Adobe Flash CS4 Professional installed, start it. Choose File > Open, and open the XFL file you just exported from After Effects.

Give yourself a pat on the back. You just completed some hard-core text animations. If you'd like to export the composition as a movie file, see Lesson 14, "Rendering and Outputting," for instructions.

Review questions

1   What are some similarities and differences between text layers and other types of layers in After Effects?

2   How can you preview a text animation preset?

3   How can you assign one layer's transformations to another layer?

4   What are text animator groups?

Review answers

1   In many ways, text layers are just like any other layer in After Effects. You can apply effects and expressions to text layers, animate them, designate them as 3D layers, and edit the 3D text while viewing it in multiple views. However, text layers are like shape layers in that you cannot open them in their own Layer panels, and that they are synthetic layers that consist entirely of vector graphics. You can animate the text in a text layer using special text animator properties and selectors.

2   You can preview text animation presets in Adobe Bridge by choosing Animation > Browse Presets. Adobe Bridge opens and displays the contents of the After Effects Presets folder. Navigate to folders containing categories of text animation presets, such as Blurs or Paths, and watch samples in the Preview panel. Then, double-click a preset to add it to the currently selected layer in the After Effects Timeline panel.

3   You can use parenting relationships in After Effects to assign one layer's transformations to another layer (except opacity transformations). When a layer is made a parent to another layer, the other layer is called the *child layer*. Creating a parenting relationship between layers synchronizes the changes in the parent layer with corresponding transformation values of the child layers.

4   Text animator groups enable you to animate the properties of individual characters in a text layer over time. Text animator groups contain one or more *selectors*. Selectors are like masks: they let you specify which characters or section of a text layer you want an animator property to affect. Using a selector, you can define a percentage of the text, specific characters in the text, or a specific range of text.

4 WORKING WITH SHAPE LAYERS

Lesson overview

In this lesson, you'll learn to do the following:

- Create custom shapes.

- Customize a shape's fill and stroke.

- Use path operations to transform shapes.

- Animate shapes.

- Repeat shapes.

- Explore design options with the Brainstorm feature.

- Add a Cartoon effect to a video layer for a distinctive look.

- Use Adobe After Effects in a DVD interface workflow.

Shape layers are created automatically when you draw a shape with any of the drawing tools. You can customize and transform an individual shape or its entire layer to create interesting results. In this lesson, you will use shape layers to build a dynamic background for the introduction of a reality series called *DJ Quad Master*. You'll also use the new Cartoon effect to change the overall look of the video. This effect performs best with video cards that support OpenGL. You may choose to skip the Cartoon effect exercise; if you do, you'll be able to finish the project, but it will not match the sample movie. This lesson will take approximately an hour to complete.

Shape layers make it easy to create expressive backgrounds and intriguing results. You can animate shapes, apply animation presets, and add Repeaters to intensify their impact.

Getting started

First, you'll preview the final movie and set up the project.

1   Make sure the following files are in the AECS4_CIB/Lessons/Lesson04 folder on your hard disk, or copy them from the *Adobe After Effects CS4 Classroom in a Book* DVD now:

   • In the Assets folder: DJ.mov, gc_adobe_dj.mp3

   • In the Sample_Movie folder: Lesson04.mov

2   Open and play the Lesson04.mov sample movie to see what you will create in this lesson. When you are done, quit QuickTime Player. You may delete this sample movie from your hard disk if you have limited storage space.

As you start After Effects, restore the default application settings. See "Restoring default preferences" on page 3.

3   Press Ctrl+Alt+Shift (Windows) or Command+Option+Shift (Mac OS) while starting After Effects. When asked whether you want to delete your preferences file, click OK.

4   Click Close to close the Welcome window.

After Effects opens to display a blank, untitled project.

5   Choose File > Save As, and then navigate to the AECS4_CIB/Lessons/Lesson04/ Finished_Project folder.

6   Name the project **Lesson04_Finished.aep**, and then click Save.

Creating the composition

Next, you'll import the files you need and create the composition.

1   Double-click an empty area of the Project panel to open the Import File dialog box.

2   Navigate to the AECS4_CIB/Lessons/Lesson04/Assets folder on your hard disk, Shift-click to select the DJ.mov and gc_adobe_dj.mp3 files, and then click Open.

3   Choose File > New > New Folder to create a new folder in the Project panel.

4   Name the folder **Assets**, press Enter or Return to accept the name, and then drag the footage items you imported into the Assets folder.

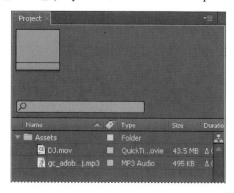

5 Press Ctrl+N (Windows) or Command+N (Mac OS) to create a new composition.

6 In the Composition Settings dialog box, name the composition **Shapes background**, make sure the NTSC DV preset is selected, and set the Duration to **10:00**. Then, click OK.

▶ **Tip:** To specify 10 seconds, type **10.** in the Duration box. The period indicates that there are no units in that position. To specify 10 minutes, type **10..** in the box.

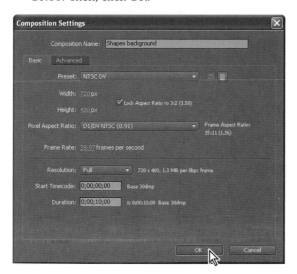

After Effects opens the new composition in the Timeline and Composition panels.

Adding a shape layer

One advantage of using a shape layer, rather than a solid layer, is that you can use the Fill option to create a linear or radial gradient. You'll use the Rectangle tool to create a gradient background for the composition.

About shapes

After Effects includes five shape tools: the Rectangle, Rounded Rectangle, Ellipse, Polygon, and Star tools. When you draw a shape directly in the Composition panel, After Effects adds a new shape layer to the composition. You can apply stroke and fill settings to a shape, modify its path, and apply animation presets. Shape attributes are all represented in the Timeline panel, and you can animate each setting over time.

The same drawing tools can create both shapes and masks. Masks are applied to layers to hide or reveal areas of an image, while shapes have their own layers. When you select a drawing tool, you can specify whether the tool draws a shape or a mask.

Drawing a shape

You'll begin by drawing the rectangle that will contain the gradient fill.

1 Select the Rectangle tool (■).

2 Choose 50% from the Magnification Ratio pop-up menu at the bottom of the Composition panel so that you can see the entire composition.

3 Click just outside the upper-left corner of the composition and drag the tool to the area just outside the bottom-right corner, so that a rectangle covers the entire composition. The shape appears in the Composition panel, and After Effects adds a shape layer named Shape Layer 1 to the Timeline panel.

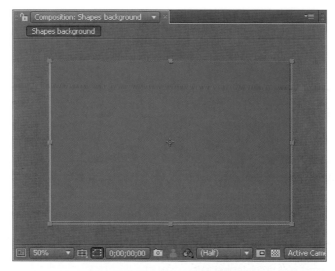

Applying a gradient fill

You can change the color of the shape by modifying its Fill settings in the Tools panel. Clicking the word *Fill* opens the Fill Options dialog box, where you can select the kind of fill, its blending mode, and its opacity. Clicking the Fill Color box opens the Adobe Color Picker if the fill is solid, or the Gradient Editor if the fill is a gradient.

1 Click the word *Fill* to open the Fill Options dialog box.

2 Select the Radial Gradient option (■), and click OK.

3 Click the Fill Color box (next to *Fill*) to open the Gradient Editor.

4 Select the white color stop, and select a light blue color. (We used RGB 100, 185, 240.)

5 Select the black color stop, and select a dark blue color. (We used RGB 10, 25, 150.)

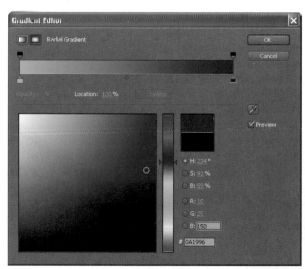

6 Click OK to apply the new gradient colors.

Modifying gradient settings

The gradient is a little small, and it falls off quickly. You'll adjust the settings for the shape layer to expand the gradient.

1 In the Timeline panel, expand Shape Layer 1 > Contents > Rectangle 1 > Gradient Fill 1.

2 Change the Start Point to **0, 225**, and the End Point to **0, 740**.

Now the gradient originates at the bottom of the screen and falls off near the top and edges of the composition.

3 Hide the Shape Layer 1 properties.

4 Select the layer name (Shape Layer 1), press Enter or Return, and type **Background**. Press Enter or Return to accept the new layer name.

5 Click the Lock column (🔒) for the Background layer to lock it so that you don't accidentally select it.

Creating custom shapes

Though there are only five shape tools, you can modify the paths you draw to create a wide variety of shapes. The Polygon tool, in particular, gives you great flexibility. You'll use it to create rotating sun shapes in the background.

Drawing a polygon

By default, the Polygon tool draws a shape using the settings of the last shape drawn with that tool. However, by adjusting the points, position, rotation, outer radius, outer roundness, and other values, you can dramatically alter the initial shape. You'll modify a simple polygon to create a much more interesting shape.

1 Select the Polygon tool (●), which is hidden behind the Rectangle tool (■).

2 Drag a polygon shape in the Composition area.

3 In the Timeline panel, expand Shape Layer 1 > Polystar 1 > Polystar Path 1.

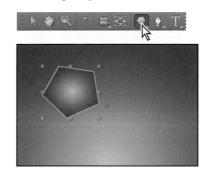

▶ **Tip:** While you're dragging the shape, you can press the spacebar to reposition the shape in the Composition panel

4 Change the Points to **6**, the Rotation to **0** degrees, and the Outer Radius to **150**.

5 Change the Outer Roundness to **-500%**.

▶ **Tip:** You can change settings to values below 0 and above 100% for more dramatic results.

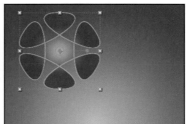

6 Hide the Polystar Path 1 properties.

7 Click the word *Fill* in the Tools panel to open the Fill Options dialog box. Select the Solid Color icon (■), and then click OK.

 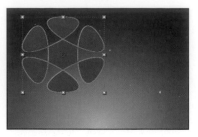

8 Click the Fill Color box, and select a bright yellow. (We used RGB 250, 250, 0.) Click OK.

9 Click the Stroke Color box and select a bright gray. (We used RGB 230, 230, 230.) Click OK.

10 Change the Stroke Width in the Tools panel to **5** pixels to emphasize the stroke.

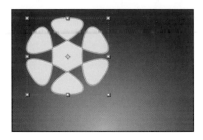

Twisting a shape

The Twist path operation rotates a path more sharply in the center than at the edges. Positive values twist clockwise; negative values twist counterclockwise. You'll use the Twist path operation to give the shape a little more definition.

1 In the Timeline panel, open the Add pop-up menu next to Contents in the Shape Layer 1 layer, and choose Twist.

2 Expand Twist 1.

3 Change the Angle to **160**.

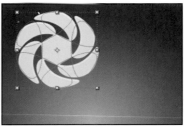

4 Hide the Polystar 1 properties.

5 Choose File > Save to save your work so far.

Repeating a shape

You've created the basic shape that you want to use in the background, but you need many more copies of it to fill the composition. You could duplicate the shape manually, but instead, you'll use the Repeater path operation to create multiple rows of the sun.

1 Select Shape Layer 1. You're selecting the layer because you want to add the Repeater to the entire shape group, not just an individual shape.

2 Open the Add pop-up menu, and then choose Repeater.

3 Expand Repeater 1.

4 Change the number of copies to **5**.

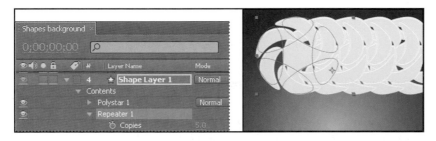

● **Note:** There are multiple Transform properties in the Timeline panel, applying to different path operators. Make sure you're selecting the appropriate Transform property for the object or layer you want to affect. In this case, you want to affect only the Repeater.

The Repeater creates four copies of the shape, overlapping each other. You'll separate them next.

5 Expand Transform: Repeater 1.

6 Change the Position to **345,0**. The first value represents the x axis. To move the shapes closer together, use a smaller value for the x axis; to move them farther apart, use a larger value.

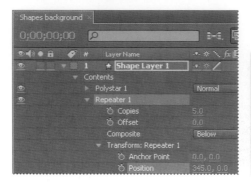 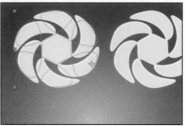

Now the shapes are farther apart. But you can't see them all at the same time. To move all of the shapes, you need to move the entire shape layer.

7 Hide the Transform: Repeater 1 properties.

8 Select Shape Layer 1, and then press **P** to display the Position property for the layer. Change the Position to **-50, 65**.

The shape layer is now in the upper-left corner of the composition. You'll scale the layer and then add more rows.

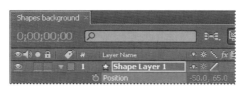

Note: Because the horizontal and vertical values are linked, both values change when you change one.

9 Select Shape Layer 1, and then press **S** to display the Scale property for the layer. Change the Scale to **50%**.

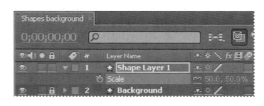 

10 Press **S** to hide the Scale property for the layer.

11 Expand Shape Layer 1 > Contents.

12 Select Shape Layer 1, and then choose Repeater from the Add pop-up menu.

13 Expand Repeater 2 > Transform: Repeater 2.

14 Change the Position to **0, 385** so that there is vertical space between the rows.

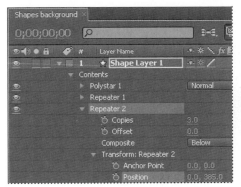 

15 Hide the Repeater 2 properties.

Rotating shapes

The suns should rotate on the background. You'll animate the Rotation property for the original shape, and the changes will automatically apply to the duplicated shapes.

1 In the Timeline panel, expand Shape Layer 1 > Contents > Polystar 1 > Transform: Polystar 1.

2 Press the Home key to make sure the current-time indicator is at the beginning of the timeline.

3 Click the stopwatch (🕑) next to the Rotation property to create an initial keyframe for the layer.

4 Press the End key to move the current-time indicator to the end of the timeline.

5 Change the Rotation to **3x+0** degrees. This setting causes the shape to rotate three times in 10 seconds.

6 Hide the properties for Shape Layer 1.

7 Drag the current-time indicator across the timeline to preview the rotation.

Blending shapes with the background

The rotating suns look good, but they contrast with the background too much. You want the character in the main video file to be the focus of attention. You'll change the blending mode and opacity for the shape layer to make the background more subtle.

1 Click Toggle Switches/Modes at the bottom of the Timeline panel.

2 Choose Overlay from the Mode pop-up menu for the Shape Layer 1 layer.

3 Select Shape Layer 1, and then press **T** to display the Opacity property for the layer.

Note: Instead of changing the opacity for the entire layer, you could change the opacity for the original shape. The value would apply to all the duplicates as well.

4 Change the Opacity to **25%**.

5 Press **T** to hide the Opacity property.

6 Select Shape Layer 1, press Enter or Return, and type **Suns** for the layer name. Press Enter or Return again to accept the new name.

7 Lock the layer to prevent accidental changes to it.

Creating stars

The Star tool is similar to the Polygon tool. A polygon is simply a star without an Inner Radius or Inner Roundness property; both tools create shapes called polystars. You'll use the Star tool to draw a star for the background, and then use the Pucker & Bloat operation to change the star's shape. Then, you'll duplicate the star and rotate the stars around the layer's anchor point.

Drawing a star

The Star tool is grouped with the other shape tools. To draw a star, drag the Star tool in the Composition panel.

1 Select the Star tool (⭐), which is hidden beneath the Polygon tool (⬤).

2 Change the fill and stroke settings for the shape before you draw the star:

- Click the Fill Color box and select a medium blue. (We used RGB 75, 120, 200.) Then, click OK.

- Click the word *Stroke*, and click None (◪) in the Stroke Options dialog box. Click OK.

3 Draw a star near the center of the composition. After Effects adds a shape layer named Shape Layer 1 to the Timeline panel.

4 In the Timeline panel, expand Shape Layer 1 > Polystar 1 > Polystar Path 1.

5 Change the Points to **6** and the Rotation to **150** degrees.

6 Change the Inner Radius to **50** and the Outer Radius to **90**. The radius values change the shape of the star.

Note: If you have trouble seeing the star in front of the background, you can temporarily hide the Suns and Background layers by clicking their visibility icons in the Timeline panel.

7 Expand the Transform: Polystar 1 properties.

8 Change the Position to **-180, -70**.

9 Collapse the Polystar 1 properties to hide them.

Applying Pucker & Bloat

After Effects includes a powerful path operation called Pucker & Bloat. You can pucker a shape by pulling the path's vertices outward while curving segments inward, or bloat a shape by pulling the vertices inward while curving segments outward. Negative values pucker a shape; positive values bloat it. You'll pucker the star to give it a distinctive look.

1 Select Shape Layer 1.

2 Choose Pucker & Bloat from the Add pop-up menu.

3 Expand Pucker & Bloat 1.

4 Change the Amount to **-125** to pucker the star.

This star shape will go well in the background. Now you can duplicate and animate it.

Duplicating shapes

You want to have multiple stars in slightly different sizes rotating around the screen. You'll use the Repeater path operation again, but this time you'll modify the Transform properties for the Repeater to get different results.

1 Select Shape Layer 1, and choose Repeater from the Add pop-up menu.

2 Expand Repeater 1, and change the number of copies to **6**.

Now there are six stars on the screen.

3 Expand Transform: Repeater 1.

4 Change the Position to **0, 0**, and change the Rotation to **230** degrees.

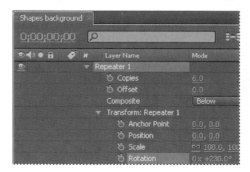 

Because you applied the rotation to the Repeater, rather than the shape, each star rotated around the layer's anchor point to a different degree. When you change the Transform properties for the Repeater, the change is multiplied by the number of copies created. For example, if there are 10 copies of a shape and you change the Rotation value to 10 degrees, the first shape retains the original value of 0, the second shape rotates 10 degrees, the third shape rotates 20 degrees, and so on. The same concept applies to each of the Transform properties.

In this project, the anchor point for the layer differs from the position of the shapes, so the chain of stars begins to wrap in on itself.

5 Change the End Opacity to **65%**. Each star is more transparent than the one before it.

6 Hide the Repeater 1 properties.

7 Select the Shape Layer 1 layer and choose Repeater from the Add pop-up menu again to add another Repeater.

8 Expand Repeater 2 > Transform: Repeater 2.

9 Change the Position to **-140, 0** and the Rotation to **40** degrees.

10 Change the Scale to **80%**.

Each duplicate star will be smaller than the one before it. Because there are three duplicates of the first group of stars, some will be 64% the size of the original.

11 Change the End Opacity to **0%**.

12 Collapse the Repeater 2 properties to hide them.

13 Choose File > Save.

Rotating shapes

You've rotated the stars around the anchor point for the layer. Now you want to animate each star to rotate around its own axis. To achieve this, you'll animate the Rotation property for the polystar shape itself, not the layer or the Repeater.

1 Expand Polystar 1 > Transform: Polystar 1.

2 Press the Home key to move the current-time indicator to the beginning of the timeline.

3 Click the stopwatch icon ( ) for the Rotation property to create an initial keyframe.

4 Press the End key to move to the end of the timeline.

5 Change the Rotation to **180** degrees.

6 Manually preview the composition by dragging the current-time indicator along the timeline. After you confirm that everything is rotating, collapse the layer.

7 Rename the Shape Layer 1 layer **Stars**, and press Enter or Return to accept the layer name.

8 Lock the Stars layer.

Incorporating video and audio layers

The background is in place. Now you can add the video of the DJ and the audio track that accompanies it.

Adding audio and video files

You imported files at the beginning of the lesson. Now you'll add them to the composition. The DJ.mov clip has no background and was rendered with a premultiplied alpha channel, so the underlying layers are visible. You'll learn about keying footage in Lesson 9, "Keying."

1 Press Home to move the current-time indicator to the beginning of the composition.

2 Open the Assets folder in the Project panel.

3 Drag the DJ.mov footage item to the Timeline panel, placing it above the other layers.

4 Drag the gc_adobe_dj.mp3 item from the Project panel to the Timeline panel, placing it beneath the other layers.

5 Lock the audio layer that you just added to the Timeline panel so that you can't accidentally select and move it later. Then, choose File > Save.

● **Note:** You can place an audio layer anywhere in the layer stack, but moving it to the bottom keeps it out of the way while you work.

Trimming the work area

The DJ.mov clip is only 5 seconds long, but the composition is 10 seconds. If you rendered this movie now, the DJ would disappear halfway through the movie. To fix the problem, you'll move the work area end point to the 5-second mark. Then, only the first 5 seconds will render.

1 Move the current-time indicator to the 5-second mark. You can drag the current-time indicator in the Timeline panel or click the Current Time box and then type **500** in the Go To Time dialog box.

2 Press **N** to move the work area end point to the current time.

● **Note:** Alternatively, if you do not want to keep the last five seconds of the composition, you can change the duration of the composition to 5 seconds. To do so, choose Composition > Composition Settings, and then type **5.00** in the Duration box.

Applying a Cartoon effect

After Effects includes a new Cartoon effect, which makes it easy to create a stylized look to your video, so that it looks more like a cartoon. Since this intro for the *DJ Quad Master* reality series is very different from other reality series, the Cartoon effect will work perfectly here.

The Cartoon effect performs best on systems with a video card that supports OpenGL. You can choose to skip this exercise and continue with "Adding a title bar."

1   Select the DJ.mov layer in the Timeline panel.

2   Choose Effect > Stylize > Cartoon.

The Cartoon effect performs three operations on a layer. First, it smooths the layer, removing a great deal of detail. Therefore, it works best on video footage rather than a graphic layer, such as the background in this project. Next, the Cartoon effect emphasizes the edges of shapes, based on their brightness values. Finally, it simplifies the color in the layer.

▶ **Tip:** For interesting results, try changing the Cartoon Render options from Fill & Edges to Fill (for a color-only effect) or Edges (for black-and-white line art).

The default settings do a pretty good job, but you'll fine-tune them in the Effect Controls panel.

3   In the Effect Controls panel, choose Fill from the Render pop-up menu.

For this project, you're only selecting Fill temporarily so that you can more easily see the results of the Fill settings as you make adjustments.

4   Change the Detail Radius amount to **20** and the Detail Threshold amount to **50**.

These settings control how much detail is removed and how it is smoothed. Higher values remove more detail.

5   In the Fill area, change the Shading Steps value to **10** and make sure the Shading Smoothness value is **70**.

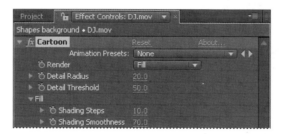

These settings determine how color is reduced and how gradients are preserved. In this project, changing these values reduces the number of colors in the DJ's shirt, creating a simpler design.

6   Choose Edges from the Render pop-up menu so you can focus on the edge controls. The layer becomes black and white temporarily.

7   In the Edge area, change the Threshold to **1.25**, and change the Width to **1**.

These settings reduce the number of black lines on the subject.

8 Leave the Softness value at its current setting, but lower the Opacity to **60%** to make the lines more subtle.

9 Choose Fill & Edges from the Render pop-up menu to restore the color.

10 Expand Advanced to see the advanced controls, which give you precise control over the edges.

11 Change the Edge Enhancement value to **50** to sharpen the edges of the layer.

12 Change the Edge Black Level to **2** to fill in more areas of the image with solid black. This makes the image even more cartoonish.

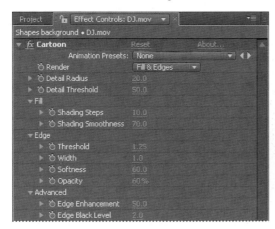 

13 Lock the DJ.mov layer to ensure you don't accidentally make changes to it as you continue the project.

Adding a title bar

You've created an exciting background and added the video of the DJ and the audio track. The only thing missing is the title to identify the program. You'll use the Rectangle tool and path operations to create a dynamic shape, and then you'll add the text.

Creating a self-animating shape

Wiggle Paths turns a standard rectangle into a series of jagged peaks and valleys. You'll use it to create a shape that looks like a soundwave. Because the operation is self-animating, you only need to change a few properties and the entire shape will move on its own.

1   Select the Rectangle tool (▤) hidden under the Star tool (★).

2   Click the Fill Color box and select a bright yellow. (We used RGB 255, 255, 130.) Click OK.

3   Click the word *Stroke*. In the Stroke Options dialog box, select Solid Color, and click OK.

4   Click the Stroke Color box and select a light gray. (We used RGB 200, 200, 200.) Click OK.

5   Change the Stroke Width to **10** pixels.

6   Draw a rectangle across the composition, near the bottom and approximately 50 pixels high.

7   In the Timeline panel, expand Rectangle 1 > Rectangle Path 1.

8   Unlink the Size values, and then change them to **680, 50**.

9   Expand Stroke 1, and then change the Stroke Opacity to **30%**.

10 Hide the Rectangle 1 properties.

11 Select Shape Layer 1, and choose Wiggle Paths from the Add pop-up menu.

12 Expand Wiggle Paths 1. Then change the Size to **150** and the Detail to **80**.

13 Select Smooth from the Points menu to make the path less jagged.

14 Change Wiggles/Second to **5** to speed up the movement.

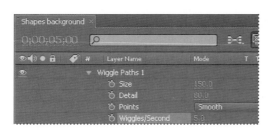 

15 Move the current-time indicator across the timeline to see the shape move. It's not exactly an audio waveform, but it's a stylistic version of one.

16 Hide all the properties for the layer.

17 Rename the layer **Lower Third**, and then lock the layer.

Adding text

All you need to do is add the title of the program. You'll use an animation preset to make the text stand out.

1 Press Home to move the current-time indicator to the beginning of the composition.

2 Select the Horizontal Type tool (T). In the Character panel, select a sans serif font, such as Arial Black, and specify a size of **60** pixels.

3 Click the Fill Color box in the Character panel, and select black (RGB 0, 0, 0). Then, click the Stroke Color box, and select white (RGB 255, 255, 255).

4 Change the Stroke Width to **2** pixels.

5 Click an insertion point in the Composition panel, and type **DJ Quad Master**.

6 Select the Selection tool, and then reposition the text over the waveform shape.

7 Select the text in the Composition panel, and choose Animation > Browse Presets. Adobe Bridge opens, displaying the animation presets that are available.

8 Navigate to the Text/3D Text folder, and then double-click the 3D Rotate In By Character thumbnail. After Effects applies the preset to the selected text.

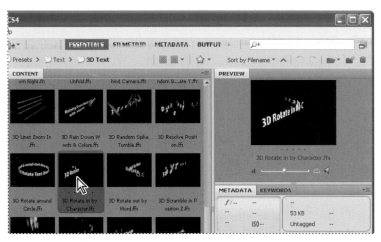

9 Make a RAM preview to see your movie! Press the spacebar to stop the preview.

● **Note:** With the Cartoon effect in place, the RAM preview may take longer than usual to render and begin playing.

Using Brainstorm to experiment

The Brainstorm feature makes it easy to try different settings for effects, and to quickly apply the one you like. To use the Brainstorm feature, select the layer or properties you want to include, and then click the Brainstorm icon. The Brainstorm dialog box displays multiple variations of your image, based on randomized settings. You can save one or more of the variants, apply one to a composition, or redo the Brainstorm operation.

The Brainstorm feature works especially well with animation presets. You'll use it to explore possibilities for the Suns layer you created for this project.

1 Save the project, and then choose File > Save As. Name the new copy of the project **Brainstorm**, and save it in the Lesson04/Finished_Project folder.

2 Unlock the Suns layer in the Timeline panel.

3 Click the Solo boxes (●) for the Suns and Background layers, so that you see only these two layers in the Composition panel.

You can isolate one or more layers for animating, previewing, or rendering by *soloing*. Soloing excludes all other layers of the same type from the Composition panel.

4 Expand the Suns layer, and then select Contents.

5 Click the Brainstorm icon (🔎) at the top of the Timeline panel to open the Brainstorm dialog box.

● **Note:** Selecting Contents selects all the properties for the layer, so that the Brainstorm feature includes them all in the operation. You can also use the Brainstorm feature to experiment with one or more specific properties.

6 Select the level of randomness Brainstorm should apply to the layer properties. The default value is 25%; for drastic changes, try **100%**.

7 Click the Brainstorm button. The feature randomizes the properties and displays variants. You can click the Brainstorm button multiple times; each time, it randomizes the settings by the percentage you've selected.

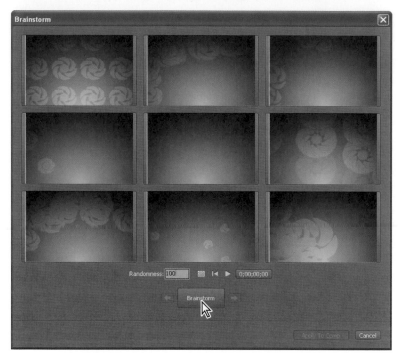

8 When you find a variation you like, move the pointer over the variant and then click the check mark icon to apply it to the composition.

Building a DVD menu

You can use After Effects to create buttons for a DVD menu you're designing in Adobe Encore. When you select a group of layers to create an Encore button, After Effects precomposes the layers and names the precomposition according to the standards Encore uses for naming buttons.

After Effects includes template projects with entire DVD menus for you to use as the basis of your own menus. To preview them in Adobe Bridge, choose File > Browse Project Templates in After Effects.

- To create a button, select the layers you want to include and choose Layer > Adobe Encore > Create Button. Name the button to match its function, such as Play Movie or Scene Selection. Then, use the menus to assign up to three highlight layers and one video thumbnail layer.

- To assign a layer to a subpicture, select the layer and choose Layer > Adobe Encore > Assign To Subpicture.

- To export the button, select the composition in the Project panel and choose Composition > Save Frame As > Photoshop Layers.

Review questions

1 What is a shape layer, and how do you create one?

2 How can you quickly create multiple copies of a shape?

3 What is the advantage of using the Brainstorm feature?

4 What does the Pucker & Bloat path operation do?

5 How does the Cartoon effect work?

Review answers

1 A shape layer is simply a layer that contains a vector graphic called a shape. To create a shape layer, draw a shape directly in the Composition panel using any of the drawing tools or the Pen tool.

2 To quickly duplicate a shape multiple times, apply a Repeater operation to the shape layer. The Repeater path operation creates copies of all paths, strokes, and fills included in the layer.

3 The Brainstorm feature creates variants of your composition based on randomized settings in the properties you selected. The feature makes it possible to explore numerous possibilities quickly and easily, and to save or apply them with a single click.

4 The Pucker & Bloat operation pulls the path's vertices outward while curving segments inward (puckering), or pulls the vertices inward while curving segments outward (bloating). Negative values pucker a shape; positive values bloat it.

5 The Cartoon effect stylizes a layer by removing some details and emphasizing others, and by simplifying color. You can change settings in the Effect Controls panel to fine-tune the effect's behavior.

5 ANIMATING A MULTIMEDIA PRESENTATION

Lesson overview

In this lesson, you'll learn how to do the following:

- Create a complex animation with multiple layers.

- Adjust the duration of a layer.

- Clip live motion video using a shape layer.

- Animate with Position, Scale, and Rotation keyframes.

- Animate a precomposed layer.

- Apply the Radio Waves effect to a solid layer.

- Add audio to a project.

- Loop an audio track using time remapping.

 In this lesson, you will work on a more complex animation project. Along the way, you'll learn to mix media, including motion video and Adobe Photoshop art; to work with audio; and to become more adept at using the Timeline panel to perform keyframe animations. The project in this lesson is an animated portfolio for a professional illustrator that can be delivered on a CD or on the web, and it is meant to be a useful, real-world self-promotion. This lesson will take 1½ to 2 hours to complete.

Illustration by Gordon Studer, www.gordonstuder.com

Adobe After Effects projects typically use a variety of imported footage, arranged in a composition, which is edited and animated using the Timeline panel. In this lesson, you'll become more familiar with animation fundamentals as you build a multimedia presentation.

Tip: If you don't see the Parent column, choose Columns > Parent from the Timeline panel menu.

2 In the Parent column for any one of the selected layers, choose 8.BG from the pop-up menu. This establishes the three selected layers as child layers to the parent layer, which is layer 8, named BG (the background).

Animating the parent layer

Now, you'll animate the position of the background layer—the parent layer—so that it moves horizontally. This, in turn, will animate the child layers in the same way.

1 Press the Home key to make sure the current-time indicator is at the beginning of the time ruler.

2 Select the BG layer in the Timeline panel and press **P** to reveal its Position property.

3 Set the BG layer's Position values to **1029, 120,** and click the stopwatch icon (●) to create a Position keyframe. This moves the background layer off to the left side of the scene, as if the camera had been moved.

Tip: A quick way to go to a frame is to press Alt+Shift+J (Windows) or Option+Shift+J (Mac OS) to open the Go To Time dialog box. Then, type the desired time without punctuation (as in **1015** for 10:15), and press Enter or Return.

4 Go to 10:15.

5 Set the BG layer's Position values to **-626, 120**. After Effects automatically creates a second keyframe and shows you the motion path of the animation in the Composition panel. The background now moves across the composition, and because the leaves, full skyline, and FG layers are child layers to the BG (parent) layer, they also move horizontally from the same starting position.

6 Select the BG layer and press **P** to hide its Position property and keep the Timeline panel neat.

Animating the bee's position

Another element of the composition that moves across the scene at the beginning of the animation is the bee. You will animate it next.

1 Press the Home key to go to 0:00.

2 Select the Bee layer in the Timeline panel and press **P** to reveal its Position property. (The bee is not visible at 0:00 in the Composition panel.)

3 Set the Position values of the Bee layer to **825, 120**, so that the bee is offscreen to the left at the beginning of the animation. Then, click the stopwatch icon (●) to create a Position keyframe.

4 Go to 1:00 and set the Bee layer's Position values to **1411, 120**, putting the bee offscreen to the right. After Effects adds a keyframe.

> ▶ **Tip:** You can also change the Bee layer's Position values by dragging the layer in the Composition panel, using the Selection tool, until the layer is in the correct position.

5 Select the Bee layer and press **P** to hide its Position property in the Timeline panel.

Trimming a layer

Because you don't want the bee to appear in the composition after 1:00, you need to *trim* the layer. Trimming (hiding) footage at the beginning or end of a layer lets you change which frames are first or last in the composition. The first frame to appear is called the *In point*, and the last frame is called the *Out point*. You can trim footage by changing the In and Out points in the Layer panel or the Timeline panel, depending on what you want to change. Here, you'll change the Out point of the Bee layer in the Timeline panel.

▶ **Tip:** You can also drag the right side of the layer duration bar to change the Out point.

- With the current-time indicator at 1:00 and the Bee layer selected in the Timeline panel, press Alt+] (Windows) or Option+] (Mac OS) to set the Out point to the current time.

Applying motion blur

To finish the bee's animation, you'll apply motion blur for more realistic movement.

1 Click the Motion Blur switch (⬤) for the Bee layer to apply motion blur.

2 Click the Enable Motion Blur button (⬤) at the top of the Timeline panel to view the motion blur in the Composition panel.

Previewing the animation

A quick manual preview will show you how the elements in the scenery move.

1 Drag the current-time indicator from 0:00 to 10:15. The animation of the background, leaves, bee, foreground objects, and the objects in the skyline makes it appear as if a camera is panning across the scene.

2 After you preview, return the current-time indicator to 0:00 and then choose File > Save to save your work.

Adjusting an anchor point

The background is moving; now it's time to animate the artist in his red car so that he appears to drive across the composition. To begin that process, you must first move the anchor point of the layer that contains the red car, without moving the layer's relative position in the composition. The red car is on the Artist layer. To edit the anchor point of the Artist layer, you need to work on the Artist layer in the Layer panel.

1 Double-click the Artist layer in the Timeline panel to open it in the Layer panel.

2 At the bottom of the Layer panel, choose Anchor Point Path from the View menu. This view displays the layer's anchor point, which by default is at the center of the layer.

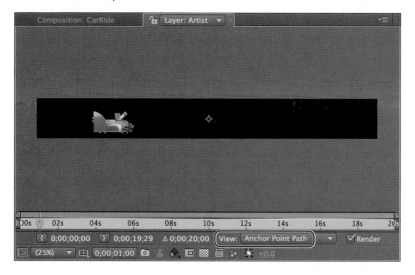

3 Select the Pan Behind tool (⌖) in the Tools panel (or press **Y** to activate it).

4 Choose Fit Up To 100% from the Magnification Ratio pop-up menu to see the entire layer, and then drag the anchor point to the lower-left corner of the car.

5 Click the Composition: CarRide tab to view the CarRide composition.

6 Select the Artist layer in the Timeline panel and press **P** to reveal its Position property.

7 Set the Position values for the Artist layer to **50, 207** so that the car is in the center of the frame, and then click the stopwatch icon () to set a Position keyframe. This is a temporary position that lets you see the car onscreen while you mask the driver into place, which is your next task. Then, you will animate the car so that it drives across the composition.

8 Select the Artist layer and press **P** to hide its Position property, and then choose File > Save to save your work.

Masking video using vector shapes

● **Note:** You'll learn much more about masking in Lesson 7.

With the car positioned onscreen, you can add the driver. You will use a custom animation preset to create a mask from a shape layer. This shape turns a frontal head shot into a side-view profile shape, which is a "Picasso-esque" signature style of the artist's work.

Creating a new composition

To help you manage the movement of this layer later, you will create a new composition, which you'll add to the main composition.

1 Drag the GordonsHead.mov clip from the Source folder in the Project panel onto the Create A New Composition button () at the bottom of the panel.

After Effects creates a new composition named GordonsHead based on the settings of the movie, and it opens the new composition in the Timeline and Composition panels.

Unfortunately, the GordonsHead movie has a different resolution than the CarRide composition. You need to fix that now.

2 Select the GordonsHead composition in the Project panel, and choose Composition > Composition Settings.

3 In the Composition Settings dialog box, change the Width to **360** pixels. If the Lock Aspect Ratio option is selected, After Effects automatically changes the Height to 240 pixels. Click OK.

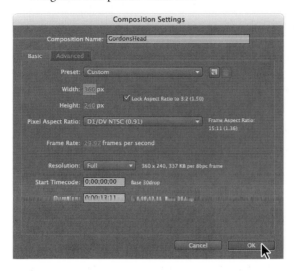

Now you'll scale the layer to fit the composition.

4 Select the GordonsHead layer in the Timeline panel, and choose Layer > Transform > Fit To Comp.

Using animation presets with shape layers

If you're the creative type, like Gordon Studer, you can create shape layers and save them as animation presets to apply to future projects. You'll apply an animation preset to a shape layer to change the appearance of Gordon's head.

1 Choose Layer > New > Shape Layer. After Effects adds a new shape layer to the composition.

2 Select Shape Layer 1 in the Timeline panel, and then choose Animation > Browse Presets. Adobe Bridge opens.

3 In Adobe Bridge, navigate to the AECS4_CIB/Lessons/Lesson05/Animation_ preset folder on your hard disk.

4 Double-click the HeadShape.ffx file to apply it to Shape Layer 1. You can close Adobe Bridge or leave it open to use later in this lesson.

Constraining a layer with an alpha matte

There are many ways to mask layers in After Effects. For example, you can use shape tools or the Pen tool to draw a mask. In this lesson, you'll use an alpha matte, which uses the alpha channel of a layer to mask another layer.

1 Click Toggle Switches/Modes at the bottom of the Timeline panel to view the Mode column.

2 In the TrkMat menu for the GordonsHead layer, choose Alpha Matte "Shape Layer 1."

The layer is now constrained by the shape layer.

Swapping a composition into a layer

Now that Gordon Studer's mug is constrained to the vector shape, you need to attach it to the car. You'll return to the main CarRide composition and swap the GordonsHead composition into the Head layer, which is currently a solid layer that serves as a placeholder.

1   Click the CarRide tab in the Timeline panel.

2   Select the head layer in the Timeline panel and then do one of the following:

  • Select the GordonsHead composition in the Project panel and press Ctrl+Alt+/ (Windows) or Command+Option+/ (Mac OS) .

  • Alt-drag (Windows) or Option-drag (Mac) the GordonsHead composition from the Project panel to the head layer in the Timeline panel.

3   Using the Selection tool (◥), drag the head layer in the Composition panel so that Gordon Studer is sitting properly in the car.

Now, use parenting again so that Gordon Studer's head will move with the car.

4 In the head layer in the Timeline panel, choose 2. Artist from the Parent menu.

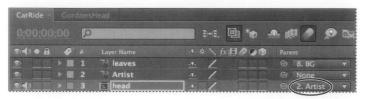

5 Choose File > Save to save your work.

Keyframing a motion path

Finally, you're ready to animate the car so that it drives onscreen at the beginning of the composition, scales larger during the middle of the composition—as if it's approaching the camera—and then pops a wheelie and drives offscreen. You'll start by keyframing the car's position to get it on the screen.

1 Press the Home key to make sure the current-time indicator is at the beginning of the time ruler.

2 Click the Video switch (👁) for the leaves layer in the Timeline panel to hide the layer so that you can clearly see the Artist layer below it.

3 Select the Artist layer in the Timeline panel and expand its Transform properties.

● **Note:** There's already a keyframe at this time from the anchor-point exercise.

4 Change its Position values to **-162, 207** to move the layer offscreen to the left (behind the leaves).

5 Go to 2:20 and change the Position values for the Artist layer to **54.5, 207**. After Effects adds a keyframe.

6 Go to 6:00 and click the Add/Remove Keyframe button (in the Switches column) for the Artist layer to add a Position keyframe for the Artist layer at the same values (54.5, 207).

When you animate the Position property, After Effects displays the movement as a motion path. You can create a motion path for the position of the layer or for the anchor point of a layer. A position motion path appears in the Composition panel; an anchor-point motion path appears in the Layer panel. The motion path appears as a sequence of dots in which each dot marks the position of the layer at each frame. A box in the path marks the position of a keyframe. The density of dots between the boxes in a motion path indicates the layer's relative speed. Dots close together indicate a slower speed; dots farther apart indicate a faster speed.

Keyframing scale and rotation transformations

The car is zooming onscreen; now, you'll make it appear as if the car is getting closer to the camera by scaling it larger. Then you'll make it pop a wheelie by keyframing the Rotation property.

1 Go to 7:15 and set the Scale values for the Artist layer to **80, 80%**. Then, click the stopwatch ( ) to set a Scale keyframe.

2 Go to 10:10 and set the Position values for the Artist layer to **28, 303**. After Effects adds a keyframe.

3 Still at 10:10, change the Scale values to **120, 120%**. After Effects adds a keyframe.

4 Still at 10:10, click the stopwatch icon (⏱) for the Rotation property to set a Rotation keyframe at the default value, 0.0˚.

5 Go to 10:13 and change the Rotation value to **0x -14.0˚**. After Effects adds a keyframe, and now the car pops a wheelie.

Now, you'll animate the car driving offscreen.

6 Go to 10:24 and set the Position values for the Artist layer to **369, 258**. After Effects adds a keyframe.

Adding motion blur

Finally, apply a motion blur to smooth out the driving sequence.

1   Hide the Artist layer properties in the Timeline panel.

2   Turn on the Motion Blur switch (⬤) for the Artist and head layers.

The blur will be visible as the car drives offscreen, and it will be visible for the flying bee as well, because you applied motion blur to that layer earlier in the lesson. You'll see all of this when you preview the composition.

Previewing your work

Now that the keyframes are set for the moving car, preview the entire clip and make sure that the driver is framed to create a pleasant composition.

1   Click the Video switch (👁) for the leaves layer to make it visible, and then click the RAM Preview button in the Preview panel to preview the animation.

2   Choose File > Save to save your work so far.

Animating additional elements

You'll get more practice creating keyframe animations as you animate the passing traffic and the buildings in the background.

Animating the passing traffic

Perhaps you noticed in the preview you just watched that the blue car is tailgating the artist in his red hot rod. The blue car is actually on a precomposed layer that also contains a yellow car. Next, you'll make the scene more dynamic by animating the blue and yellow cars so that they drive past the artist's car in the background.

● **Note:** Remember, a precomposition is simply a layer with nested layers in it. In this example, the vehicles layer contains one nested layer with a blue car and one nested layer with a yellow car.

1   Select the vehicles layer in the Timeline panel, and click the Solo switch (◉) to isolate it as you work. Then, press the **P** key to reveal the layer's Position property.

2   Go to 3:00.

3   Using the Selection tool (⬚), drag the vehicles layer in the Composition panel so that both cars are offscreen to the right. Press Shift after you start to drag to constrain the movement vertically. Or, simply set the vehicles layer's Position values to **684, 120**.

4 Click the stopwatch icon (⏱) to create a Position keyframe for the vehicles layer.

5 Go to 4:00, and drag the vehicles layer in the Composition panel so that both cars are offscreen to the left. Or, simply set the layer's Position values to **93, 120**. After Effects adds a keyframe.

6 Turn on motion blur for the vehicles layer.

7 Select the vehicles layer in the Timeline panel, and press **P** to hide its Position property.

8 Unsolo the vehicles layer, and then manually preview the passing traffic by dragging the current-time indicator from about 2:25 to 4:06.

Animating the buildings

Animated buildings? You bet. You'll animate a couple of buildings rising and "jumping" in the background as the artist cruises through downtown San Francisco. Once again, you'll be working with a precomposition (full skyline), but you'll open it to animate its nested layers individually.

1 Double-click the full skyline composition in the Project panel to open it in its own Timeline and Composition panels. Notice that this composition has three layers: skyline, building, and buildings. You'll start with the buildings layer.

2 Go to 5:10, select the buildings layer in the Timeline panel, and press **P** to reveal its Position property.

3 Click the stopwatch icon (🖉) to set a Position keyframe for the buildings layer at the default values (160, 120).

4 Go to 4:20 and in the Composition panel, use the Selection tool (➤) to drag the buildings layer down, off the bottom of the composition, until its y Position value is 350. Press Shift after you start to drag to constrain the horizontal axis. After Effects adds a keyframe.

▶ **Tip:** Dragging the layer into position is good practice, but you can also directly enter the y coordinates in steps 4 and 5 if you don't want to drag the layer in the Composition panel.

5 Go to 5:02 and drag the buildings layer up in the Composition panel until its y coordinate is 90. After Effects adds a keyframe.

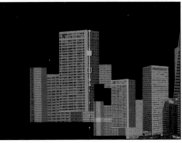

Great. You've got your first animated building. Next, you'll finesse the movement at the high point of the jump to make it more natural. (Naturally jumping buildings? Aw, come on. This is fun.)

Adding Easy Ease

Finesse the movement at the high point of the jump by adding Easy Ease.

1 Right-click (Windows) or Control-click (Mac OS) the keyframe at 5:02 and choose Keyframe Assistant > Easy Ease. This adjusts the speed of change as the motion approaches and retreats from the keyframe.

2 Drag the current-time indicator from 4:20 to 5:10 to preview the jumping building.

Copying the building animation

To animate the other layers in the full skyline composition, you'll copy and paste the buildings layer's keyframes to those other layers—but at different times—so that the elements jump in sequence.

1 Click the Position property name for the buildings layer to select all of the property's keyframes, and then choose Edit > Copy or press Ctrl+C (Windows) or Command+C (Mac OS).

2 Go to 5:00 and select the building layer in the Timeline panel. Choose Edit > Paste or press Ctrl+V (Windows) or Command+V (Mac OS) to paste the keyframes to this layer. (You won't see the pasted keyframes if the Position property isn't visible.)

3 Go to 5:10 and select the skyline layer. Choose Edit > Paste or press Ctrl+V (Windows) or Command+V (Mac OS) again to paste the keyframes to this layer, too.

4 Select the building layer name and press the **P** key to see the copied keyframes. Do the same for the skyline layer.

5 Apply motion blur to all three layers, and then switch to the CarRide Timeline panel and turn on motion blur for the full skyline precomposed layer. This applies motion blur to all of the nested layers.

You've done a lot of work. Take a look at the animation from the beginning.

6 Watch a RAM preview.

7 Choose File > Save to save your work.

Applying an effect

You've created several keyframed animations in this project. You'll switch gears now and apply an effect in this next exercise. The effect will animate some radio waves emitting from the Transamerica Pyramid building.

Adding a solid-color layer

You need to apply the radio wave effect on its own layer, which will be a solid-color layer.

About solid-color layers

You can create solid images of any color or size (up to 30,000 x 30,000 pixels) in After Effects. After Effects treats solids as it does any other footage item: You can modify the mask, transform properties, and apply effects to a solid layer. If you change settings for a solid that is used by more than one layer, you can apply the changes to all layers that use the solid or to only the single occurrence of the solid. Use solid layers to color a background or to create simple graphic images.

1 Make sure the CarRide Timeline panel is open.

2 Choose Layer > New > Solid. In the Solid Settings dialog box, name the layer **radio waves**, and then click the Make Comp Size button. Then click OK to create the layer.

3 Drag the radio waves layer in the Timeline panel so that it sits directly above the BG layer.

By default, the radio waves layer lasts the duration of the composition. However, it needs to be only a few seconds long, to last the length of the effect. So you'll change the layer's duration.

4 Click the Expand Or Collapse The In/Out/Duration/Stretch Panes button (⇕) in the lower-left corner of the Timeline panel to view those four columns.

5 Click the orange Duration value for the radio waves layer.

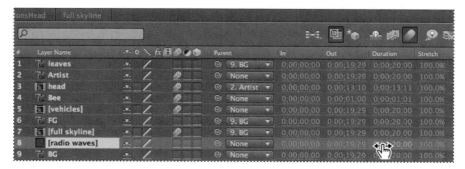

6 In the Time Stretch dialog box, set the New Duration to **8:00**. Then, click OK.

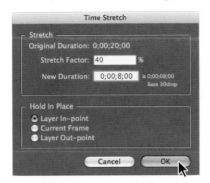

7 In the time ruler, drag the radio waves layer duration bar (from the center) so that it starts at 6:00. Watch the In value for the layer to see when it's at 6:00.

8 Go to 6:00, the first frame of the radio waves effect.

Applying the effect

Now, you're ready to apply the radio waves effect to the solid layer.

1 With the radio waves layer selected in the Timeline panel, choose Effect > Generate > Radio Waves. Nothing changes in the Composition panel, because the first wave hasn't emitted yet.

2 In the Effect Controls panel, expand the Wave Motion and Stroke properties, if they aren't already visible. Then, do the following:

- Choose Each Frame from the Parameters Are Set At menu.

- Set the Expansion to **0.40**.

- Set the Velocity to **1.00**.

- Set the Color to white (RGB **255**, **255**, **255**).

- Set the Opacity to **0.50**.

- Set both the Start Width and End Width to **3.00**.

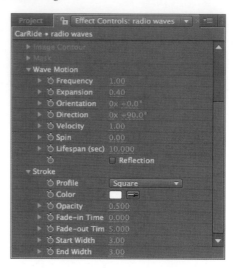

3 Still in the Effect Controls panel, click the cross-hair button for the Producer Point setting near the top of the panel. Then, in the Composition panel, click to set the producer point at the top of the pyramid.

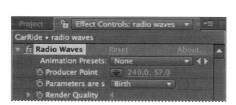

Radio waves with the settings you specified will now emit from the top of the pyramid building. You just need to parent the radio waves layer to the full skyline layer so that the waves travel with the building across the composition.

4 In the Parent column of the radio waves layer, choose 7. full skyline from the pop-up menu.

5 Go to 5:28, just before the Radio Waves effect begins, and in the Preview panel, select From Current Time. (You may need to expand the Preview panel to see all the options.)

6 Click the RAM Preview button (▶) to view a RAM preview from the point that the Radio Waves effect begins.

After watching the preview, tidy up the Timeline panel.

7 Click the Expand Or Collapse The In/Out/Duration/Stretch Panes button (⏸) to hide those columns, and then press the Home key to go to the beginning of the time ruler.

8 Choose File > Save to save your work.

Creating an animated slide show

Now that you've completed this complex animation of the artist driving through a stylized cityscape, it's time to add samples of his work to the easel. The point, after all, is to show off the artist's work to potential new clients. However, this slide-show technique could easily be adapted to other uses, such as presenting family photos or making a business presentation.

Importing the slides

The artist has provided a folder of sample artwork, but you'll use only some of the images. To help you choose, use Adobe Bridge to preview them.

1 Choose File > Browse In Bridge to jump to Adobe Bridge.

2 In the Folders panel, navigate to the AECS4_CIB/Lessons/Lesson05/Assets folder on your hard disk.

3 Click the various "studer_" images and study them in the Preview panel.

4 Ctrl-click (Windows) or Command-click (Mac OS) to select your five favorite images, and then double-click to add them to the After Effects Project panel. We chose studer_Comcast.jpg, studer_Map.jpg, studer_music.jpg, studer_Puzzle.jpg, and studer_Real_Guys.jpg.

5 Leave Adobe Bridge open in the background.

Making a new composition

You'll put these images into their own composition, which will make it easier to turn them into a slide show, complete with transition effects between slides.

1 In After Effects, click the Project tab to view the Project panel.

2 Deselect all items in the Project panel. Then, Shift-click to select the five Studer images, and drag them onto the Create A New Composition button (🖻) at the bottom of the panel.

3 In the New Composition From Selection dialog box, do the following:

- In the Create area, select Single Composition.
- In the Options area, set the Still Duration to **2:00**.
- Select the Sequence Layers and Overlap options.
- Set the Duration to **0:10**.
- Choose Cross Dissolve Front And Back Layers from the Transition menu.
- Click OK.

The transition option creates a sequence of still images that dissolve from one to the next. When you click OK, After Effects opens the new composition, named for the Studer image at the top of the list in the Project panel, in the Composition and Timeline panels. Before continuing, you'll give the composition a more intuitive name.

4 Choose Composition > Composition Settings and rename the composition **Artwork**. Then, click OK.

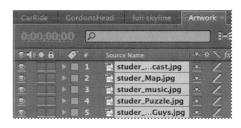
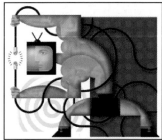

Positioning the slide show

Wasn't it easy to make the slide show? Now, you'll position the slide show on the canvas of the easel. The slides are actually larger than the canvas, but because they're in a composition, you can size them as a unit.

1 Switch to the CarRide Timeline panel and go to 11:00, which is when the canvas is centered in the composition.

2 Drag the Artwork composition from the Project panel into the CarRide Timeline panel, placing it at the top of the layer stack.

Currently, the Artwork layer is set to start at 0:00. You need to adjust the timing of the layer so that it appears at 11:00.

3 Drag the layer duration bar (from the center) for the Artwork layer in the time ruler so that its In point is at 11:00.

Now, you'll scale the slides to fit the canvas.

4 With the Artwork layer selected in the Timeline panel, press **S** to reveal its Scale property.

5 Set the Scale values to **45, 45%**.

6 Select the Artwork layer in the Timeline panel and choose Layer > Blending Mode > Darken. This drops out the pure white in each image and replaces it with the softer white of the canvas.

7 Click the RAM Preview button (▶) in the Preview panel to watch a RAM preview of the slide show. (Make sure From Current Time is selected to start the RAM preview at 11:00.)

Fading in the first slide

As it stands, the first slide instantly appears in the easel at 11:00. You'll animate the Artwork layer's opacity so that the first slide fades in.

1 Select the Artwork layer in the Timeline panel and press **T** to reveal its Opacity property.

2 Go to 11:00.

3 Set the Artwork layer's Opacity to **0%**, and click the stopwatch icon (⏱) to set an Opacity keyframe.

4 Go to 11:03 and set the Artwork layer's Opacity to **100%**. After Effects adds a keyframe. That should do the trick.

5 Manually preview the animation from 11:00 to 11:03 to see the first slide fade in.

  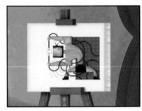

6 Select the Artwork layer in the Timeline panel and press **T** to hide its Opacity property. Then, choose File > Save to save your work.

Using SWF and FLV files in After Effects

Adobe Flash CS4 Professional and Adobe After Effects CS4 work well together. Each has unique tools to help you achieve different creative results.

Importing SWF files

If you've created animations in Flash, you can import them into After Effects as SWF files and then composite them with other video or render them as video with additional creative effects. SWF files are small files that are often used to deliver animated vector graphics (such as cartoons), audio, and other data types over the Internet. When After Effects imports a SWF file, it preserves the keyframes in the root timeline, so you can continue to use them for timing other effects.

Each SWF file imported into After Effects is flattened into a single continuously rasterized layer, with its alpha channel preserved. Continuous rasterization means that graphics stay sharp as they are scaled up. This import method lets you use the root layer or object of your SWF file as a smoothly rendered element in After Effects, bringing together the best capabilities of each tool.

Exporting XFL files

You can export an After Effects composition to an XFL file, which contains the composition's layers and keyframes from any Transform properties, so that you can continue working on the file in Flash. You exported a project to an XFL file in Lesson 3, "Animating Text."

Exporting FLV and F4V files

FLV and F4V files contain only pixel-based (rasterized) video, not vector graphics, and they aren't interactive. To play a movie in the FLV format, you must import the FLV file into Flash and publish it in an SWF file.

The FLV and F4V formats are container formats, each of which is associated with a set of video and audio formats. FLV files generally contain video data that is encoded using the On2 VP6 or Sorenson Spark codec and audio data encoded using an mp3 audio codec. F4V files generally contain video data that is encoded using an H.264 video codec and the AAC audio codec.

After Effects markers can be included as cue points in an output FLV file. To transfer keyframes or global property values into Flash from After Effects, run the Convert Selected Properties To Markers.jsx script before rendering and exporting an FLV file.

To learn more about using Flash and After Effects together, see After Effects Help.

Adding an audio track

Give yourself a hand. You've done a lot of animating in this project. But you're not quite done. Gordon Studer speaks to the viewer while he drives the car across the composition, but you'll add some polish by dropping in a background audio track.

1 Choose File > Browse In Bridge to jump to Adobe Bridge.

2 In the Content panel, select the piano.wav thumbnail preview. Adobe Bridge lets you preview audio.

3 If the file doesn't automatically play when you select it, click the Play button (▶) in the Preview panel to hear the track. Click the Pause button (❚❚) or press the spacebar to stop.

4 Double-click the piano.wav file to import it into the After Effects Project panel.

5 Drag the piano.wav item from the Project panel into the CarRide Timeline panel, placing it at the bottom of the layer stack.

Supported audio file formats

You can import any of the following types of audio files into After Effects:

- Adobe Sound Document (ASND; multi-track files imported as merged single track)
- Advanced Audio Coding (AAC, M4A)
- Audio Interchange File Format (AIF, AIFF)
- MP3 (MP3, MPEG, MPG, MPA, MPE)
- Video for Windows (AVI, WAV; requires QuickTime on Mac OS)
- Waveform (WAV)

Looping the audio track

The duration of the piano layer isn't as long as the composition, so you'll need to loop it. Luckily, this music track has been composed to loop cleanly. You're going to loop the audio clip using the time remapping feature. You'll learn to use time remapping in more depth in Lesson 6, "Animating Layers."

1   Select the piano.wav layer in the Timeline panel.

2   Choose Layer > Time > Enable Time Remapping. A Time Remap property appears for the layer in the Timeline panel, and two Time Remap keyframes appear for the layer in the time ruler.

3   Alt-click (Windows) or Option-click (Mac OS) the stopwatch icon (⏱) for the layer's Time Remap property. This sets the default expression for time remapping; it has no immediate effect in the Composition panel.

4   In the Expression: Time Remap property for thepPiano layer, click the Expression Language pop-up menu and choose Property > loopOut(type = "cycle", numKeyframes = 0).

The audio is now set to loop in a cycle, repeating the clip endlessly. All you need to do is extend the Out point of the layer to the end of the composition.

5   Select the piano layer in the Timeline panel and press the End key to go to the end of the time ruler. Then, press Alt+] (Windows) or Option+] (Mac OS) to extend the layer to the end of the composition.

You'll preview the entire composition soon.

6   Hide the piano layer's properties, and then choose File > Save to save your work.

Zooming in for a final close-up

Everything is looking good, but zooming in for a final close-up of the slide show will really focus the viewer's attention on the artwork.

1 In the Project panel, drag the CarRide composition onto the Create A New Composition button (■) at the bottom of the panel. After Effects creates a new composition, named CarRide 2, and opens it in the Timeline and Composition panels. You'll rename the composition to avoid confusion.

2 Select the CarRide 2 composition in the Project panel, press Enter or Return, and type **Lesson05**. Then, press Enter or Return again to accept the new name.

3 In the Lesson05 Timeline panel, go to 10:24, the first frame where the car clears the right side of the composition.

4 Select the CarRide layer in the Lesson05 Timeline panel and press **S** to reveal its Scale property.

5 Click the stopwatch icon (●) to set a Scale keyframe at the default values, 100, 100%.

6 Go to 11:00 and change the Scale values to **110, 110%**. After Effects adds a keyframe, and for the rest of the composition, the slide show will be prominent and eye-catching.

7 Select the CarRide layer and press **S** to hide its Scale property.

Previewing the entire composition

It's time to see how the whole thing comes together.

1 In the Preview panel, deselect From Current Time, and then click the RAM Preview button (▶) to watch a RAM preview of the entire composition.

2 Press the spacebar to stop playback when you're done.

3 Choose File > Save.

Sending the project to reviewers

If you're working for a client, collaborating on a larger project with colleagues, or simply want input from other video professionals, send the project out for review. The Clip Notes feature in After Effects CS4 lets you export the composition as a PDF file. Reviewers can open the file in Adobe Acrobat or Adobe Reader and add notes that are attached to specific points in the timeline.

Exporting the composition as a PDF file

You'll create a PDF file of the current composition for reviewers.

1 Select the CarRide composition in the Project panel, and then choose File > Export > Adobe Clip Notes.

▶ **Tip:** On the Clip Notes tab, you can customize the instructions that the reviewer receives, and you can add your e-mail address so the reviewer knows where to send comments. If you want comments uploaded to an ftp site, enter the site information on the Others tab.

2 In the Adobe Clip Notes dialog box, select Clip Notes: QuickTime from the Format menu and NTSC Source To 512kbps from the Preset menu. Select both Export Video and Export Audio.

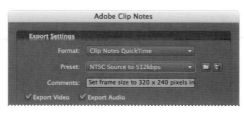

3 Click OK to close the Adobe Clip Notes dialog box. After Effects opens the Render Queue panel.

4 In the Render Queue panel, click the underlined filename next to Output To.

5 Navigate to the Lesson05/Finished_Project folder, and name the movie File_for_review.pdf. Click Save.

● **Note:** If you do not want to render the file now, you can continue working with the completed PDF file in the Lesson05/ End_Project_File folder.

6 Click Render. After Effects renders and exports the file. You can send the resulting PDF file to reviewers, who can open the PDF file, add notes, click Export, and send a small file (containing only the notes and the information about their location) to you.

7 Close the Render Queue panel.

Importing Clip Notes into After Effects projects

You can import the Clip Notes comments directly into your After Effects project. Imported comments appear as markers in the Timeline panel. If you double-click a marker, the Composition Marker dialog box opens to reveal the comments.

In this lesson, your client added some comments to this composition, and you'll import them here.

1 Open the Lesson05_Finished.aep project file in After Effects, if it isn't already open.

2 In the Project panel, select the CarRide composition, which is the composition you rendered the PDF file from.

3 Choose File > Import > Adobe Clip Notes Comments.

4 Navigate to the Lesson05/End_Project_File folder and select the Final_for_ review_data.xfdf file. Then, click Open.

5 Double-click comment markers in the Timeline panel to view the comments.

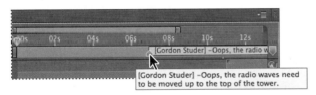

Congratulations. You've just created a complex animation, practicing all kinds of After Effects techniques and capabilities along the way, from parenting to audio looping to importing Clip Notes. Although you're not going to render it for final output right now, this project is used for Lesson 14, "Rendering and Outputting." You can skip to that lesson now if you'd like to learn how to output this project for a few different media, or you can proceed sequentially through the book and render it later.

Review questions

1 How does After Effects display an animation of the Position property?

2 What is a solid-color layer and what can you do with it?

3 What types of audio can you import into an After Effects project?

4 How can you send a composition out for review?

Review answers

1 When you animate the Position property, After Effects displays the movement as a motion path. You can create a motion path for the position of the layer or for the anchor point of a layer. A position motion path appears in the Composition panel; an anchor-point motion path appears in the Layer panel. The motion path appears as a sequence of dots, where each dot marks the position of the layer at each frame. A box in the path marks the position of a keyframe.

2 You can create solid images of any color or size (up to 30,000 x 30,000 pixels) in After Effects. After Effects treats solids as it does any other footage item: you can modify the mask, transform properties, and apply effects to the solid layer. If you change settings for a solid that is used by more than one layer, you can apply the changes to all layers that use the solid or to only the single occurrence of the solid. Use solid layers to color a background or create simple graphic images.

3 You can import any of the following types of audio files into After Effects: Adobe Sound Document (ASND; multi-track files imported as merged single track), Advanced Audio Coding (AAC, M4A), Audio Interchange File Format (AIF, AIFF), MP3 (MP3, MPEG, MPG, MPA, MPE), Video for Windows (AVI, WAV; requires QuickTime on Mac OS), and Waveform (WAV).

4 To send a composition out for review, render it and export it in Adobe Clip Notes format. Then, e-mail the resulting PDF file to reviewers, who can open it in Adobe Acrobat or Adobe Reader, make comments, and export the comments in a small file for you. When you receive the comments, import them into After Effects to view them.

6 ANIMATING LAYERS

Lesson overview

In this lesson, you'll learn how to do the following:

- Animate a layered Adobe Photoshop file.

- Duplicate an animation using the pick whip.

- Work with imported Photoshop layer styles.

- Apply a track matte to control the visibility of layers.

- Animate a layer using the Corner Pin effect.

- Apply the Lens Flare effect to a solid layer.

- Use time remapping and the Layer panel to dynamically retime footage.

- Edit Time Remap keyframes in the Graph Editor.

 Adobe After Effects provides several tools and effects that let you simulate motion video using a layered Photoshop file. In this lesson, you will import a layered Photoshop file of the sun appearing through a window, and then you will animate it to simulate the motion of the sun rising through the panes of glass. This is a stylized animation in which the motion is first accelerated, and then slows down as clouds and birds move through the window's frame at the end. This lesson will take approximately an hour to complete.

Animation is all about making changes over time—
changes to an object or image's position, opacity,
scale, and other properties. This lesson provides more
practice animating the layers of a Photoshop file,
including dynamically remapping time.

Getting started

First, you'll preview the final movie, and set up the project.

1 Make sure the following files are in the AECS4_CIB/Lessons/Lesson06 folder on your hard disk, or copy them from the *Adobe After Effects CS4 Classroom in a Book* DVD now.

    • In the Assets folder: clock.mov, sunrise.psd

    • In the Sample_Movies folder: Lesson06_regular.mov, Lesson06_retimed.mov

2 Open and play the Lesson06_regular.mov file to see the straightforward time-lapse animation you will create in this lesson.

3 Open and play the Lesson06_retimed.mov file to see the same animation after time has been remapped, which you will also do in this lesson.

4 When you're done, quit QuickTime Player. You may delete the sample movies from your hard disk if you have limited storage space.

When you begin the lesson, restore the default application settings for After Effects. See "Restoring default preferences" on page 3.

5 Press Ctrl+Alt+Shift (Windows) or Command+Option+Shift (Mac OS) while starting After Effects. When asked whether you want to delete your preferences file, click OK. Click Close to close the Welcome window.

After Effects opens to display an empty, untitled project.

6 Choose File > Save As.

7 In the Save As dialog box, navigate to the AECS4_CIB/Lessons/Lesson06/ Finished_Project folder.

8 Name the project **Lesson06_Finished.aep**, and then click Save.

Importing the footage

You need to import one source item for this lesson.

1 Double-click an empty area of the Project panel to open the Import File dialog box.

2 Navigate to the AECS4_CIB/Lessons/Lesson06/Assets folder on your hard disk and select the sunrise.psd file.

3 Choose Composition – Cropped Layers from the Import As menu, so the dimensions of each layer will match the layer's content.

4 Click Open.

5 In the Sunrise.psd dialog box, make sure Composition – Cropped Layers is selected in the Import Kind menu, and click OK.

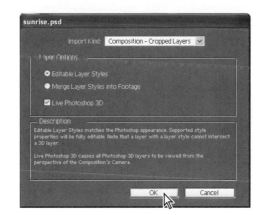

Before continuing, take a moment to study the layers of the file you just imported.

6 In the Project panel, expand the sunrise Layers folder to see the Photoshop layers. Resize the Name column to make it wider and easier to read, if necessary.

Each of the elements that you will animate in After Effects—the shadows, birds, clouds, and sun—is on a separate layer. In addition, there is one layer representing the initial, pre-dawn lighting conditions in the room (Background), and a second layer that represents the final, bright daylight conditions in the room (Background Lit). Similarly, there are two layers for the two lighting conditions outside the window: Window and Window Lit. The Window Pane layer includes a Photoshop layer style that simulates a pane of glass.

After Effects preserves the layer order, transparency data, and layer styles from the source Photoshop document. It also preserves other features, such as adjustment layers and type, which you don't happen to be using in this project.

Preparing layered Photoshop files

Before you import a layered Photoshop file, name its layers carefully to reduce preview and rendering time, and to avoid problems importing and updating the layers:

- Organize and name layers. If you change a layer name in a Photoshop file after you have imported it into After Effects, After Effects retains the link to the original layer. However, if you delete an imported layer, After Effects will be unable to find the original layer and will list it as missing in the Project panel.

- Make sure that each layer has a unique name to avoid confusion.

Creating the composition

For this lesson, you'll use the imported Photoshop file as the basis of the composition.

1 Double-click the sunrise composition in the Project panel to open it in the Composition panel and in the Timeline panel.

2 Choose Composition > Composition Settings.

3 In the Composition Settings dialog box, change the Duration to **10:00** to make the composition 10 seconds long, and then click OK.

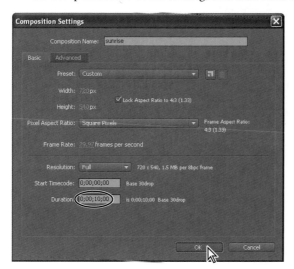

About Photoshop layer styles

Adobe Photoshop provides a variety of layer styles—such as shadows, glows, and bevels—that change the appearance of a layer. After Effects can preserve these layer styles when you import Photoshop layers. You can also apply layer styles in After Effects.

Though layer styles are referred to as effects in Photoshop, they behave more like blending modes in After Effects. Layer styles follow transformations in the standard render order, whereas effects precede transformations. Another difference is that each layer style blends directly with the underlying layers in the composition, whereas an effect is rendered on the layer to which it's applied, the result of which then interacts with the underlying layers as a whole.

The layer style properties are available for the layer in the Timeline panel.

To learn more about working with layer styles in After Effects, see After Effects Help.

Simulating lighting changes

The first part of the animation involves lightening the dark room. You'll use Opacity keyframes to animate the light.

1   In the Timeline panel, click the Solo switch (●) for both the Background Lit and Background layers. Soloing the layers isolates them to speed animating, previewing, and rendering.

Currently, the lit background is on top of the regular (darker) background, obscuring it and making the initial frame of the animation light. However, you want the animation to start dark, and then lighten. To accomplish this, you will make the Background Lit layer initially transparent, and have it "fade in" and appear to lighten the background over time.

2   Go to 5:00.

3   Select the Background Lit layer in the Timeline panel and press **T** to reveal its Opacity property.

4   Click the stopwatch icon (●) to set an Opacity keyframe. Note that the Opacity value is 100%.

5 Press the Home key to go to 0:00, and then set the Opacity for the Background Lit layer to **0%**. After Effects adds a keyframe. Now, when the animation begins, the Background Lit layer is transparent, which allows the dark Background layer to show through.

6 Click the Solo switches (●) for the Background Lit and Background layers to restore the view of the other layers, including Window and Window Lit. Make sure to leave the Opacity property for the Background Lit layer visible.

7 Expand the Window Pane layer's Transform properties. The Window Pane layer has a Photoshop layer style that creates a bevel on the window.

8 Go to 2:00 and click the stopwatch next to the Opacity property for the Window Pane layer to create a keyframe at the current value, 30%.

9 Press the Home key to go to the beginning of the time ruler, and change the Opacity property to **0%**.

10 Hide the Window Pane properties.

11 Click the Play/Pause button (▶) in the Preview panel, or press the spacebar to preview the animation. The interior of the room transitions gently from dimly to brightly lit.

12 Press the spacebar to stop playback at any time after 5:00.

13 Choose File > Save.

Duplicating an animation using the pick whip

Now, you need to lighten the view through the window. To do this, you'll use the pick whip to duplicate the animation you just created. You can use the pick whip to create expressions that link the values of one property or effect to another.

About expressions

When you want to create and link complex animations, such as multiple car wheels spinning, but want to avoid creating tens or hundreds of keyframes by hand, you can use expressions instead. With expressions, you can create relationships between layer properties and use one property's keyframes to dynamically animate another layer. For example, if you set rotation keyframes for a layer and then apply the Drop Shadow effect, you can use an expression to link the Rotation property's values with the Drop Shadow effect's Direction values; that way, the drop shadow changes accordingly as the layer rotates.

Expressions are based on the JavaScript language, but you do not need to know JavaScript to use them. You can create expressions by using simple examples and modifying them to suit your needs, or by chaining objects and methods together.

You work with expressions in the Timeline panel or the Effect Controls panel. You can use the pick whip to create expressions, or you can enter and edit expressions manually in the expression field, a text field in the time graph under the property.

For more about expressions, see After Effects Help.

1 Press the Home key to go to the beginning of the time ruler.

2 Select the Window Lit layer and press **T** to reveal its Opacity property.

3 Alt-click (Windows) or Option-click (Mac OS) the Opacity stopwatch for the Window Lit layer to add an expression for the default Opacity value, 100%. The words *transform.opacity* appear in the time ruler for the Window Lit layer.

4 With the transform.opacity expression selected in the time ruler, click the pick whip icon (🔘) on the Window Lit Expression: Opacity line and drag it to the Opacity property name in the Background Lit layer. When you release the mouse, the pick whip snaps, and the expression in the Window Lit layer time ruler now reads "thisComp.layer("Background Lit").transform.opacity." This means that the Opacity value for the Background Lit layer (0%) replaces the previous Opacity value (100%) for the Window Lit layer.

5 Drag the current-time indicator from 0:00 to 5:00. Notice that the Opacity values for the two layers match.

6 Press the Home key and then the spacebar to preview the animation again. Notice that the sky outside the window lightens as the room inside the window does.

7 Press the spacebar to stop playback.

8 Hide the Window Lit and Background Lit layers' properties to keep the Timeline panel tidy for your next task.

9 Choose File > Save to save your project.

Animating movement in the scenery

The scenery outside the window is unrealistically static. For one thing, the sun should actually rise. In addition, shifting clouds and flying birds would bring this scene to life.

Animating the sun

To make the sun rise in the sky, set keyframes for its Position, Scale, and Opacity properties.

1 In the Timeline panel, select the Sun layer and expand its Transform properties.

2 Go to 4:07 and click the stopwatch icons ( ) to set keyframes for the Position, Scale, and Opacity properties at their default values.

3 Go to 3:13.

4 Still working with the Sun layer, set its Scale to **33, 33%** and its Opacity to **10%**. After Effects adds a keyframe for each property.

5 Press the End key to go to the end of the composition.

6 For the Position property of the Sun layer, set the y value to **18**, and then set the Scale values to **150, 150%**. After Effects adds two keyframes.

You've just set keyframes that instruct the sun to move up and across the sky, and to become slightly larger and brighter as it rises.

7 Hide the Sun layer's properties.

Animating the birds

Next, you'll animate the motion of the birds flying by.

1 Select the Birds layer in the Timeline panel and press **P** to reveal its Position property.

2 Go to 4:20 and set the Position values for the Birds layer to **200, 49**. Then, click the stopwatch ( ) to add a Position keyframe.

3 Go to 4:25 and set the Position values of the Birds layer to **670, 49**. After Effects adds a keyframe.

4 Select the Birds layer and press **P** to hide its Position property.

Animating the clouds

Next, you'll animate the shifting and drifting of the clouds in the sky.

1 Select the Clouds layer in the Timeline panel and expand its Transform properties.

2 Go to 5:22 and click the stopwatch icon ( ) for the Position property to set a Position keyframe at the current value (406.5, 58.5).

3 Still at 5:22, set the Opacity for the Clouds layer to **33%**, and click the stopwatch icon to set an Opacity keyframe.

4 Go to 5:02 and set the Clouds layer Opacity value to **0%**. After Effects adds a keyframe.

5 Go to 9:07 and set the Clouds layer Opacity value to **50%**. After Effects adds a keyframe.

6 Press the End key to go to the last frame of the composition.

7 Set the Position of the Clouds layer to **456.5, 48.5**. After Effects adds a keyframe.

Previewing the animation

Now, see how it all comes together.

1 Press the Home key to go to 0:00.

2 Press F2 to deselect everything, and then press the spacebar to preview the animation. The sun rises in the sky, the birds fly by (very quickly), and the clouds drift. However, there's a fundamental problem: these elements all overlap the window frame—the birds even appear to be flying inside the room. You'll solve this next.

3 Press the spacebar to stop playback.

4 Hide the Clouds layer's properties, and then choose File > Save.

Adjusting the layers and creating a track matte

To solve the problem of the sun, birds, and clouds overlapping the window frame, you must first adjust the hierarchy of the layers within the composition, and then you will use an alpha track matte to allow the outside scenery to show through the window, but not appear to be inside the room.

Precomposing layers

You'll start by precomposing the Sun, Birds, and Clouds layers into one composition.

1 Shift-click to select the Sun, Birds, and Clouds layers in the Timeline panel.

2 Choose Layer > Pre-compose.

3 In the Pre-compose dialog box, name the new composition **Window Contents**. Make sure the Move All Attributes Into The New Composition option is selected, and select Open New Composition. Then, click OK.

A new Timeline panel named Window Contents appears. It contains the Sun, Birds, and Clouds layers you selected in step 1 of this exercise. The Window Contents composition appears in the Composition window, as well.

4 Click the Sunrise Timeline panel to see the contents of the main composition. Notice that the Sun, Birds, and Clouds layers have been replaced by the Window Contents layer, which refers to the Window Contents composition.

Creating the track matte

Now, you will create the track matte to hide the outside scenery behind all areas of the image except the window pane. To do that, you'll duplicate the Window Lit layer and use its alpha channel.

About track mattes and traveling mattes

When you want one layer to show through a hole in another layer, set up a *track matte*. You'll need two layers—one to act as a matte, and another to fill the hole in the matte. You can animate either the track matte layer or the fill layer. When you animate the track matte layer, you create a *traveling matte*. If you want to animate the track matte and fill layers using identical settings, you can precompose them.

You define transparency in a track matte using values from either its alpha channel or the luminance of its pixels. Using luminance is useful when you want to create a track matte using a layer without an alpha channel, or a layer imported from a program that can't create an alpha channel. In both alpha-channel mattes and luminance mattes, pixels with higher values are more transparent. In most cases, you use a high-contrast matte so that areas are either completely transparent or completely opaque. Intermediate shades should appear only where you want partial or gradual transparency, such as along a soft edge.

After Effects preserves the order of a layer and its track matte after you duplicate or split the layer. Within the duplicated or split layers, the track matte layer remains on top of the fill layer. For example, if your project contains Layers A and B, where A is the track matte and B the fill layer, duplicating or splitting both of these layers results in the layer order ABAB.

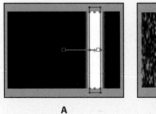 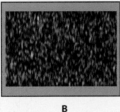 

A   B   C

Traveling matte
A. *Track matte layer: a solid with a rectangular mask, set to Luma Matte. The mask is animated to travel across the screen.*
B. *Fill layer: a solid with a pattern effect.*
C. *Result: The pattern is seen in the track matte's shape and added to the image layer, which is below the track matte layer.*

1 In the Sunrise Timeline panel, select the Window Lit layer.

2 Choose Edit > Duplicate.

3 Drag the duplicate layer, Window Lit 2, up in the layer stack so that it's above the Window Contents layer.

4 Click Toggle Switches/Modes in the Timeline panel to display the TrkMat column so you can apply the track matte.

5 Select the Window Contents layer and choose Alpha Matte "Window Lit 2" from the TrkMat pop-up menu. The alpha channel of the layer above (Window Lit 2) is used to set transparency for the Window Contents layer, so that the scenery outside the window shows through the transparent areas of the window pane.

6 Press the Home key and then press the spacebar to preview the animation. Press the spacebar again when you're done.

7 Choose File > Save to save your project.

Adding motion blur

The birds will look more authentic if they include motion blur. You'll add the motion blur and then set the shutter angle and phase, which control the intensity of the blur.

1 Switch to the Window Contents Timeline panel.

2 Go to 4:22—the middle of the birds animation. Then, select the Birds layer, and choose Layer > Switches > Motion Blur to turn on the motion blur for the Birds layer.

3 Click the Enable Motion Blur button (⬤) at the top of the Timeline panel to display the motion blur for the Birds layer in the Composition panel.

4 Choose Composition > Composition Settings.

5 In the Composition Settings dialog box, click the Advanced tab and reduce the Shutter Angle to **30˚**. This setting imitates the effect of adjusting a shutter angle on a real camera, which controls how long the camera aperture is open, gathering light. Larger values create more motion blur.

6 Change the Shutter Phase to **0˚**, and then click OK.

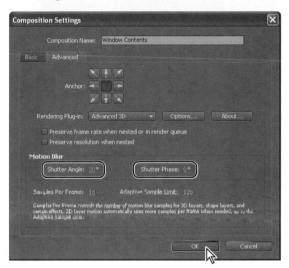

Animating the shadows

It's time to turn your attention to the shadows cast on the table by the clock and the vase. In a realistic time-lapse image, they would shorten as the sun rises.

There are a few ways to create and animate shadows in After Effects. For example, you could use 3D layers and lights. In this project, however, you will use the Corner Pin effect to distort the Shadows layer of the imported Photoshop image. Using the Corner Pin effect is like animating with the Photoshop Free Transform tool. The effect distorts an image by repositioning each of its four corners. You can use it to stretch, shrink, skew, or twist an image, or to simulate perspective or movement that pivots from the edge of a layer, such as a door opening.

1 Switch to the Sunrise Timeline panel and press the Home key to make sure you're at the beginning of the time ruler.

Note: If you don't see the controls, choose View Options from the Composition panel menu. In the View Options dialog box, select Handles and Effect Controls, and then click OK.

2 Select the Shadows layer in the Timeline panel and then choose Effect > Distort > Corner Pin. Small circles appear around the corner points of the Shadows layer in the Composition panel.

You'll start by setting the four corners of the Shadows layer to correspond to the four corners of the glass tabletop. Begin about midway into the animation, when the sun is high enough to start affecting the shadow.

▶ **Tip:** The lower-right corner of the Shadows layer is offscreen. To adjust that corner, switch to the Hand tool (🖑) and drag up in the Composition panel so that you can see some of the pasteboard below the image. Then, switch back to the Selection tool (🔖) and drag the lower-right corner-pin handle to the approximate location of the lower-right corner of the glass tabletop.

3 Go to 6:00 and then drag each of the four corner-pin handles to the respective corners of the glass table top. Notice that the x, y coordinates update in the Effect Controls panel.

If you have trouble getting the shadows to look right, you can enter the values manually, as shown in the figure below.

4 Set a keyframe for each corner at 6:00 by clicking the stopwatch icon (⏱) for each position in the Effect Controls panel.

5 Press the End key to go to the last frame of the composition.

6 Using the Selection tool (↖), drag the two lower corner-pin handles to shorten the shadows: drag them about 25% closer to the back edge of the tabletop. You may also need to move the two upper corners in slightly so that the bases of the shadows still align properly with the vase and clock. Your corner pin values should be similar to those in the following figure; you can enter the values directly if you prefer not to drag the corners. After Effects adds keyframes.

7 If necessary, select the Hand tool (✋) and drag the composition down to center it vertically in the Composition panel. Then, switch back to the Selection tool (↖) and deselect the layer.

8 Press the Home key to go to 0:00, and then press the spacebar to preview the entire animation, including the corner-pin effect. When you're done, press the spacebar again.

9 Choose File > Save to save your project.

Adding a lens flare effect

In photography, when bright light (such as sunlight) reflects off the lens of a camera, it causes a flare effect. Lens flares can be bright, colorful circles and halos, depending on the type of lens in the camera. After Effects offers a few lens flare effects. You'll add one now to enhance the realism of this time-lapse photography composition.

1 Go to 5:10, where the sun is shining brightly into the lens of the camera.

2 Choose Layer > New > Solid.

3 In the Solid Settings dialog box, name the layer **Lens Flare** and click the Make Comp Size button. Then, set the Color to black by clicking the swatch and setting the RGB values to 0 in the Color Picker dialog box. Click OK to close the Color Picker and return to the Solid Settings dialog box.

4 Click OK to create the Lens Flare layer.

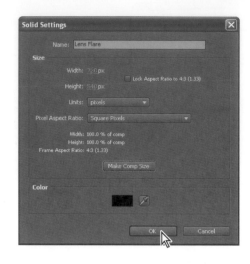

5 With the Lens Flare layer selected in the Sunrise Timeline panel, choose Effect > Generate > Lens Flare. The Composition panel and the Effect Controls panel display the visual and numeric default Lens Flare settings, respectively; you'll customize the effect for this composition.

▶ **Tip:** You can also enter the Flare Center values directly in the Effect Controls panel.

6 Drag the Flare Center cross-hair icon (⊕) in the Composition panel to the center of the sun. You cannot see the sun in the Composition panel; the x, y coordinates, which you can read in the Effect Controls or Info panel, are approximately 455, 135.

7 In the Effect Controls panel, change the Lens Type to 35mm Prime, a more diffuse flare effect.

8 Make sure you're still at 5:10. In the Effect Controls panel, click the stopwatch icon (⏱) for the Flare Brightness property to set a keyframe at the default value of 100%.

9 Now, adjust the brightness of the lens flare to peak when the sun is highest.

- Go to 3:27 and set the Flare Brightness value to **0%**.

- Go to 6:27 and set the Flare Brightness value to **0%**, also.

- Go to 6:00 and set the Flare Brightness to **100%**.

10 Finally, with the Lens Flare layer selected in the Timeline panel, choose Layer > Blending Mode > Screen to change the blending mode.

▶ **Tip:** You can also choose Screen from the Mode pop-up menu in the Timeline panel.

11 Press the Home key and then the spacebar to preview the Lens Flare effect. When you're done, press the spacebar again.

12 Choose File > Save to save your project.

Animating the clock

The animation now looks very much like a time-lapse photo—except the clock isn't working yet! The hands of the clock should be spinning quickly to show the progress of time. To show this, you will add an animation that was created specifically for this scene. The animation was created in After Effects as a set of 3D layers that are lit, textured, and masked to blend into the scene.

● **Note:** You'll learn more about 3D layers in Lessons 11 and 12.

1 Bring the Project panel forward. Close the sunrise Layers folder, and then double-click an empty area in the panel to open the Import File dialog box.

2 In the AECS4_CIB/Lessons/Lesson06/Assets folder, select the clock.mov file and click Open.

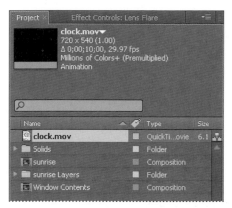

The QuickTime movie clock.mov appears at the top of the Project panel.

3 Click in the Sunrise Timeline panel to make it active and then press the Home key to go to the beginning of the time ruler. Then, drag the clock.mov footage item from the Project panel to the top of the layer stack in the Timeline panel.

4 Preview the animation by pressing the spacebar. Press the spacebar to stop playback when you're done.

5 Choose File > Save to save the project.

Rendering the animation

To prepare for the next task, retiming the composition, you need to render the sunrise composition and export it as a movie.

1 Select the sunrise composition in the Project panel and then choose Composition > Add to Render Queue.

The Render Queue panel opens.

2 Choose Maximize Frame from the Render Queue panel menu to make the panel larger.

3 Accept the default Render Settings in the Render Queue panel, and then click the orange, underlined words *Not Yet Specified* next to the Output To pop-up menu.

4 Navigate to the AECS4_CIB/Lessons/Lesson06/Assets folder and name the file **Lesson06_retime.avi** (Windows) or **Lesson06_retime.mov** (Mac OS). Then, click Save.

5 Expand the Output Module group, and then choose Import from the Post-Render Action menu. This will import the movie file when it's done.

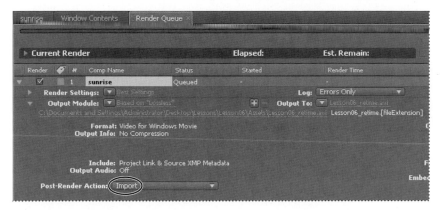

6 Hide the Output Module section.

7 Click the Render button in the Render Queue panel.

After Effects displays a progress bar as it renders and exports the composition, and it plays an audio alert when it is finished. It also imports the resulting movie file into the project.

8 When After Effects has finished rendering and exporting the composition, choose Restore Frame Size from the Render Queue panel menu, and then close the Render Queue panel.

Retiming the composition

So far, you have created a straightforward time-lapse simulation. That's fine, but After Effects offers more ways to play with time using the time-remapping feature. Time remapping lets you dynamically speed up, slow down, stop, or reverse footage. You can also use it to do things like create a freeze-frame result. The Graph Editor and the Layer panel are a big help when remapping time, as you'll see in the following exercise, when you retime the project so that the time-lapse speed changes dynamically.

For this exercise, you'll use the movie that you just imported as the basis of a new composition, which will be easier to remap.

1 Drag the Lesson06_retime movie onto the Create A New Composition button () at the bottom of the Project panel. After Effects creates a new composition named Lesson06_retime, and displays it in the Timeline and Composition panels. Now you can remap all of the elements of the project at once.

2 With the Lesson06_retime.mov layer selected in the Timeline panel, choose Layer > Time > Enable Time Remapping. After Effects adds two keyframes, at the first and last frames of the layer, visible in the time ruler. A Time Remap property also appears under the layer name in the Timeline panel; this property lets you control which frame is displayed at a given point in time.

3 Double-click the Lesson06_retime layer name in the Timeline panel to open it in the Layer panel. The Layer panel provides a visual reference of the frames you change when you remap time. It displays two time rulers: The time ruler at the bottom of the panel displays the current time. The Source Time ruler, just above the time ruler, has a remap-time marker that indicates which frame is playing at the current time.

4 Drag the current-time indicator across the time ruler in the Timeline panel, and notice that the source-time and current-time markers in the two Layer panel rulers are synchronized. That will change as you remap time.

5 Go to 4:00 and change the Time Remap value to **2:00**. This remaps time so that frame 2:00 plays at 4:00. In other words, the composition now plays back at half-speed for the first 4 seconds of the composition.

6 Press the spacebar to preview the animation. The composition now runs at half-speed until 4:00, and at a regular speed thereafter. Press the spacebar again when you have finished previewing the animation.

Viewing time remapping in the Graph Editor

Using the Graph Editor, you can view and manipulate all aspects of effects and animations, including effect property values, keyframes, and interpolation. The Graph Editor displays changes in effects and animations as a two-dimensional graph, with playback time represented horizontally (from left to right). In layer bar mode, in contrast, the time ruler represents only the horizontal time element, without showing a visual representation of changing values.

• Make sure the Time Remap property is selected for the Lesson06_retime layer in the Timeline panel, and then click the Graph Editor button (⊠) to display the Graph Editor.

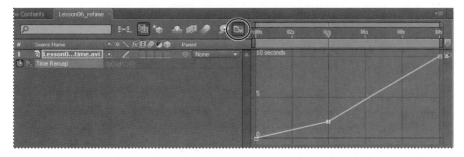

The Graph Editor displays a time-remap graph that shows a white line connecting the keyframes at 0:00, 4:00, and 10:00. The angle of the line is shallow up to 4:00, and then it becomes steeper. The steeper the line, the faster the playback time.

Using the Graph Editor to remap time

When remapping time, you can use the values in the time-remap graph to determine and control which frame of the movie plays at which point in time. Each Time Remap keyframe has a time value associated with it that corresponds to a specific frame in the layer; this value is represented vertically on the time-remap graph. When you enable time remapping for a layer, After Effects adds a Time Remap keyframe at the start and end points of the layer. These initial Time Remap keyframes have vertical time values equal to their horizontal position.

By setting additional Time Remap keyframes, you can create complex motion effects. Every time you add a Time Remap keyframe, you create another point at which you can change the playback speed or direction. As you move the keyframe up or down in the time-remap graph, you adjust which frame of the video is set to play at the current time.

Have some fun with the timing of this project.

▶ **Tip:** Watch the Info panel as you drag to help you pinpoint the exact value of the keyframe.

1 In the time-remap graph, drag the middle keyframe vertically from 2 up to 10 seconds.

2 Drag the last keyframe down to 0 seconds.

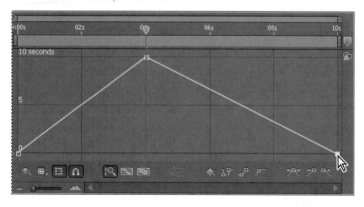

3 Press the Home key to go to 0:00 and then press the spacebar to preview the results. Watch the time ruler and Source Time ruler in the Layer panel to see which frames are playing at any given point in time. Now the animation progresses rapidly over the first 4 seconds of the composition and then plays in reverse for the rest of the composition.

4 Press the spacebar to stop the preview.

Having fun yet? Keep going.

5   Ctrl-click (Windows) or Command-click (Mac OS) the last keyframe to delete it. The composition is still in fast-forward mode for the first 4 seconds, but now it holds on a single frame (the last frame) for the rest of the composition.

6   Press the Home key and then the spacebar to preview the animation. Press the spacebar again when you're done.

7   Ctrl-click (Windows) or Command-click (Mac OS) the dotted line at 6:00 to add a keyframe at 6:00 with the same value as the keyframe at 4:00.

● **Note:** Pressing Ctrl or Command temporarily activates the Add Vertex tool.

8   Ctrl-click (Windows) or Command-click (Mac OS) at 10:00 to add another keyframe, and then drag it down to 0 seconds. Now the animation progresses rapidly, holds for two seconds on the last frame, and then runs in reverse.

9   Press the Home key and then the spacebar to preview the change. Press the spacebar again when you're done.

Adding an Easy Ease Out

Soften the shift in time that occurs at 6 seconds with an Easy Ease Out.

*   Click to select the keyframe at 6:00 and then click the Easy Ease Out button ( ) at the bottom of the Graph Editor. This slows the shift into reverse—the footage runs slowly in reverse at first, and then gradually speeds up.

▶ **Tip:** You can refine the amount of ease on this transition further by dragging the Bezier handle that appears out of the right side of the keyframe at 6:00. If you drag it to the right, the transition is softer; if you drag it down or to the left, the transition is more pronounced.

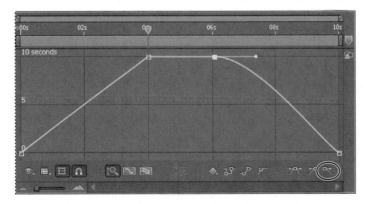

Scaling the animation in time

Finally, use the Graph Editor to scale the entire animation in time.

1   Click the Time Remap property name in the Timeline panel to select all of the Time Remap keyframes.

2   Make sure the Show Transform Box button ( ) at the bottom of the Graph Editor is on; a free transform selection box should be visible around all of the keyframes.

▶ **Tip:** If you press Ctrl (Windows) or Command (Mac OS) while you drag, the entire free transform box scales around the center point, which you can also drag to offset. If you press Alt (Windows) or Option (Mac OS) and drag one corner of the free transform box, the animation is skewed in that corner as you drag. You can also drag one of the right transform handles to the left to scale the entire animation so that it happens more quickly.

3 Drag one of the upper transform handles from 10 seconds to 5 seconds. The entire graph shifts, reducing the top keyframe values and slowing playback.

4 Press the Home key and then the spacebar to preview the change. Press the spacebar again when you're done.

5 Choose File > Save.

Congratulations. You've completed a complex animation, complete with shifts in time. You can render and export the time-remap project if you'd like. Follow the instructions in "Rendering the animation" in this lesson, or see Lesson 14, "Rendering and Outputting," for detailed instructions on rendering and exporting a composition.

Review questions

1 How does After Effects import Photoshop files?

2 What is the pick whip and how do you use it?

3 What is a track matte and how do you use it?

4 How do you remap time in After Effects?

Review answers

1 When you import a layered Photoshop file into After Effects as a composition, After Effects preserves the layer order, transparency data, and layer styles from the source Photoshop document. It also preserves other features, such as adjustment layers and type. When you import a layered Photoshop file as a single footage item, however, After Effects flattens and merges the Photoshop layers into one image.

2 The pick whip creates expressions that link the values of one property or effect to another layer. To use the pick whip, simply drag the pick whip icon from one property to another.

3 When you want one layer to show through a hole in another layer, you can use a track matte. To create a track matte, you need two layers: one to act as a matte, and another to fill the hole in the matte. You can animate either the track matte layer or the fill layer. When you animate the track matte layer, you create a traveling matte.

4 There are several ways to remap time in After Effects. Time remapping lets you dynamically speed up, slow down, stop, or reverse footage. When remapping time, you can use the values in the time-remap graph in the Graph Editor to determine and control which frame of the movie plays at which point in time. When you enable time remapping for a layer, After Effects adds a Time Remap keyframe at the start and end points of the layer. By setting additional Time Remap keyframes, you can create complex motion effects. Every time you add a Time Remap keyframe, you create another point at which you can change the playback speed or direction.

7 WORKING WITH MASKS

Lesson overview

In this lesson, you'll learn how to do the following:

- Create a mask using the Pen tool.

- Change a mask's mode.

- Edit a mask shape by controlling vertices and direction handles.

- Feather a mask edge.

- Replace the contents of a mask shape.

- Adjust the position of a layer in 3D space to blend it with the rest of the shot.

- Create a reflection effect.

- Create a vignette.

- Use Auto Levels to correct the color of the shot.

In this lesson, you will create a mask for the screen of a desktop computer and replace the screen's original content with a TV news promo. Then, you will adjust the positioning of the new footage so that it fits the perspective of the shot. Finally, you will polish the scene by adding a reflection, creating a vignette effect, and adjusting the color. This lesson will take approximately an hour to complete.

There will be times when you won't need (or want) everything in the shot to be included in the final composite. Use masks to control what appears.

About masks

A mask in Adobe After Effects is a path, or outline, that is used to modify layer effects and properties. The most common use of masks is to modify a layer's alpha channel. A mask consists of segments and vertices. Segments are the lines or curves that connect vertices. Vertices define where each segment of a path starts and ends.

A mask can be either an open or a closed path. An open path has a beginning point that is not the same as its end point; a straight line is an open path. A closed path is continuous and has no beginning or end, such as a circle. Closed-path masks can create transparent areas for a layer. Open paths cannot create transparent areas for a layer, but are useful as parameters for an effect. For example, you can generate a running light around a mask using the Vegas effect.

A mask belongs to a specific layer. Each layer can contain multiple masks.

You can draw masks in common geometric shapes—including polygons, ellipses, and stars—with the shape tools, or you can use the Pen tool to draw an arbitrary path.

Getting started

Begin by previewing the movie and setting up the project.

1 Make sure the following files are in the AECS4_CIB/Lessons/Lesson07 folder on your hard disk, or copy them from the *Adobe After Effects CS4 Classroom in a Book* DVD now.

  • In the Assets folder: news_promo.mov, office_mask.mov

  • In the Sample_Movie folder: Lesson07.mov

2 Open and play the Lesson07.mov sample movie to see what you will create in this lesson. When you are done, quit QuickTime Player. You may delete the sample movie from your hard disk if you have limited storage space.

When you begin the lesson, restore the default application settings for After Effects. See "Restoring default preferences" on page 3.

3 Press Ctrl+Alt+Shift (Windows) or Option+Command+Shift (Mac OS) while starting After Effects CS4 to restore default preferences settings. When asked whether you want to delete your preferences file, click OK. Click Close to close the Welcome window.

After Effects opens to display a new, untitled project.

4 Choose File > Save As, and navigate to the AECS4_CIB/Lessons/Lesson07/ Finished_Project folder.

5 Name the project **Lesson07_Finished.aep**, and then click Save.

Importing the footage

You need to import two footage items for this exercise.

1   Double-click an empty area of the Project panel to open the Import File dialog box.

2   Navigate to the AECS4_CIB/Lessons/Lesson07/Assets folder, Shift-click to select the news_promo.mov and office_mask.mov files, and then click Open.

3   In the Interpret Footage dialog box that appears, select Ignore, and then click OK. There is an alpha channel in the news_promo movie, but it isn't needed for this project.

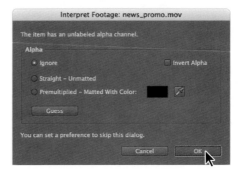

About the Interpret Footage dialog box

After Effects uses a set of internal rules to automatically interpret footage that you import. Generally, you don't need to change these settings. However, if your footage isn't standard, After Effects may interpret it incorrectly. In this case, you can use the settings in the Interpret Footage dialog box to reinterpret your footage. The settings in the Interpret Footage dialog box should match your source footage settings; don't use it to specify settings for your final rendered output.

When you choose Ignore, you instruct After Effects to disregard all transparency data in the file.

For more information on the settings in the Interpret Footage dialog box, see After Effects Help.

You'll start by organizing the files in the Project panel.

4   Choose File > New > New Folder to create a new folder in the Project panel, or click the Create A New Folder button (▬) at the bottom of the Project panel.

5   Type **mov_files** to name the folder, press Enter (Windows) or Return (Mac OS) to accept the name, and then drag the two movies into the mov_files folder.

6 Click the triangle to expand the folder so that you can see the footage items inside.

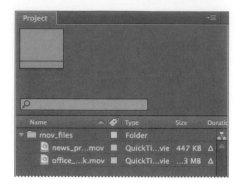

Creating the composition

Now, you'll create the composition based on the aspect ratio and duration of one of the footage items.

1 Select the office_mask.mov footage item in the Project panel and drag it to the Create A New Composition button (■) at the bottom of the panel.

After Effects creates a composition named office_mask and opens it in the Composition and Timeline panels.

2 Choose File > Save to save your work so far.

Creating a mask with the Pen tool

The computer screen currently contains a word-processing document. To replace it with the news promo, you need to mask the screen.

1 Press the Home key to make sure the current-time indicator is at the beginning of the time ruler.

2 Zoom into the Composition panel until the monitor screen nearly fills the view. You may need to use the Hand tool (🖐) to reposition the view in the panel.

3 Select the Pen tool (✒) in the Tools panel. The Pen tool creates straight lines or curved segments. The monitor appears to be square, so you'll try using straight lines first.

4 Click the upper-left corner of the monitor screen to place the first vertex.

5 Click the upper-right corner of the monitor to place the second vertex. After Effects connects the two points with a segment.

6 Click to place a third vertex in the lower-right corner of the monitor, and then click to place a fourth vertex in the lower-left corner of the monitor.

7 Move the Pen tool over the first vertex (in the upper left corner) When a circle appears next to the pointer (as in the middle image below), click to close the mask path.

Editing a mask

The mask looks pretty good, but instead of masking the information *inside* the monitor, the mask has removed everything *outside* the monitor. So you need to invert the mask. Alternatively, you could change the mask mode, which is set to Add by default.

About mask modes

Blending modes for masks (mask modes) control how masks within a layer interact with one another. By default, all masks are set to Add, which combines the transparency values of any masks that overlap on the same layer. You can apply one mode to each mask, but you cannot change a mask's mode over time.

The first mask you create interacts with the layer's alpha channel. If that channel doesn't define the entire image as opaque, then the mask interacts with the layer frame. Each additional mask that you create interacts with masks located above it in the Timeline panel. The results of mask modes vary depending on the modes set for the masks higher up in the Timeline panel. You can use mask modes only between masks in the same layer. Using mask modes, you can create complex mask shapes with multiple transparent areas. For example, you can set a mask mode that combines two masks and sets the opaque area to the areas where the two masks intersect.

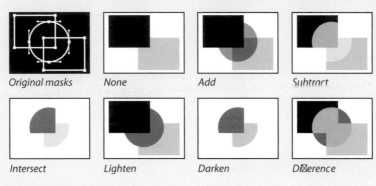

Original masks *None* *Add* *Subtract*

Intersect *Lighten* *Darken* *Difference*

Inverting the mask

For this project, you need everything inside the mask to be transparent and everything outside the mask to be opaque. You'll invert the mask now.

▶ **Tip:** Pressing the **M** key twice in quick succession displays all mask properties for the selected layer.

1   Select the office_mask layer in the Timeline panel, press the **M** key to see the Mask Path property for the mask.

There are two ways to invert this mask: by choosing Subtract from the Mask Mode pop-up menu, or by selecting the Inverted option.

2 Select the Inverted option for Mask 1.

The mask inverts.

3 Press F2 to deselect the office_mask layer.

If you look closely at the monitor, you will probably see portions of the screen still appearing around the edges of the mask.

These errors will certainly call attention to changes being made to the layer, and they need to be fixed. To fix them, you'll change the straight lines to curves.

Creating curved masks

Curved or freeform masks use Bezier curves to define the shape of the mask. Bezier curves give you the greatest control over the shape of the mask. With them, you can create straight lines with sharp angles, perfectly smooth curves, or a combination of the two.

1 In the Timeline panel, select Mask 1, the mask for the office_mask layer. Selecting Mask 1 makes the mask active and also selects all the vertices.

2 In the Tools panel, select the Convert Vertex tool (⊾), which is hidden behind the Pen tool.

▶ **Tip:** The keyboard shortcut for the Pen tool is **G**. Press the **G** key multiple times to cycle through the Pen tools.

3 In the Composition panel, click any of the vertices. The Convert Vertex tool changes the corner vertices to smooth points.

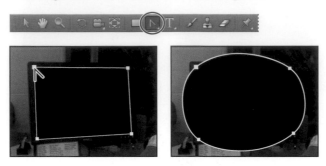

4 Switch to the Selection tool (▶) and click anywhere in the Composition panel to deselect the mask, and then click the first vertex that you created.

Two direction handles extend off the smooth point. The angle and length of these handles control the shape of the mask.

5 Drag the right handle of the first vertex around the screen. Notice how this changes this shape of the mask. Notice also that the closer you drag the handle to another vertex, the less the shape of the path is influenced by the direction handle of the first vertex, and the more it is influenced by the direction handle of the second vertex.

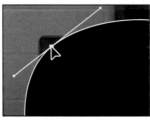

Click the vertex   Drag the handle

> **Tip:** Press Ctrl+Z (Windows) or Command+Z (Mac OS) to undo a change if you make a mistake. You can also change the zoom level and use the Hand tool to reposition the image in the Composition panel as you work.

6 Once you are comfortable moving the handles, position the handle of the upper-left vertex as in the preceding figure. As you have seen, you can create very fluid shapes.

Breaking direction handles

By default, the direction handles of any smooth point are connected to one another. As you drag one handle, the opposite handle moves as well. However, you can break this connection to get greater control over the shape of the mask, and you can create sharp points or long, smooth curves.

1 Select the Convert Vertex tool (⊾) in the Tools panel.

2 Drag the right direction handle of the upper-left vertex. The left direction handle remains stationary.

3 Adjust the right direction handle until the top segment of the mask shape more closely follows the curve of the monitor in that corner. It doesn't have to be perfect.

4 Drag the left direction handle of the same vertex until the left segment of the shape more closely follows the curve of the monitor in that corner.

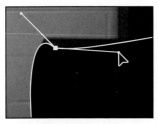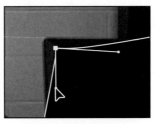

Drag the right direction handle of the upper-left vertex, and then
the left direction handle to follow the curve of the monitor.

5 Repeat steps 2–4 for the other three corner points of the mask until the shape of the mask more closely matches the curvature of the monitor.

6 When you're done, deselect the office_mask layer in the Timeline panel to check the edge of your mask. You should not see any of the monitor screen.

▶ **Tip:** Again, you may need to adjust your view in the Composition panel as you work. You can drag the image with the Hand tool. To temporarily switch to the Hand tool, press and hold the spacebar.

7 Choose File > Save to save your work.

Creating a Bezier mask

You used the Convert Vertex tool to change a corner vertex to a smooth point with Bezier handles, but you could create a Bezier mask in the first place. To do so, click in the Composition panel with the Pen tool where you want to place the first vertex. Then, click where you want to place the next vertex, and drag in the direction you want to create a curve. When you are satisfied with the curve, release the mouse button. Continue to add points until you've created the shape you want.
Close the mask by either clicking on the first vertex or double-clicking the last vertex. Then, switch to the Selection tool to refine the mask.

Feathering the edges of a mask

The mask looks good, but you need to soften the edges a bit.

1 Choose Composition > Background Color.

2 Click the color swatch and choose white for the background color (RGB **255, 255, 255**). Then click OK to close the Color Picker, and OK again to close the Background Color dialog box.

The white background allows you to see that the edge of the monitor screen looks a little too sharp and unrealistic. To address this, you'll feather, or soften, the edges.

3 Select the office mask layer in the Timeline panel and press the F key to display the Mask Feather property for the mask.

4 Increase the Mask Feather amount to **1.5, 1.5** pixels.

5 Hide the properties for the office_mask layer, and then choose File > Save to save your work.

Replacing the content of the mask

You are now ready to replace the background with the TV news promo movie and blend it with the overall shot.

1 In the Project panel, select the news_promo.mov file and drag it to the Timeline panel, placing it below the office_mask layer.

2 Choose Fit Up To 100% from the Magnification Ratio pop-up menu at the bottom of the Composition panel so that you can see the whole composition.

3 Using the Selection tool (↖), drag the news_promo layer in the Composition panel until the anchor point is centered in the monitor screen.

Repositioning and resizing the news clip

The news promo clip is too big for the monitor screen, so you'll resize it as a 3D layer, which will give you more control over its shape and size in this shot.

1 With the news_promo layer selected in the Timeline panel, turn on the 3D switch for the layer.

2 Press the **P** key to show the Position property for the news_promo layer.

The Position property for a 3D layer has three values: From left to right they represent the x, y, and z axes of the image. The z axis controls the depth of the layer. You can see these axes represented in the Composition panel.

● **Note:** You'll learn more about 3D layers in Lessons 11 and 12.

3 Position the pointer in the Composition panel over the red arrow so that a small *x* appears. The red arrow controls the x (horizontal) axis of the layer.

4 Drag left or right as necessary to center the clip horizontally in the monitor screen.

5 Position the pointer in the Composition panel over the green arrow so that a small *y* appears. Then, drag up and down as necessary to position the clip vertically in the monitor screen.

6 Position the pointer in the Composition panel over the blue cube where the red and green arrows meet so that a small *z* appears. Then, drag down and to the right to increase the depth of field.

▶ Tip: You can also enter the Position values directly in the Timeline panel instead of dragging in the Composition panel.

7 Continue to drag the x, y, and z axes until the entire clip fits into the monitor screen, as shown in the following image. The final x, y, and z values should be approximately 114, 219, 365.

Rotating the clip

The news clip fits better, but you need to rotate it slightly to improve the perspective.

1 Select the news_promo layer in the Timeline panel and press the **R** key to reveal its Rotation properties. Again, since this is a 3D layer, you can control rotation on the x, y, and z axes.

2 Change the Y Rotation value to **-10°**. This swivels the layer to match the perspective of the monitor.

3 Change the Z Rotation value to **-2°**. This aligns the layer with the monitor.

Your composition should now resemble the preceding image.

4 Hide the properties for the news_promo layer, and then choose File > Save to save your work.

Adding a reflection

The masked image looks convincing, but you can make it look even more realistic by adding a reflection to the monitor.

1   Choose Layer > New > Solid.

2   In the Solid Settings dialog box, name the layer **Reflection**, click the Make Comp Size button, change the Color to white, and then click OK.

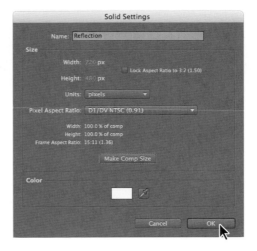

Instead of trying to exactly re-create the shape of the office_mask layer's mask, it is easier to copy it to the Reflection layer.

3   Select the office_mask layer in the Timeline panel and press the **M** key to display the Mask Path property for the mask.

4   Select Mask 1, and then choose Edit > Copy or press Ctrl+C (Windows) or Command+C (Mac OS).

5   Select the Reflection layer in the Timeline panel, and then choose Edit > Paste or press Ctrl+V (Windows) or Command+V (Mac OS).

This time, you want to keep the area inside the mask opaque and make the area outside the mask transparent.

6   Select the office_mask layer, and then press **U** to hide the mask properties.

7   Select the Reflection layer in the Timeline panel and press the **M** key to reveal the Mask 1 Mask Path property for the layer.

8 Deselect the Inverted option. The Reflection layer now obscures the news_promo layer.

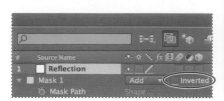

9 Zoom in to see the screen, and then select the Selection tool (➤). In the Composition panel, select the lower-right vertex of the Reflection layer's mask and drag it toward the upper-left corner of the mask.

10 Adjust the other vertices and direction handles until your shape resembles the following figure.

11 With the Reflection layer selected in the Timeline panel, press the **F** key to display the Mask Feather property for the mask.

12 Increase the Feather amount to **90, 90** pixels.

This creates an apparent reflection on the monitor, but because of the layers' stacking order, the reflection spills onto the whole shot.

13 Select the Reflection layer in the Timeline panel and drag it below the office_mask layer.

14 With the Reflection layer selected, press **T** to reveal its Opacity property.

15 Reduce the Opacity value to **65%** to reduce the intensity of the reflection.

16 Press **T** to hide the Opacity property, and then press F2 to deselect all layers.

Applying a blending mode

To create unique interactions between layers, you may want to experiment with blending modes. Blending modes control how each layer blends with, or reacts to, layers beneath it. Blending modes for layers in After Effects are identical to blending modes in Adobe Photoshop.

1 In the Timeline panel menu, choose Columns > Modes to display the Mode pop-up menu.

2 Choose Add from the Reflection layer's Mode pop-up menu.

This creates a hard glare on the monitor screen image and boosts the colors underneath.

3 Choose File > Save to save your work.

Adding a 3D light layer

Instead of creating the reflection using a solid layer and a feathered mask, you could also use a 3D light layer to create realistic surface reflection. As noted earlier, you'll learn more about 3D layers, including using 3D light layers, in Lessons 11 and 12. If you're ambitious, however, you can follow these steps to create a 3D light layer now with this project. This exercise is optional.

1   Hide the Reflection layer by clicking its Video switch.

2   Choose Layer > New > Light.

3   Click OK to accept the default values in the Light Settings dialog box.

4   With the Light 1 layer selected in the Timeline panel, press **P** to display its Position property. The Position property affects the placement of the light in the scene.

5   Set the Position values for the Light 1 layer to **260**, **-10**, **-350**, which moves the light above the monitor and off the image.

6   Select the Light 1 layer in the Timeline panel and press **A** to reveal its Point Of Interest property. The point of interest determines where the light is "looking."

7   Set the Point Of Interest values to **135**, **200**, **0**.

8   Select the news_promo.mov layer in the Timeline panel and press **AA** to reveal the layer's Material Options properties. Material Options properties determine how a 3D layer interacts with light and shadow, both of which are important components of realism and perspective in 3D animation.

9   Increase the Specular value to **75%** and the Shininess value to **50%**.

10 Lower the Metal value to **50%**. The Metal value determines how much of the layer's color reflects the light. Because there are dark blues in the layer, little light is being reflected. Because you are simulating glass in front of the layer, lowering this value causes the reflection to take on the same color as the light.

11 Hide the properties for the news_promo.mov layer.

That's it. You've created the same effect using a 3D light layer.

Creating a vignette

A popular effect in motion graphic design is to apply a vignette to the composition. This is often done to simulate light variations of a glass lens. It creates an interesting look that focuses the attention on the subject and sets the shot apart.

1 Zoom out to see the whole image.

2 Choose Layer > New > Solid.

3 In the Solid Settings dialog box, name this layer **Vignette**, click the Make Comp Size button, change the Color to black (RGB 0, 0, 0), and then click OK.

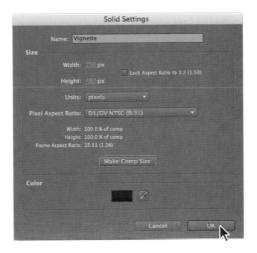

In addition to the Pen tool, After Effects provides tools that let you easily create square and elliptical masks.

4 In the Tools panel, select the Ellipse tool (●), hidden behind the Rectangle tool (■).

5 In the Composition panel, position the cross-hair pointer in the upper-left corner of the image. Drag to the opposite corner to create an elliptical shape that fills the image. Adjust the shape and position using the Selection tool, if necessary.

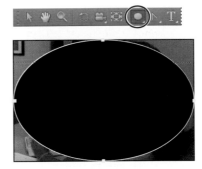

Using the Rectangle and Ellipse tools

The Rectangle tool, as the name suggests, creates a rectangle or square. The Ellipse tool creates an ellipse or circle. You create mask shapes with these tools by dragging them in the Composition or Layer panel.

If you want to draw a perfect square or circle, press the Shift key as you drag with the Rectangle tool or the Ellipse tool. To create your mask from the center, press Ctrl (Windows) or Command (Mac OS) after you start to drag. Press Ctrl+Shift or Command+Shift after you start to drag to create a perfect square or circle mask from a center anchor point.

Be careful! If you use these tools without a layer selected, you'll draw a shape, not a mask.

6 Expand the Mask 1 property in the Vignette layer to display all of the mask properties for the layer.

7 Choose Subtract from the Mask 1 Mode pop-up menu.

8 Increase the Mask Feather amount to **200, 200** pixels.

Your composition should now resemble the following figure.

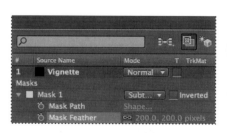 

Even with this large feather amount, the vignette is a bit intense and constricting. You can give the composition more breathing room by adjusting the Mask Expansion property. The Mask Expansion property represents, in pixels, how far from the original mask edge you are expanding or contracting the adjusted edge.

9 Increase Mask Expansion to **90** pixels.

10 Hide the properties for the Vignette layer and then choose File > Save.

Tip for creating masks

If you have worked with other programs such as Adobe Illustrator or Photoshop, you're probably familiar with masks and Bezier curves. If not, here are a few additional tips to help you create them effectively:

- Use as few vertices as possible.

- As you saw in this lesson, you can close a mask by clicking the starting vertex. You can also open a closed mask: click a mask segment, choose Layer > Mask And Shape Path, and deselect Closed.

- To add points to an open path, press Ctrl (Windows) or Command (Mac OS), and click the last point on the path. When the point is selected, you can continue adding points.

Adjusting the color

The shot is looking quite polished, but the color of the office_mask.mov layer is rather dull. Warming it up will make the image really pop.

1 Select the office_mask.mov layer in the Timeline panel.

2 Choose Effect > Color Correction > Auto Levels. The Auto Levels effect sets highlights and shadows by defining the lightest and darkest pixels in each color channel as white and black, and then it redistributes intermediate pixel values proportionally. Because Auto Levels adjusts each color channel individually, it may remove or introduce color casts.

Why apply this effect? Sometimes video cameras favor a certain color channel that makes the image cooler (bluer) or warmer (redder). The Auto Levels effect sets the black and white pixels for each channel, with the end result looking much more natural.

The color of the office_mask.mov layer should look much better now.

3 Choose File > Save to save the finished project.

In this lesson you have worked with the mask tools to hide, reveal, and adjust portions of a composition to create a stylized inset shot. Next to keyframes, masks are probably the most-used feature of After Effects.

You can preview the clip now, if you'd like, or render and export it following the steps in Lesson 14, "Rendering and Outputting."

Review questions

1 What is a mask?

2 Name two ways to adjust the shape of a mask.

3 What is a direction handle used for?

4 What is the difference between an open mask and a closed mask?

Review answers

1 A mask in After Effects is a path, or outline, that is used to modify layer effects and properties. The most common use of masks is to modify a layer's alpha channel. A mask consists of segments and vertices.

2 You can adjust the shape of a mask by dragging individual vertices, or by dragging a segment.

3 A direction handle is used to control the shape and angle of a Bezier curve.

4 An open mask can be used to control effects or the placement of text; it does not define a region of transparency. A closed mask defines a region that will affect the alpha channel of a layer.

8 DISTORTING OBJECTS WITH THE PUPPET TOOLS

Lesson overview

In this lesson, you'll learn how to do the following:

- Place Deform pins using the Puppet Pin tool.

- Define areas of overlap using the Puppet Overlap tool.

- Stiffen part of an image using the Puppet Starch tool.

- Animate the position of Deform pins.

- Smooth motion in an animation.

- Record animation using the Puppet Sketch tool.

The Puppet tools in Adobe After Effects let you quickly add natural motion to raster images and vector graphics. Three tools create pins to define the point of deformation, areas of overlap, and areas that should remain more rigid. An additional tool, the Puppet Sketch tool, lets you record animation in real time. In this lesson, you'll use the Puppet tools to animate a character slipping on a banana peel. This lesson will take approximately an hour to complete.

Pull, squash, stretch, and otherwise deform objects on the screen using the Puppet tools. Whether you're creating realistic animations, fantastic scenarios, or modern art, the Puppet tools expand your creative freedom.

Getting started

Start by previewing the final movie, and then setting up the project.

1. Make sure the following files are in the AECS4_CIB/Lessons/Lesson08 folder on your hard disk, or copy them from the *Adobe After Effects CS4 Classroom in a Book* DVD now:

   - In the Assets folder: backdrop.psd, banana.psd, man.psd

   - In the Sample_Movie folder: Lesson08.mov

2. Open and play the Lesson08.mov file to see what you will create in this lesson. When you are done, quit QuickTime Player. You may delete this sample movie from your hard disk if you have limited storage space.

When you begin this lesson, restore the default application settings for After Effects. See "Restoring default preferences" on page 3.

3. Press Ctrl+Alt+Shift (Windows) or Command+Option+Shift (Mac OS) while starting After Effects. When asked whether you want to delete your preferences file, click OK. Click Close to close the Welcome window.

After Effects opens to display a blank, untitled project.

4. Choose File > Save As.

5. In the Save As dialog box, navigate to the AECS4_CIB/Lessons/Lesson08/Finished_Project folder.

6. Name the project **Lesson08_Finished.aep**, and then click Save.

Importing footage

You'll import three Adobe Photoshop files, which you'll use to create the scene.

1. Choose File > Import > File.

2. Navigate to the AECS4_CIB/Lessons/Lesson08/Assets folder. Shift-click to select the backdrop.psd, banana.psd, and man.psd files, and then click Open. The footage items appear in the Project panel.

3. Click the Create A New Folder button at the bottom of the Project panel.

4. Name the folder **Assets**, and then drag the footage items into the folder.

5. Expand the Assets folder to see its contents.

Creating the composition

As with any project, you need to create a new composition.

1 Choose Composition > New Composition.

2 Name the composition **Walking Man**.

3 Make sure the Preset pop-up menu is set to NTSC DV. The preset automatically sets the width, height, pixel aspect ratio, and frame rate for the composition.

4 In the Duration field, type **500** to specify 5 seconds, and then click OK.

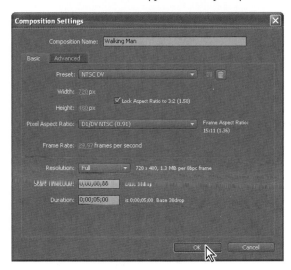

After Effects opens the new composition in the Timeline and Composition panels.

Adding the background

It's easier to animate a character in context, so first you'll add the background to the composition.

1 Press the Home key to ensure the current-time indicator is at the beginning of the composition.

2 Drag the backdrop.psd file to the Timeline panel.

3 Lock the layer to prevent accidental changes to it.

Scaling an object

Next, you'll add the banana peel. At its default size, it's large enough to do real damage to anyone who slips on it. You'll scale it to a more proportional size for the scene.

1   Drag the banana.psd file from the Project panel to the top layer in the Timeline panel.

2   Select the banana.psd layer in the Timeline panel and press **S** to display its Scale property.

3   Change the Scale to **15%**.

4   Press **P** to display the layer's Position property.

5   Change the Position to **160, 420**. The banana peel moves to the left side of the composition.

6   Hide the properties for the banana.psd layer.

Adding the character

The last element in the scene is the character himself. You'll add him to the composition and then scale and position him appropriately.

1   Drag the man.psd footage item from the Project panel to the Timeline panel at the top of the layer stack.

2   Select the man.psd layer, and press **S** to display its Scale property.

3   Change the Scale to **15%**.

Note: In the original drawing, the character has already slipped on the banana peel and was falling. To make it easier to animate, the character has been modified to be more upright. Sometimes you can make your work easier by making some adjustments before animation.

4 Press **P** to display the Position property, and change the Position to **575, 300**.

5 Press **P** again to hide the Position property for the layer.

About the Puppet tools

The Puppet tools turn raster and vector images into virtual marionettes. When you move the string of a marionette, the body part attached to that string moves; pull the string attached to the hand and the hand goes up. The Puppet tools use pins to indicate where strings would be attached.

The Puppet effect deforms parts of an image based on the position of pins that you place and animate. These pins determine which parts of the image should move, which parts should remain rigid, and which parts should be in front when areas overlap.

There are three kinds of pins, each placed by a different tool:

- The Puppet Pin tool (🖈) places and moves Deform pins, which deform a layer.

- The Puppet Overlap tool (🔺) places Overlap pins, which indicate the parts of an image that should be in the front when areas overlap.

- The Puppet Starch tool (▣) places Starch pins, which stiffen parts of the image so that they are distorted less.

As soon as you place a pin, the area within an outline is automatically divided into a mesh of triangles. Each part of the mesh is associated with the pixels of the image, so as the mesh moves, so do the pixels. When you animate a Deform pin, the mesh deforms more in the area closest to the pin, while keeping the overall shape as rigid as possible. For example, if you animate a pin in a character's hand, the hand and arm will be deformed, but most of the character will remain in place.

● **Note:** The mesh is calculated at the frame where the Deform pins are applied. If you add more pins anywhere in the timeline, they are placed based on the original position of the mesh.

Adding Deform pins

Deform pins are the main component of the Puppet effect. Where you place those pins and how you position them determine how the objects move on the screen. You'll place Deform pins and display the mesh that After Effects creates to determine the area of influence for each pin.

When you select the Puppet Pin tool, the Tools panel displays the Puppet tool options. Each pin has its own properties in the Timeline panel, and After Effects automatically creates an initial keyframe for each pin.

1 Select the Puppet Pin tool (✎) in the Tools panel.

● **Note:** Be careful! The character's right arm is on the left side of the image, and vice versa. Pin the character according to his left and right, not yours!

2 In the Composition panel, place a Deform pin in the character's right arm, near the wrist. You may find it helpful to zoom in to see the character more clearly. A yellow dot representing the Deform pin appears in the Composition panel.

If you used the Selection tool (▸) to move the Deform pin, the entire character would move with it. You need more pins to keep the other parts of the mesh in place.

3 Using the Puppet Pin tool, place another Deform pin in the left arm near the wrist.

Now you can move the right hand with the Selection tool. The more pins you place, the smaller the area of influence for each pin, and the less each area will stretch. Undo any stretching by pressing Ctrl+Z (Windows) or Command+Z (Mac OS).

4 Place additional Deform pins in the man's right and left legs (near the ankles), the torso (near the bottom of the tie), and forehead.

5 In the Timeline panel, expand the Mesh 1 > Deform properties. Each Deform pin is listed. To keep track of each pin, you'll rename them.

6 Select Puppet Pin 1, press Enter (Windows) or Return (Mac OS), and rename the pin **Right Arm**. Press Enter or Return again to accept the new name.

7 Rename the remaining pins (Puppet Pin 2 through Puppet Pin 6) **Left Arm**, **Right Leg**, **Left Leg**, **Torso,** and **Head**, respectively.

8 Select Show in the options section of the Tools panel to display the distortion mesh.

9 Change the Triangles value in the options section of the Tools panel to **300**. This setting determines how many triangles are included in the mesh. Increasing the number of triangles results in a smoother animation, but also increases rendering time.

▶ **Tip:** You can extend the mesh beyond the outline of the layer in order to ensure a stroke is included in the deformation. To expand the mesh, increase the Expansion property in the options section of the Tools panel.

Defining areas of overlap

Normal human movement requires the arms to swing, so as the character walks across the screen, portions of his right arm and leg will be behind other areas of his body. You'll use the Puppet Overlap tool to define the areas that should appear in front when areas overlap.

1 Select the Puppet Overlap tool (🔨), which is hidden behind the Puppet Pin tool in the Tools panel.

2 Select Show in the options area of the Tools panel to view the distortion mesh.

3 Zoom in and use the Hand tool (✋) to position the man in the Composition window, so that you can see his torso and legs clearly. Then, select the Puppet Overlap tool again.

4 In the options area of the Tools panel, change In Front to **100%**. The In Front value determines the apparent proximity to the viewer; changing the value to 100% prevents those parts of the body that are overlapped from showing through.

● **Note:** You must select the Show option separately for each Puppet tool. You can also place pins without viewing the mesh.

▶ **Tip:** If the mesh doesn't appear when you select Show, click outside the path shape in the Composition panel.

5 Click in the mesh to place Overlap pins on the character's torso and left leg, which are the areas that should remain in the front. As you add a pin, adjust its Extent value in the options area of the Tools panel. The Extent value determines how far the overlap influence extends for the pin; the affected area appears lighter in the Composition panel. Use this image as a guide.

Stiffening an area

The character's arms and legs should move as he walks, but his torso should stay fairly firm. You'll use the Puppet Starch tool to add Starch pins where you want the character to be stiffer.

1 Select the Puppet Starch tool (⬚), hidden behind the Puppet Overlap tool in the Tools panel.

2 Select Show in the options area of the Tools panel to display the distortion mesh.

3 Place Starch pins in the lower half of the torso, as in this image.

4 Hide the properties for the man.psd layer in the Timeline panel.

> ● **Note:** The Amount value determines how rigid the area will be. Typically, a low value is fine; higher values make the area more rigid. You can also use negative numbers to reduce the rigidity of another pin.

Animating pin positions

The Deform, Overlap, and Starch pins are in place. Now you can change the Deform pin positions to animate the character. The Overlap pins keep the front areas in the front, and the Starch pins keep specific areas (in this case, the torso) from moving too much.

Creating a walking cycle

Initially, the character should be walking across the screen. To create a realistic walking cycle, keep in mind that as humans walk, wave patterns develop in the motion path. You'll create a wave pattern in the pin positions. However, the values will vary slightly to add a bit of randomness, and to keep the character from looking too much like a robot.

1   Select the man.psd layer in the Timeline panel, and then press **U** to display all the keyframes for the layer.

2   Press Home to move the current-time indicator to the beginning of the timeline.

3   In the Timeline panel, change the position of the Deform pins as follows:

- Head: **845, 295**

- Torso: **821.5, 1210**

- Left Leg: **1000.5, 1734**

- Right Leg: **580.5, 1734**

- Left Arm: **1384.5, 1214.7**

- Right Arm: **478.5, 1108**

● **Note:** After Effects automatically creates keyframes when you place Deform pins, so you do not need to click the stopwatch for each pin before setting its initial position.

4 To complete the walking cycle, move the pins to the following positions at the times indicated in the chart below.

TIME	HEAD	TORSO	LEFT LEG	RIGHT LEG	LEFT ARM	RIGHT ARM
0:07	593, 214	570.5, 1095	604, 1614.5			
0:15	314, 295	312.5, 1210	118.5, 1748.3	580.5, 1734	886.5, 1208	-325.5, 1214.7
0:18	-6, 217	37.5, 1098.3		352.5, 1618.6		
1:00	-286, 295	253.5, 1210	118.5, 1748.3	-561.5, 1734	-121.5, 1234.7	-325.5, 1214.7
1:07	-614, 218.3	-530, 1094	-70.3, 1628.8			
1:15	-883, 300.7	-803.5, 1213.3	-1003.5, 1728.7	-561.5, 1734	-121.5, 1234.7	-1309.5, 1101.3
1:23	-1153, 212.7	-1055.5, 1099.7	-789.3, 1609.4			
2:00	-1412, 319.3	-1283.5, 1213	-1003.4, 1728.7	-1545.5, 1740.7	-1147.5, 1241.3	-1309.5, 1101.3
2:08	-1622, 246	-1505.5, 1099.7	-996, 1617	-1926.5, 1677.1		

▶ **Tip:** The Timeline panel measures time in seconds and frames, depending on the frames-per-second (fps) rate. So 0:07 equals frame 7, and 1:15 equals 1 second and 15 frames. At 29.97 fps, 1:15 is frame 45 in the composition.

Squash and stretch

As the character moves, his body squashes and stretches. Squash and stretch is a traditional animation technique that adds realism and weight to objects. It's an exaggeration of the effect that occurs in real life when a moving object comes into contact with a stationary object, such as the ground. When squashing and stretching are applied correctly, the volume of the character doesn't change.

The easiest way to understand the principle of squash and stretch is to view an animation of a bouncing ball. As the ball lands, it partially flattens, or squashes. As it bounces up, it stretches.

To see squash and stretch in action, open the Squash_and_stretch.aep project file in the Lesson08/End_Project_Files folder.

Animating a slip

The character steps on a banana peel, loses his balance, and falls. The falling movements occur more quickly than the walking cycle. To surprise the viewer, you'll animate the character to fall off the screen.

1   Move the current-time indicator to 2:11, and then change the position of the Left Leg pin to **-2281**, **1495.3**.

2   At 2:15, move the Deform pins to the following positions:
    *   Head: **-1298, 532.7**
    *   Torso: **-1667.5, 1246.3**
    *   Left Leg: **-2398.8, 1282.7**
    *   Right Leg: **-2277.5, 874**
    *   Left Arm: **-1219.5, 1768**
    *   Right Arm: **-1753.5, 454.7**

3   At 2:20, make the character fall off the screen by moving the Deform pins to the following positions:
    *   Head: **-1094, 2452.7**
    *   Torso: **-1643.5, 3219.7**
    *   Left Leg: **-2329.5, 2682**
    *   Right Leg: **-2169.5, 2234**
    *   Left Arm: **-1189.5, 3088**
    *   Right Arm: **-1597.5, 2654.7**

4   Hide the properties for the man.psd layer.

Moving an object

Of course, when the man slips on the banana peel, the banana peel moves, too. It should slide out from beneath the man's feet and fly off the screen. You didn't add any pins to the banana, and you don't need them. Instead, you'll move the entire layer, using its Position and Rotation properties.

1   Move the current-time indicator to 2:00.

2   Select the banana.psd layer in the Timeline panel, and press **P** to display its Position property.

▶ **Tip:** To view multiple layer properties at the same time, press the Shift key while you press the keyboard shortcut for the additional layer property.

3 Press Shift+**R** to display the layer's Rotation property.

4 Click the stopwatches next to Position and Rotation to create initial keyframes for each property.

5 Move to 2:06, and change the Position to **80**, **246** and the Rotation to **19**°.

6 Move to 2:15, and change the Position to **-59**, **361**, so that the banana peel moves completely off the screen.

7 At 2:15, change the Rotation to **42**° so that the peel continues to rotate slightly as it moves off the screen.

8 Make a RAM preview and view your animation. If necessary, adjust the Position property for Deform pins in the Timeline panel. Then choose File > Save.

Extra credit: Smoothing motion

The character in this animation walks, but his movement is a little stiff. You can make movement flow more naturally using the Easy Ease and roving keyframe features.

You've used Easy Ease in other lessons. The Easy Ease In, Easy Ease Out, and Easy Ease options adjust the speed of an object.

Roving keyframes create smooth movement across several keyframes at once. They are not linked to a specific time; their speed and timing are determined by the keyframes near them. To create a roving keyframe, right-click (Windows) or Control-click (Mac OS) the keyframe, and then select Rove Across Time in the keyframe menu.

Note: *The first and last keyframes cannot be roving keyframes.*

To smooth the character's movement, use Easy Ease and roving keyframes. You can experiment with the features, but start by trying to make your keyframes match those in the following image.

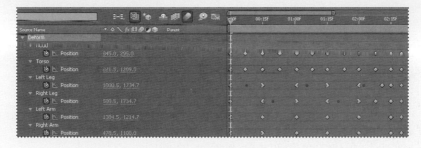

Recording animation

Changing the Position property for each pin at each keyframe worked, but you probably found it slow and tedious. If you were creating a much longer animation, you'd quickly tire of entering precise numbers for each keyframe. Instead of manually animating keyframes, you can use the Puppet Sketch tool to drag the objects into position in real time. After Effects starts recording the motion as soon as you begin dragging a pin, and it stops recording when you release the mouse button. The composition moves forward through time as you move the pin. When you stop recording, the current-time indicator returns to the point at which you began recording, so that you can record the path for another pin during the same time period.

Experiment with this method of animation as you re-create the slipping motion using the Puppet Sketch tool.

1   Choose File > Save As, and name the project **Motionsketch.aep**. Save it in the Lesson08/Finished_Project folder.

2   Delete all keyframes in the man.psd layer after 2:08. The walking cycle remains, but you've removed the keyframes that animate the character slipping and falling.

3   Move the current-time indicator to 2:08.

4   Select the Puppet Pin tool in the Tools panel.

5   In the Timeline panel, expand the man.psd layer, and then expand Effects. Select Puppet to see the pins in the Composition panel.

6   Select a pin in the Composition panel, and press Ctrl (Windows) or Command (Mac OS) to activate the Puppet Sketch tool (a clock icon appears next to the pointer).

7   Continue to press Ctrl or Command as you drag the pin into a new position. Release the mouse button when you've finished. The current-time indicator returns to 2:08

8   Press Ctrl or Command and drag another pin into position. Use the outline of the character to guide you.

9   Continue using the Puppet Sketch tool to move all the pins through the animation until you're satisfied with the movement.

10 Create a RAM preview to view the final animation.

Now you've used all the Puppet tools to create a realistic, engaging animation. Remember that you can use the Puppet tools to deform and manipulate many kinds of objects, not just drawn art. And watch out for banana peels!

Review questions

1 What's the difference between the Puppet Pin tool and the Puppet Overlap tool?

2 When would you use the Puppet Starch tool?

3 How can you make your animation more fluid?

4 Describe two methods of animating pin positions.

Review answers

1 The Puppet Pin tool creates Deform pins, which define the position of a portion of the image as the image is deformed. The Puppet Overlap tool creates Overlap pins, which determine which areas of an object remain in front when two areas overlap.

2 Use the Puppet Starch tool to add Starch pins to an area that you want to remain more rigid while other areas of the object are distorted.

3 To make your animation more fluid, you can use the Easy Ease feature or roving keyframes. Additionally, you can create smoother movement by increasing the number of triangles in the distortion mesh, but increasing the number of triangles also increases the time it takes to render the animation.

4 You can manually animate pin positions by changing the value of the Position property for each pin in the Timeline panel. To animate pin positions more quickly, use the Puppet Sketch tool: with the Puppet Pin tool selected, press Ctrl or Command and drag a pin to record its movement.

9 KEYING

Lesson overview

In this lesson, you'll learn how to do the following:

- Create a garbage mask.

- Use the Color Difference Key effect to key an image.

- Check an image's alpha channel for errors in a key.

- Choke a matte to refine a key.

- Use the Spill Suppressor effect to remove unwanted light spill.

- Key out a background using the Keylight effect.

- Adjust the contrast of an image using the Levels effect.

- Prepare a project for mobile devices using Adobe Device Central.

 In this lesson, you will create an introductory menu for a fictional sports network, called Mobile Sports Network, which provides sports scores and stats on mobile phones. You'll work with live-action footage of an actor captured on a greenscreen stage. You will learn how to use keying effects to remove the green background and clean up the edge of the key to remove any lingering green spill. Then, you'll add titles to the intro. Because some customers will receive the information on phones and others on other mobile devices and personal computers, the company wants to ensure the video looks good on both low-resolution and high-resolution screens. You'll use Adobe Device Central to ensure the project works well on a variety of mobile devices. This lesson will take approximately an hour to complete.

The word *keying* might conjure up images of a weather person on the evening news, or a shooting technique used in major motion pictures. With Adobe After Effects, even the simplest, least-expensive project can benefit from this technique.

About keying

Keying is defining transparency by a particular color value (with a color key or chroma key) or brightness value (with a luminance key) in an image. When you *key out* a value, all pixels that have similar colors or luminance values become transparent.

Keying makes it easy to replace a background of a consistent color or brightness with another image, which is especially useful when working with objects that are too complex to mask easily. The technique of keying out a background of a consistent color is often called *bluescreening* or *greenscreening*, although you do not have to use blue or green; you can use any solid color for a background.

Difference keying defines transparency with respect to a particular baseline background image. Instead of keying out a single-color screen, you can key out an arbitrary background.

Why might you use keying? There are a variety of reasons, including the following:

- A stunt may be too dangerous for an actor to perform on location.

- The location may be too hazardous for cast and crew.

- In the case of science-fiction movies, the location may not exist at all.

- You are working with a limited budget and cannot shoot any other way.

The best way to ensure a good key is to know what format works best. While uncompressed footage will always provide the highest quality, MiniDV and the newer HDV formats are popular. In this lesson, you'll use HDV footage, which uses the same compression scheme as MiniDV. Any compression can create artifacts, such as blocky regions or aliasing along the curves and diagonals of your subject. The greater the digital compression, the harder it is to pull a clean key. After Effects can help you solve these and other keying problems.

▶ **Tip:** You will have greater success when pulling a key in an HDV or MiniDV format if your backdrop is green instead of blue. Luminance information, which makes up 60% of the video signal, is encoded into the green channel. The green channel is also the least compressed of the RGB color channels. Blue, on the other hand, tends to be the noisiest channel.

Getting started

Before you begin, preview the movie you're creating.

1   Make sure the following files are in the AECS4_CIB/Lessons/Lesson09 folder on your hard disk, or copy them from the *Adobe After Effects CS4 Classroom in a Book* DVD now.

- In the Assets folder: MobileSportsIntro.mov, mobilesportsbackground.mov

- In the Sample_Movie folder: Lesson09.mov

2   Open and play the Lesson09.mov sample movie to see what you will create. When you are done, quit QuickTime Player. You may delete this sample movie from your hard disk if you have limited storage space.

Creating compositions in Device Central

Screen dimensions, video frame rates, and color gamuts vary greatly from one mobile device to another. Adobe Device Central contains device profiles that provide information about these characteristics. Using this information, you can create movies that play correctly and look as you intend on the mobile devices you choose. You create your compositions in Device Central—a Device Master composition, and a composition for each of the mobile devices you select. You design, animate, and prepare your movie in the Device Master composition, and then use the device-specific compositions for previews and to render and export for final output.

Because you're preparing this project for mobile devices as well as high-resolution devices, you'll begin by creating the compositions in Device Central, which is installed when you install After Effects.

1 Start Adobe Device Central CS4.

2 In the Welcome window, click After Effects File under the Create New Mobile heading. This creates a new composition in Device Central. No specific devices are targeted yet.

● **Note:** If the Welcome window doesn't appear, choose File > New Document In > After Effects to create the new composition.

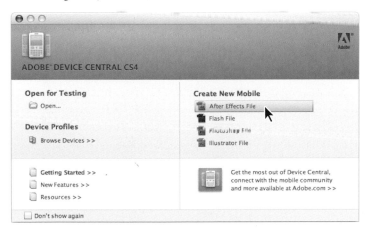

Available mobile devices are listed in the Online Library panel, but only Flash Lite is in the Local Library. In this lesson, you'll use the Nokia 3120 and Sony Ericsson K630i phones, as well as Flash Lite 2.1. You'll need to add the phones to your local library first.

3 In the Online Library panel, click the triangle next to the Nokia group to see its contents.

4 Expand the Nokia group, and then double-click Nokia 3120 to add it to your local library. Then, collapse the Nokia group.

5 Expand the Sony Ericsson group, and then double-click K630i. Collapse the Sony Ericsson group.

6 In the Local Library panel, expand each group to display the devices you want to target.

7 Press Ctrl (Windows) or Command (Mac OS) as you select the three devices (Flash Lite 2.1 16k 320 x 480, Nokia 3120, and Sony Ericsson K630i) in the Local Library panel.

The devices are added to the New Composition panel.

8 Select Create Master Composition at the top of the New Composition panel. This option creates a composition that contains the selected devices as well as a Master Devices composition.

9 Click Create. After Effects CS4 opens.

10 Click Close to close the Welcome window in After Effects.

The Project panel contains two folders: Device Central Comps and Solids.

11 Double-click the Device Central
   Comps folder to see its contents.
   It contains a Device Master
   composition, a composition for
   each of the devices you selected, a
   Preview composition, and a Guide
   Comps folder. Collapse the Device
   Central Comps folder, and click an
   empty area of the Project panel to
   deselect all items.

12 Choose File > Save As.

13 In the Save As dialog box, navigate to the AECS4_CIB/Lessons/Lesson09/
   Finished_Project folder, and name the project **Lesson09_Finished.aep**.

Importing the footage

You need to import two footage items for this lesson.

1 Choose File > Import > File.

2 Navigate to the AECS4_CIB/Lessons/Lesson09/Assets folder. Ctrl-click
   (Windows) or Command-click (Mac OS) to select the MobileSportsIntro.mov
   and mobilesportsbackground.mov files, and then click Open. The footage items
   appear in the Project panel. You will organize them before getting underway.

3 Choose File > New > New Folder to
   create a new folder in the Project
   panel, or click the Create A New
   Folder button (■) at the bottom of
   the panel.

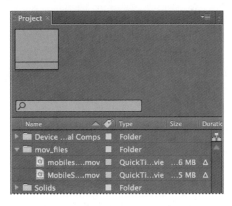

4 Type **mov_files** to name the folder,
   press Enter or Return to accept
   the name, and then drag the two
   footage items into the mov_files
   folder.

5 Expand the folder so that you can
   see the items inside.

Creating a composition for keying

Device Central created several compositions for you, but it can be difficult to see keying errors or subtle changes using compositions created by Device Central, which are at a lower resolution. Because you will also be preparing this project for viewing on larger screens, you'll create a separate composition for keying.

1 Choose Composition > New Composition.

2 In the Composition Settings dialog box, type **Color Difference Key** in the Composition Name box.

3 Make sure the Preset pop-up menu is set to NTSC DV. This automatically sets the width, height, pixel aspect ratio, and frame rate for the composition.

4 In the Duration field, type **1023** to specify 10 seconds and 23 frames, which matches the length of the MobileSportsIntro.mov footage item, and then click OK.

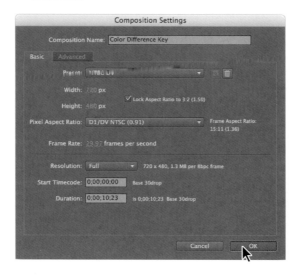

After Effects opens the new composition in the Timeline and Composition panels.

Changing the background color

The default background in After Effects is black, which makes it hard to see holes or other errors when pulling a key. So you'll start by changing the background to something other than black or white. In this lesson, you will use orange.

1 Choose Composition > Background Color.

2 Click the color swatch and select a bright orange hue, such as RGB 255, 175, 0. Then click OK to close the Color Picker, and OK again to close the Background Color dialog box.

▶ **Tip:** Instead of changing the background color, you can also click the Toggle Transparency Grid button (▨) at the bottom of the Composition panel. This displays a checkerboard background that reveals transparency, which is another good way to spot errors in a key.

Adding the foreground subject

You're ready to add the subject to the composition.

1 Press the Home key to make sure the current-time indicator is at the beginning of the time ruler.

2 Drag the MobileSportsIntro.mov item from the Project panel to the Timeline panel. The MobileSportsIntro.mov image appears in the foreground of the Composition panel.

This is a simple greenscreen shot. If you manually preview the shot by dragging the current-time indicator, you'll notice that the shot is too big for the composition. The project was shot on an HDV camera and captured at a resolution of 1440 x 1080. You'll need to resize the clip to use it in a standard definition (SD) project.

3 Select the MobileSportsIntro.mov item in the Timeline panel, and press **S** to display its Scale property.

4 Change the Scale amount to **45%**.

5 Move the current-time indicator to 4:00.

The actor has overshot her mark slightly and needs to be re-centered in the frame.

6 Select the MobileSportsIntro.mov item again, and press **P** to display its Position property.

Note: You can also reposition an item using the proportional grid. Click the Choose Grid And Guide Options button, and choose Proportional Grid to display it in the Composition panel.

7 Change the position to **417, 240** to shift the layer slightly to the right.

The clip is still too wide for the composition, but it will work because it lets you reposition the actor. You may notice in the movie that not everything is out of the frame, as a small portion of a light reflector remains.

Using garbage masks

This greenscreen shot is typical of a lower-budget production. Though the screen is evenly lit, the cloth is wrinkled, which could cause some problems when you pull the key.

When After Effects pulls a key, it looks at the entire frame. The larger the area that must be analyzed and the larger the variation in color, the greater the risk that you won't be able to remove all of the background color. You can reduce this risk and remove unwanted distractions by using a *garbage mask*.

As the name implies, a garbage mask (or matte) is used to mask out the bad, or unnecessary, parts of an image. When you create a garbage mask for a layer, it's a good idea to keep it fairly loose. If the foreground subject is moving, you need to leave enough room in the garbage mask to accommodate the motion. If you make it too tight, your subject may move outside the mask. Remember, a garbage mask is used to help solve problems, not create new ones.

There is no limit to the number of garbage masks you can have in a composition. In fact, on some complex shots it is not uncommon to have multiple garbage masks isolate limbs, faces, hair, or different subjects in the scene.

Creating a garbage mask

You'll create a garbage mask to limit the area you need to key.

1 Move the current-time indicator to 2:00 in the Timeline panel. This is the point at which the actor has stepped fully into the frame, and it's where she moves furthest to the left.

2 Select the Pen tool (✎) in the Tools panel.

3 Using the Pen tool, click to place vertices around the actor as in the following illustration. Be sure to leave room so that she can enter from the right of the screen. Close the mask by double-clicking the last vertex.

4 To make sure that your garbage mask isn't too tight, drag the current-time indicator across the time ruler and make sure the actor does not move out of the masked area. If she does, switch to the Selection tool (▶) and adjust the vertices.

Animating a garbage mask

Because you needed to leave room for the actor to enter from the right, a lot of wrinkled greenscreen remains. You'll remove more of this area by animating the garbage mask over time.

1 Move the current-time indicator to 1:15 in the Timeline panel.

2 Select the MobileSportsIntro.mov layer in the Timeline panel, and press **M** to display the Mask properties for the layer.

3 Click the stopwatch icon (⏱) next to the Mask Path property to set an initial keyframe for the mask.

4 Move the current-time indicator to 2:00.

5 Select the Selection tool (▸).

6 Click outside the mask, and then adjust the vertices on the right side of the screen, reducing the amount of greenscreen visible. You can add points using the Pen tool for more flexibility.

7 Manually preview the clip to ensure the actor doesn't move outside of the masked area. If she does, make adjustments to the vertices again.

8 Press **M** to hide the Mask property.

9 Choose File > Save to save your work so far.

Applying the Color Difference Key effect

There are many keying effects in After Effects. The Color Difference Key effect creates transparency from opposite starting points by dividing an image into two mattes, Matte Partial A and Matte Partial B. Matte Partial B bases the transparency on the specified key color, and Matte Partial A bases transparency on areas of the image that do not contain a second, different color. By combining the two mattes into a third matte, called the *alpha matte*, the Color Difference Key creates well-defined transparency values.

Confused yet? Many people who come across the Color Difference Key stop right there and run away in terror. But you don't need to fear the Color Difference Key.

1 Select the MobileSportsIntro.mov layer in the Timeline panel, and choose Effect > Keying > Color Difference Key.

2 In the Effect Controls panel, click the eyedropper for the Key Color setting. Then, click the green background color in the Composition panel.

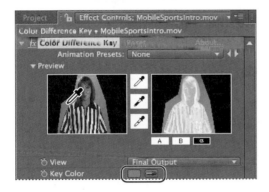

3 Click the A button under the right thumbnail preview to view Matte Partial A.

Portions of the background are still visible in the Matte Partial A preview. This is actually a good thing, because it allows you to refine your key, which you'll do now.

4 Using the Black eyedropper (the middle one between the two thumbnail previews), click the brightest portion of background that did not key out in the Composition panel. This will be near the top of the actor's head.

5 Click the B button under the right thumbnail preview to see Matte Partial B, which is the inverse of Matte Partial A.

6 Using the Black eyedropper again, click the brightest portion of the remaining background in the Composition panel (near the bottom). This should remove any remaining traces of the background.

7 Click the Alpha button under the right thumbnail preview. If this were a clean matte, the actor would be completely white. She's not, so you need to make some adjustments to the effect.

8 In the Effect Controls panel, decrease the Matte In White amount to **53**. You can think of the Matte In Black and Matte In White as being similar to the Levels effects.

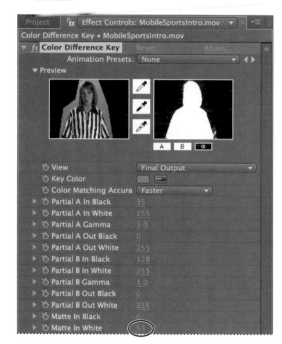

● **Note:** Don't despair if your results look different from ours. Because the shades of green vary across the greenscreen, you may need to reset the effect and select a different shade. It's common to try different shades when keying out greenscreens. We used RGB values of 113, 151, and 34. You can double-click the swatch next to Key Color to set RGB values.

Adjusting these two controls cleans up the alpha channel of the image. The result is a clean key accomplished with just a few clicks of the mouse.

Checking the alpha channel for errors

The orange (or transparent) background of the composition makes it easy to see any lingering bits of the greenscreen, but it may still be difficult to see any holes that may have been created with the actor. To double-check your key, switch to the alpha-channel view to see the resulting matte.

1   At the bottom of the Composition panel, click the Show Channel button (🌑) and choose Alpha from the pop-up menu.

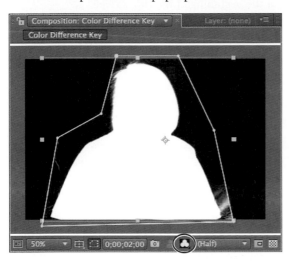

You can now see the black-and-white matte of your key. The black portion of the image represents the area that is transparent. The white portion represents the area that is opaque. Gray areas of the alpha channel (the feathered edge around the actor's head and hair) are semi-transparent.

2   Make sure no portion of the actor is black or gray. If you have followed the steps so far, you should be in good shape.

3   Click the Show Channel button again, and choose RGB to return to RGB view.

4   Manually preview the clip to make sure no background is visible at any point.

5   Hide the Color Difference Key properties in the Effect Controls panel.

6   Choose File > Save to save your work.

Choking the matte

Because the Color Difference Key removes color only from the clip, the edge of the actor still has an unwanted fringe. To refine the edge of your matte, you need to *choke*, or tighten, it.

Additionally, just before the actor walks on, a small area of greenscreen may appear. The garbage mask takes care of this problem area once the actor is in position, but choking the matte will remove it at the beginning of the clip, as well.

1 Select the MobileSportsIntro.mov layer in the Timeline panel, and choose Effect > Matte > Matte Choker.

This effect gives you more control over the edge of the matte than the Simple Choker effect. The main difference between the two is that the Simple Choker allows you only to tighten up the matte, while the Matte Choker also allows you to smooth, or feather, the edges.

In the Effect Controls panel, the top three Matte Choker controls—Geometric Softness 1, Choke 1, and Gray Level Softness 1—let you spread the matte as far as possible without changing its shape. The next three controls can be used to choke the matte.

In this lesson, most of the default settings work well. Consider yourself fortunate if this is the case on all your future keying projects. The only setting you need to adjust is the Geometric Softness 2 setting, which you'll use to create a slight blur along the edge of the matte.

2 Increase the Geometric Softness 2 amount to **10**.

3 Check the matte by clicking the Show Channel button at the bottom of the Composition panel and choosing Alpha from the pop-up menu. Preview the beginning of the clip to make sure the background is gone.

The matte looks great!

4 Switch back to the RGB view to get ready to remove some green spill.

5 Hide the Matte Choker properties to keep the Effect Controls panel tidy.

Removing spill

If you look closely at the actor's hair, you will see green highlights. This is the result of green light bouncing off the background and onto the subject. You can remove this and any unwanted green fringes around the actor with the Spill Suppressor effect. Typically, the Spill Suppressor is used to remove key color spills from the edges of a matte. It is essentially a simple desaturation filter.

It's easier to select the spill color if you temporarily turn off the Color Difference Key effect.

1   Select the MobileSportsIntro.mov layer in the Timeline panel and choose Effect > Keying > Spill Suppressor.

2   At the top of the Effect Controls panel, click the effect icon (🎇) next to the Color Difference Key effect to turn it off.

3   In the Spill Suppressor area at the bottom of the Effect Controls panel, select the Color To Suppress eyedropper and click a green region near the actor's hair. It's easiest to select at the top of the screen.)

4   Turn the Color Difference Key effect back on. The subject is now keyed out and the unwanted green in and around her hair is gone.

5   Hide the Spill Suppressor properties.

6   Choose File > Save.

Key out a background with the Keylight effect

There are many ways to pull a key in After Effects. In addition to using the Color Difference keyer, another good alternative is to use the Keylight effect. Keylight is a plug-in effect, licensed from The Foundry, that comes with After Effects CS4 Professional. It is a powerful keyer with numerous controls, and it is also one of the few effects that can pull a clean key in just one click.

If you'd like to try the Keylight effect, start this lesson over and complete the following exercise instead of the "Applying the Color Difference Key effect," "Choking the matte," and "Removing spill" exercises.

1 With the MobileSportsIntro.mov layer selected in the Timeline panel, choose Effect > Keying> Keylight (1.2).

As with the Color Difference Key, the first step is to select the key color.

2 In the Effect Controls panel, select the Screen Colour eyedropper.

3 In the Composition panel, click a green area of the background near the actor's shoulder.

The results are instantaneous, and for many keying projects, one click will produce the desired result. Still, you need to check for possible errors or holes. The effect's View pop-up menu will help you find and correct errors.

4 In the Effect Controls panel, choose Status from the View pop-up menu.

This shows an exaggerated view of the matte that is generated by the key color selection. Opaque areas appear white, transparent regions appear black, and semi-transparent pixels are gray. You can see that large areas of the image are not keyed correctly.

5 In the Effect Controls panel, increase the Screen Gain amount to **120**. Most of the background is knocked out.

6 Increase the Screen Pre-Blur to **10** so that the background appears to wrap around the actor.

7 Expand the Screen Matte property. Decrease the Clip White value to **50**, and change the Screen Shrink/Grow value to **-2** to contract the matte. Then, increase the Screen Softness to **5**.

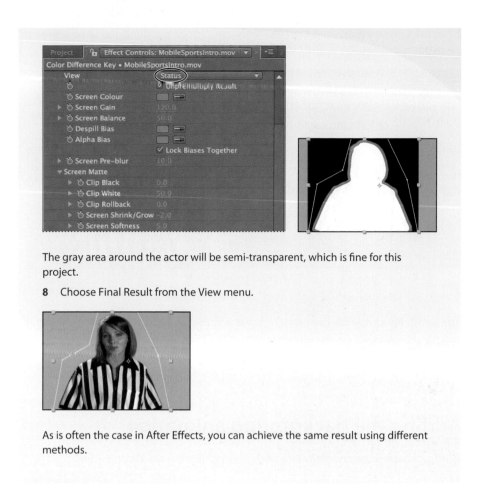

The gray area around the actor will be semi-transparent, which is fine for this project.

8   Choose Final Result from the View menu.

As is often the case in After Effects, you can achieve the same result using different methods.

Adjusting contrast

You can make the image stand out more by adjusting the levels.

1   Select the MobileSportsIntro.mov layer in the Timeline panel, and then choose Effect > Color Correction > Levels.

2 In the Levels area of the Effect Controls panel, decrease the Input White amount to **225**.

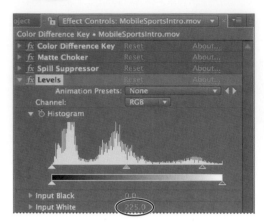 

3 Choose File > Save.

The Levels effect remaps the range of input color levels onto a new range of output color levels and changes the gamma correction curve. The Levels effect is useful for basic image quality adjustment. It works the same way as the Levels adjustment in Adobe Photoshop.

Adding the background animation

With a clean key, you're ready to add the background to the composition.

1 Press the Home key to make sure the current-time indicator is at the beginning of the time ruler.

2 Click the Project tab, and drag the mobilesportsbackground.mov item from the Project panel to the Timeline panel, placing it at the bottom of the layer stack.

3 Watch a RAM preview of the composition.

If you have a sharp eye, you may still notice a few aliasing artifacts here and there around the actor. Remember, you are working with footage that originated in HDV format, which is compressed and susceptible to some errors. Also, keep in mind that the computer monitor has a better resolution than a television set. To accurately judge the results of your key, you need to connect your system to a video monitor and view the results there. You'll preview how the keying appears on mobile devices soon.

4 When you are done watching the RAM preview, press the spacebar to stop playback.

5 Choose File > Save to save your work.

Adding text

Now, you'll add a text layer and create the menu items that appear in the intro.

1 Move the current-time indicator to 5:15. This is the point where the actor tells the viewer to press 1 to select "basketball."

2 Select the Horizontal Type tool (T) in the Tools panel. After Effects opens the Character and Paragraph panels.

The company logo, which appears at the beginning of the animated background, uses Gill Sans font, and the company would like you to use that for the menu, if possible. Because this intro will be viewed on the small screens of mobile devices, you'll make the text large and bold.

3 In the Character panel, do the following:

- Choose Gill Sans Bold if you have it; otherwise, select a bold sans serif font such as Helvetica Bold.

- Increase the Font Size to **60** pixels.

- Click the Fill Color swatch and choose a yellow hue, such as RGB 225, 225, 0.

- Click the Stroke Color swatch and select black.

- Increase the Stroke Width to **8** pixels.

- Choose Fill Over Stroke from the pop-up menu for the stroke behavior.

4 Click in the Composition panel, near the bottom of the screen, and type **1 - Basketball**.

Positioning the text

You'll reposition the text to ensure it appears within the title-safe area for TV and mobile devices. The title-safe area is the area that will be visible to viewers. The text appears on the screen for only a short time, so you'll also set In and Out points for the layer.

1 Click the Choose Grid And Guide Options button (⊞) at the bottom of the Composition panel and choose Title/Action Safe from the pop-up menu.

▶ **Tip:** Turn on the proportional grid if you want to center the text precisely.

2 Use the Selection tool to center the title within the title-safe area.

3 With the current-time indicator at 5:15, press the [key to move the layer's In point to the current time.

4 Go to 7:00, and press Alt+] (Windows) or Option+] (Mac OS) to trim the layer's Out point to the current time.

Adding a drop shadow

The text looks pretty good, but you can make it even better by adding a drop shadow.

1 With the 1 - Basketball text layer selected in the Timeline panel, choose Layer > Layer Styles > Drop Shadow.

2 In the Timeline panel, double-click the Drop Shadow layer style to see its properties.

3 Reduce the Distance (the distance of the shadow from the text) to **0.0**, increase the Spread to **25%**, and increase the Size to **25**.

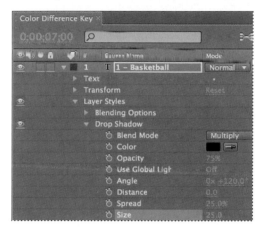 

Now, the text stands out against the background, making it easier to read on small screens.

4 Hide the Layer Styles properties.

5 Choose File > Save to save your work.

Animating text

Next, you'll add a transition to fade the text out.

1 Select the 1 - Basketball text layer, and then move the current-time indicator to 6:20.

2 In the Effects & Presets panel, navigate to Animation Presets > Text > Animate Out.

3 Double-click the Fade Out Slow preset to apply it to the current layer. It starts at the current time.

Expand the Text properties for the 1 - Basketball layer to see the preset, which is listed as Animator 1. Its ending keyframe is far beyond the layer's Out point. You'll fix that, and in the process, make the slow effect a fast fade-out.

4 With the 1 - Basketball layer selected in the Timeline panel, press the U key to reveal all of the keyframes for the selected layer.

5 Drag the ending keyframe for the Offset property to the Out point for the layer (7:00).

6 Manually preview the text animation.

Duplicating the text

You've created the first menu item. You could create each of the three remaining menu items the same way, but it's easier to duplicate the layer and its properties.

1 Select the 1 - Basketball layer in the Timeline panel, and press Ctrl+D (Windows) or Command+D (Mac OS) to duplicate the layer.

A new layer, named 1 - Basketball 2, appears in the Timeline panel.

2 Move the current-time indicator to 8:09, which is where the second menu item should end on the screen.

3 Press the] key to move the Out point of the layer to the current time.

4 Move to 7:00 in the time ruler, and press Alt+[(Windows) or Option+[(Mac OS) to trim the In point of the layer to the current time.

5 Double-click the new layer (1 - Basketball 2). The text is selected and After Effects switches to the Horizontal Type tool.

6 Type **2 - Soccer**.

7 Use the Selection tool to center the text in the title-safe area. Press the Shift key as you move the text to keep it from shifting vertically.

8 Select the 2 - Soccer layer in the Timeline panel, and press Ctrl+D (Windows) or Command+D (Mac OS) to duplicate the layer.

9 Move the current-time indicator to 9:11, where the third menu item should end on the screen, and press] to move the Out point to the current time.

10 Move to 8:09, and press Alt+[(Windows) or Option+[(Mac OS) to trim the In point to the current time.

11 Double-click the duplicate layer (2 - Soccer 2), and type **3 - Golf**. Use the Selection tool to center the text in the title-safe area as you hold down the Shift key.

12 Repeat steps 8–11 to duplicate the 3 - Golf layer, set the Out point of the duplicated layer to the end of the time ruler and the In point to 9:11, and replace the text with **4 - Tennis**. Center the text in the title-safe area.

13 Click in an empty area of the Timeline panel to deselect all the layers.

All the text is in place!

14 Choose File > Save to save your work.

● **Note:** You can run a RAM preview of the text effects more quickly if you turn off the visibility of the other layers. As long as the audio icon appears next to the MobileSportsIntro.mov layer, you'll hear the actor's voice.

Preparing the composition for mobile devices

The main work of the composition is done. You're ready to move it into the compositions you created using Device Central.

1 In the Project panel, expand the Device Central Compositions folder, and then double-click the Device Master composition to open it in the Timeline panel.

The composition contains three layers called *guide layers*. Each guide layer contains a masked solid that displays the safe area for a mobile device you selected in Device Central.

2 Press the Home key to make sure the current-time indicator is at the beginning of the time ruler.

3 In the Project panel, drag the Color Difference Key composition to the Timeline panel. Place it at the bottom of the layer stack.

The Color Difference Key composition is too large for any of the selected devices. Most mobile devices have a frame size of 320 x 240 pixels. The Color Difference Key composition has a frame size of 720 x 480 pixels. You'll need to resize it.

4 With the Color Difference Key layer selected, press **S** to display its Scale property.

5 Change the Scale amount to **50%**. Now the layer fits nicely inside all the guide areas.

There's one more change to make. Device Central used the default length of 10 seconds for its compositions, but the Color Difference Key composition is 10 seconds and 23 frames. You'll change the settings for the device compositions.

6 Select the Device Master composition in the Project panel, and then choose Composition > Composition Settings.

7 Change the Duration to **10:12**, and then click OK.

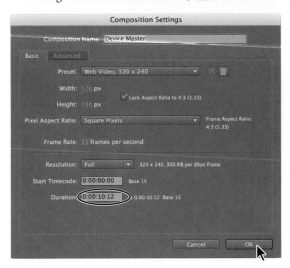

The Device Central compositions have a frame rate of 15 frames per second, half the frame rate of the Color Difference Key composition. Therefore, instead of 23 additional frames, you need only 12.

8 Change the Duration for each of the other compositions in the Device Central Comps folder in the Project panel. (There are four more compositions in that folder: Flash Lite 2.1 16 320 x 240, Nokia 3120, Preview, and Sony Ericsson K630i.)

9 Double-click the Preview composition in the Project panel to open it. The Preview composition shows you how your final composition will look on each of the devices. If you identify any problems with positioning, or if it is difficult to read the text on any of the devices, open the composition for that device and make the necessary adjustments.

10 Choose File > Save to save your work.

Congratulations. You've not only completed a difficult keying project, but you developed it for both mobile devices and larger screens. If you want to render and export these compositions, see Lesson 14, "Rendering and Outputting," for instructions.

Review questions

1 What is *keying* and when do you use it?

2 What is the purpose of using a garbage mask?

3 How can you check for errors in a color key?

4 What is *spill* and how can you fix it in After Effects?

5 How can you use Device Central to prepare compositions in After Effects?

Review answers

1 *Keying* is defining transparency by a particular color value (with a color key or chroma key) or brightness value (with a luminance key) in an image. When you *key out* a value, all pixels that have similar colors or luminance values become transparent. Keying makes it easy to replace a background of a consistent color or brightness with another image, which is especially useful when working with objects that are too complex to mask easily.

2 A garbage mask is used to remove unwanted portions of the image. This limits the region After Effects must search when keying, thus speeding up the keying calculations and increasing the chances for a cleaner key.

3 Use the alpha channel to check for errors in a color key. Make sure the background is a contrasting color, or toggle on the transparency grid, and then click the Show Channel button at the bottom of the Composition panel and choose Alpha. This displays a black-and-white matte. The black portion represents the area that is transparent; the white portion represents the area that is opaque; gray areas are semi-transparent.

4 Light spill occurs when light illuminating the background reflects onto the subject and colors the shadows and highlights. You can remove spill using the Spill Suppressor effect. Select the keyed layer and choose Effect > Keying > Spill Suppressor.

5 Use Device Central to create compositions with the appropriate settings for multiple mobile devices, and to preview the compositions on those devices.

10 PERFORMING COLOR CORRECTION

Lesson overview

In this lesson, you'll learn how to do the following:

- Use the Levels effect to correct the color in a shot.

- Replace the sky with a different image.

- Use the Auto Levels effect to introduce a color shift.

- Correct a range of colors using Synthetic Aperture Color Finesse 2.

- Apply the Photo Filter effect to warm portions of an image.

- Remove unwanted elements with the Clone Stamp tool

As the name implies, color correction is a way of altering or adapting the color of the captured image. Color correction is performed to optimize source material, to focus attention on a key element in a shot, to correct errors in white balance and exposure, to ensure color consistency from one shot to another, or to create a color palette for a specific visual look desired by a director. In this lesson, you will improve the color of a video clip that was shot without the proper white balance setting. You'll apply a variety of color-correction effects to clean up and enhance the image. Finally, you will remove an unwanted portion of the shot with the Clone Stamp tool. This lesson will take approximately an hour to complete.

Most shots require some degree of color correction.
With Adobe After Effects, you can transform a dull,
lifeless shot into a bright, sharp clip in no time.

Getting started

First, you'll preview the final movie, and set up your project.

1 Make sure the following files are in the AECS4_CIB/Lessons/Lesson10 folder on your hard disk, or copy them from the *Adobe After Effects CS4 Classroom in a Book* DVD now.

- In the Assets folder: Albertson_Hall.mov, storm_clouds.jpg

- In the Sample_Movie folder: Lesson10.mov

2 Open and play the Lesson10.mov file to see what you will create in this lesson. When you're done, quit QuickTime Player. You may delete the sample movie from your hard disk if you have limited storage space.

When you begin this lesson, restore the default application settings for After Effects. See "Restoring default preferences" on page 3.

3 Press Ctrl+Alt+Shift (Windows) or Command+Option+Shift (Mac OS) while starting After Effects. When asked whether you want to delete your preferences file, click OK. Click Close to close the Welcome window.

After Effects opens to display an empty, untitled project.

4 Choose File > Save As.

5 In the Save As dialog box, navigate to the AECS4_CIB/Lessons/Lesson10/ Finished_Project folder.

6 Name the project **Lesson10_Finished.aep**, and then click Save.

> **Note:** This lesson uses the SA Color Finesse 2 effect, which requires a serial number that is included with your application. If you open the Lesson10_end file, you may be prompted to register the effect and enter your serial number.

Importing the footage

You need to import two footage items for this lesson.

1 Choose File > Import > File.

2 Navigate to the AECS4_CIB/Lessons/Lesson10/Assets folder, Shift-click to select the Albertson_Hall.mov and storm_clouds.jpg files, and then click Open.

3 Choose File > New > New Folder to create a new folder in the Project panel, or click the Create A New Folder button (▦) at the bottom of the panel.

4 Type **Movies** to name the folder, press Enter or Return to accept the name, and then drag the Albertson_Hall.mov item into the Movies folder.

5 Create another new folder and name it **Images**. Then, drag the storm_clouds.jpg item into the Images folder.

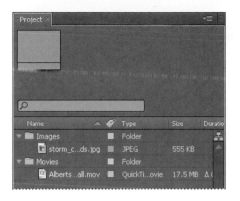

6 Expand the folders so that you can see their contents.

Creating the composition

Now, you will create a new composition based on the Albertson_Hall.mov file.

1 Drag the Albertson_Hall.mov item onto the Create A New Composition button (▣) at the bottom of the Project panel. After Effects creates a new composition named for the source file and displays it in the Composition and Timeline panels.

2 (Optional) Choose Composition > Composition Settings to check the composition's aspect ratio and duration. This is an NTSC DV composition that is 5 seconds long. Click Cancel to close the Composition Settings dialog box.

3 Drag the Albertson_Hall composition to an empty area of the Project panel to move it out of the Movies folder.

4 Drag the current-time indicator across the time ruler to preview the shot. There is an unappealing blue cast to the entire image. You'll correct that first.

5 Choose File > Save to save your work.

Previewing your project on a video monitor

If possible, perform color correction on a video monitor instead of a computer monitor. The gamma values between a computer monitor and a broadcast monitor vary greatly. What may look good on a computer screen may be too bright and washed out on a broadcast monitor.

You can view After Effects compositions on a broadcast monitor via the IEEE 1394 (FireWire) port on your computer. One way to accomplish this is to use a video tape recorder that accepts FireWire. You can loop the signal from your computer to the video tape recorder and then run a cable to your video monitor via the monitor/video output on the video tape recorder.

1 With a video monitor connected to your computer system, start After Effects CS4.

2 Do one of the following, depending on your platform:

   • In Windows, choose Edit > Preferences > Video Preview. Then, choose IEEE 1394 (OHCI Compliant) from the Output Device pop-up menu.

   • In Mac OS, choose After Effects > Preferences > Video Preview. Then, choose FireWire from the Output Device pop-up menu.

3 For Output Mode (Windows and Mac OS), choose the appropriate format for your system, which is NTSC in North America.

4 To view the composition you are working on, select the Previews, Mirror On Computer Monitor, Interactions, and Renders options. With all of these options selected, you will be able to see every update and change you make to the composition on the video monitor.

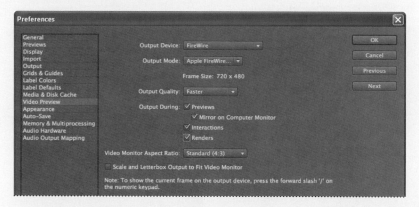

5 Click OK to close the Preferences dialog box.

Always be sure your video or computer monitor is properly calibrated before performing color correction. For instructions on calibrating a computer monitor, see After Effects Help.

Adjusting color balance

After Effects provides several tools for color correction. Some may do the job with a single click, but understanding how to adjust colors manually gives you the greatest freedom to achieve the look you want. You'll use the Levels effect to darken the shadows, remove the blue cast, and make the image pop a little more.

1 Press the Home key to make sure the current-time indicator is at the beginning of the time ruler.

2 Select the Albertson_Hall.mov layer in the Timeline panel.

3 Press Enter or Return, rename the layer **Building**, and then press Enter or Return to accept the new name.

4 With the Building layer selected, choose Effect > Color Correction > Levels (Individual Controls).

The Levels (Individual Controls) effect may be a little intimidating at first, but it can give you great control over your shot. It remaps the range of input color or alpha channel levels onto a new range of output levels, functioning much the same as the Levels adjustment in Adobe Photoshop.

The Channel menu specifies the channel to be modified, and the histogram shows the number of pixels with each luminance value in the image. When the selected channel is RGB, you can adjust the overall brightness and contrast of the image. That's a good place to start.

5 In the Effect Controls panel, make sure RGB is selected in the Channel menu. Then click the triangle next to RGB to expand its properties.

6 Enter **2** for the Input Black value, slightly darkening the shadows. The Input Black slider under the histogram moves accordingly.

7 Enter **0.85** for the Gamma value, increasing the contrast so that it pops a little more. The Gamma value represents the midtones.

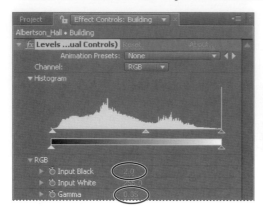 

To correct the blue cast, you must first determine what areas are supposed to be gray (or white or black) in the image. In this shot, the building is supposed to be a neutral color.

8 Move the cursor over the concrete areas of the building and note the RGB values in the Info panel.

In a region near the door, the RGB value is 70, 95, 125. To determine what the values should be, divide 255 (the highest RGB value) by the highest of the gray values. That gives you 255 divided by 125 (the blue value near the door), or *2.04*. To equalize the colors, so that blue is no longer prominent, you need to multiply 2.04 by the original red and green values (70 and 95, respectively). The new values are 142.8 for red and 193.8 for green.

9 In the Effect Controls panel, expand the Red and Green properties.

10 For the Red Input White value, enter **142.8**; for the Green Input White value, enter **193.8**.

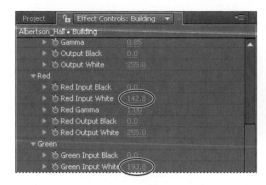

The blue cast is gone, revealing a much more realistic scene.

For each channel, the Input settings increase the value, while the Output settings decrease the value. For example, lowering the Input Red value adds red to the highlights in the shot, and increasing the Output Red value adds red to the shadows or dark areas in the shot.

Performing the math lets you home in on the appropriate settings quickly. If you prefer, you could experiment with the settings to find the best values for your purpose.

11 Hide the Levels properties in the Effect Controls panel.

Replacing the background

This shot was taken on a clear day with a cloudless sky. To add a little drama, you'll key out the sky and replace it with storm clouds.

Keying out an area with the Color Range effect

The Color Range effect keys out a specified range of colors. This key effect is especially useful where the color to be keyed is unevenly lit. The current sky ranges in color from light blue to dark blue, a perfect candidate for the Color Range effect.

1 Press the Home key to make sure the current-time indicator is at the beginning of the time ruler.

2 With the Building layer selected in the Timeline panel, choose Effect > Keying > Color Range.

Changing the background color of the composition can help you spot any keying errors.

3 Choose Composition > Background Color, and select red (RGB **255, 0, 0**). Click OK to close the dialog box.

4 In the Effect Controls panel, choose RGB from the Color Space menu.

5 Select the Key Color eyedropper, next to the Preview window in the Effect Controls panel. Then, in the Composition panel, select a midtone blue color in the sky. The keyed out area appears red in the Composition panel, and black in the Preview window in the Effect Controls panel.

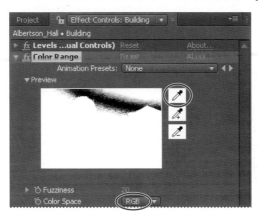

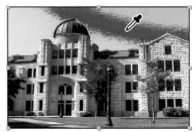

6 Select the Add To Key Color eyedropper in the Effect Controls panel, and then click another area of the sky in the Composition panel.

7 Repeat step 6 until the entire sky has been keyed out.

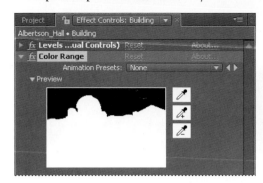 

Even with the sky keyed out, a slight fringe of color remains around the building. You can remove that fringe by choking the matte.

8 Hide the Color Range properties in the Effect Controls panel.

9 Choose Effect > Matte > Matte Choker.

10 In the Effect Controls panel, lower the Geometric Softness 1 value to **2** and increase the Geometric Softness 2 value to **2.5**.

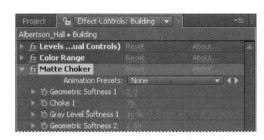 

11 Hide the Matte Choker properties in the Effect Controls panel, and save your work so far.

Adding a new background

With the original sky keyed out, you're ready to add the clouds to the scene.

1 Click the Project tab to display the Project panel. Then, drag the storm_clouds.jpg item from the Project panel to the Timeline panel, placing it below the Building layer.

2 Select the storm_clouds.jpg layer, press Enter or Return, rename the layer
   Clouds, and press Enter or Return again.

3 Click the Video switch (👁) for the Building layer to hide it. Now, you can fully
   see the storm clouds layer. You need to scale and reposition the clouds to fit the
   sky area of the image.

4 With the Clouds layer selected in the Timeline panel, press the **S** key to display
   its Scale property.

5 Decrease the Scale values to **60, 60%**.

▶ **Tip:** If you're typing
the values, press Tab to
jump between the
fields.

6 Make sure the Clouds layer is selected in the Timeline panel and press **P** to
   display its Position property.

7 Change the Position values to **360, 145**.

8 Press **P** to hide the Position property.

Color-correcting the clouds

Although the storm clouds are dramatic, the contrast of the image and the color cast don't really match the building. You'll use the Auto Levels effect to correct that.

The Auto Levels effect automatically sets highlights and shadows by defining the lightest and darkest pixels in each color channel as white and black, and then it redistributes intermediate pixel values proportionately. Because Auto Levels adjusts each color channel individually, it may remove or introduce a color cast. In this case, with the default settings applied, Auto Levels introduces a blue color cast that makes the clouds more intense.

1 With the Clouds layer selected in the Timeline panel, choose Effect > Color Correction > Auto Levels.

2 Turn on the Video switch (👁) for the Building layer so you can see the building with the clouds.

3 Choose File > Save to save your work.

Removing unwanted elements

The color is looking great, but you're not quite done. The director wants you to remove the lamp post that appears directly in front of the doors to the building, as she believes it is distracting. You'll use the Clone Stamp tool to paint out this unwanted element of the scene. Cloning in After Effects is similar to cloning in Photoshop, but you can clone across the entire timeline, rather than in a single image.

Because the lamp post doesn't move, you can touch up a single frame and apply it to the entire movie.

1 Press the Home key to make sure the current-time indicator is at the beginning of the time ruler.

2 Double-click the Building layer in the Timeline panel to open it in the Layer panel. You can paint only on individual layers—not the composition as a whole.

3 Zoom in to see the area around the doors clearly.

4 Select the Clone Stamp tool (🖋) in the Tools panel.

The Clone Stamp tool samples the pixels on a source layer and applies the sampled pixels to a target layer; the target layer can be the same layer or a different layer in the same composition.

When you select the Clone Stamp tool, After Effects opens the Brushes and Paint panels.

5 In the Brushes panel, select a hard, 5-pixel brush.

6 In the Paint panel, choose Constant from the Duration menu. The Constant setting applies the Clone Stamp effect from the current time forward. Because you're starting at the beginning of the composition, the changes you make will affect every frame in the composition.

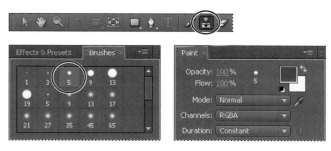

7 In the Layer panel, position the cursor to the right of the top of the lamp post. Alt-click (Windows) or Option-click (Mac OS) to designate a source point for cloning.

8 Click on the lamp post to clone an area, and then continue clicking to remove the entire lamp post.

▶ **Tip:** If you make a mistake, just press Ctrl+Z (Windows) or Command+Z (Mac OS) to undo the stroke, and then try again.

 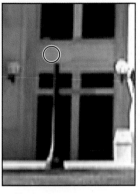 

9 When the lamp post is gone, select the Selection tool, and then close the Building layer panel.

Correcting a range of colors

You've corrected the overall color for the scene, but you can also enhance a specific area as a secondary color correction. In this shot, the color correction caused the grass in front of the building to look like a mature bluegrass instead of a welcoming green lawn. For this, you will use the Synthetic Aperture Color Finesse 2 effect, a third-party effect that installs with After Effects and offers the capability to isolate a color range and adjust only those colors.

● **Note:** Synthetic Aperture Color Finesse 2 is a powerful color-correction plug-in. Once you're familiar with it, you can use it to perform a wide variety of color corrections.

Color Finesse 2 applies its effect to the original layer, ignoring other effects you've applied. Because you've already performed some color correction, you'll precompose the layer to include the results of the effects you've applied.

1 Select the Building layer in the Timeline panel, and then press Ctrl+D (Windows) or Command+D (Mac OS) to duplicate the layer.

2 With the duplicate layer (Building 2) selected, choose Layer > Pre-compose.

3 In the Pre-compose dialog box, name the new composition **Grass Enhance**, select Move All Attributes Into The New Composition, and click OK.

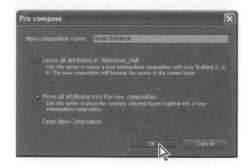

You've created the precomposed layer, so you'll retain the color-correction effects you've applied. However, to avoid any issues with the cloning you performed to remove the lamp post, you'll mask the grass area. The mask will ensure that only the grass is affected.

4 With the Grass Enhance layer selected in the Timeline panel, select the Pen tool (✒) in the Tools panel. Click around the grass area to create a mask.

5 With the Grass Enhance layer selected in the Timeline panel, press the **F** key to display the Mask Feather property, and change the amount to **2, 2** pixels. Feathering blends the layers more naturally.

6 Press the **F** key again to hide the Mask Feather property.

Now you're ready to use Color Finesse 2.

● **Note:** SA Color Finesse 2 may prompt you to enter a serial number. Use the one provided in your software package.

7 With the Grass Enhance layer selected, choose Effect > Synthetic Aperture > SA Color Finesse 2.

8 In the SA Color Finesse 2 area of the Effect Controls panel, click Full Interface.

SA Color Finesse 2 opens in its own window.

9 Check the box in the Secondary tab to activate secondary color correction, and then click the Secondary tab to open the Secondary color-correction controls.

SA Color Finesse 2 enables you to perform up to six different secondary color-correction operations. You'll need only one for this project, however.

10 Check the box on the A tab to perform your color-correction operation.

11 Using the four Sample eyedroppers, make four color selections in the grass area. Try to sample various shades of green from light to dark; zoom in if necessary to help you select a range of hues.

Four samples don't encompass the entire contrast range of the grass, but SA Color Finesse 2 has controls to refine the color selection.

12 Still on the A tab, choose Mask from the Preview menu. Now you can see the areas that are selected and those that are masked (shaded in red).

13 Adjust the Chroma Tolerance, Luma Tolerance, and Softness sliders until all of the grass is selected. It's okay if trees or shrubs are selected; the mask you applied earlier ensures that those adjustments will not appear in the final composition.

14 Increase the Saturation amount to **150**.

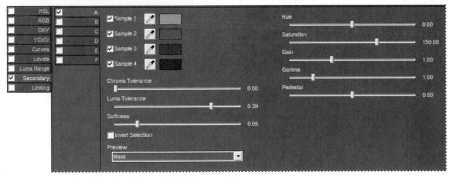

15 Choose Off from the Preview menu, and then click OK to apply the correction and to close the SA Color Finesse 2 window.

16 Choose File > Save to save your work.

● **Note:** To learn more about SA Color Finesse 2, read the manual included with the After Effects software.

Warming colors with the Photo Filter effect

Finally, you'll warm up the entire shot to make it more inviting with the Photo Filter effect.

The Photo Filter effect mimics the technique of using a colored filter on a camera lens to adjust the color balance and color temperature of the light transmitted through the lens and exposing the film. You can choose a color preset to apply a hue adjustment to an image, or you can specify a custom color using the Color Picker or the eyedropper.

To apply the warming filter to all the elements in the shot, you'll apply the Photo Filter effect to an adjustment layer.

1   Click an empty area in the Timeline panel to deselect all layers.

2   Choose Layer > New > Adjustment Layer. The new adjustment layer should be the first layer in the layer stack.

3   With the Adjustment layer selected in the Timeline panel, choose Effect > Color Correction > Photo Filter.

4   In the Effect Controls panel, choose Warming Filter (81) from the Filter menu.

5   Choose File > Save.

If you'd like to output the composition, see Lesson 14, "Rendering and Outputting," for details.

Congratulations. You've transformed the color of this composition and removed a distracting element.

Review questions

1 Why do you need to color-correct a shot?

2 What does the SA Color Finesse 2 effect do?

3 What effect can you use to warm up the colors in an image?

4 How can you clone an area across an entire timeline?

Review answers

1 Color correction is performed to optimize the source material, to focus attention on a key element in the shot, to correct errors in white balance and exposure, to ensure color consistency from one shot to another, or to create a color palette to match the visual look the director prefers.

2 SA Color Finesse 2 is a third-party plug-in installed with After Effects CS4. It performs a wide variety of color-correction effects, including the ability to isolate a color range for enhancement. SA Color Finesse 2 affects the original layer, ignoring any effects that have already been applied.

3 You can use the Photo Filter color-correction effect to warm up the color of an image. The Photo Filter effect mimics the technique of using a colored filter over the lens of a camera to adjust the color balance and color temperature of light transmitted through the lens and exposing the film. Choose the Warming Filter in the Photo Filter Effect Controls panel to warm up the color of an image.

4 To ensure that cloning occurs across the entire timeline, move the current-time indicator to the beginning of the time ruler, and then choose Constant from the Duration menu in the Paint panel.

11 BUILDING 3D OBJECTS

Lesson overview

In this lesson, you'll learn how to do the following:

- Create a 3D shape from a solid layer.

- Create 3D text with expressions.

- Look at a 3D scene from multiple views.

- Create a guide layer to aid in object placement.

- Control the way a layer animates by moving its anchor point.

- Rotate and position layers along x, y, and z axes.

 Adobe After Effects can work with layers in two dimensions (x, y) or three dimensions (x, y, z). So far in this book, you've worked almost exclusively in two dimensions. When you specify a layer as three-dimensional (3D), After Effects adds the z axis, which provides control over the layer's depth. By combining this depth with a variety of lights and camera angles, you can create animated 3D projects that take advantage of the full range of natural motion, lighting and shadows, perspective, and focusing effects. In this lesson, you'll explore how to create and control basic 3D layers. Then, in Lesson 12, "Using 3D Features," you'll continue working with this project, adding lights, effects, and other elements to animate the 3D objects and complete the composition, a promotional video for a book. This lesson will take approximately 1½ hours to complete.

By clicking a single switch in the Timeline panel in
After Effects, you can turn a 2D layer into a 3D layer,
opening up a whole new world of creative
possibilities.

Getting started

First, preview the movie you're creating, and then set up the project.

1   Make sure the following files are in the AECS4_CIB/Lessons/Lesson11 folder on your hard disk, or copy them from the *Adobe After Effects CS4 Classroom in a Book* DVD now:

  • In the Assets folder: AEBack.jpg, AEFront.jpg, AESpine.jpg

  • In the Sample_Movie folder: Lesson11.mov

2   Open and play the Lesson11.mov file to see what you will create in this lesson. When you are done, quit QuickTime Player. You may delete this sample movie from your hard disk if you have limited storage space.

When you begin this lesson, restore the default application settings for After Effects. See "Restoring default preferences" on page 3.

3   Press Ctrl+Alt+Shift (Windows) or Command+Option+Shift (Mac OS) while starting After Effects. When asked whether you want to delete your preferences file, click OK. Click Close to close the Welcome window.

After Effects opens to display an empty, untitled project.

4   Choose File > Save As.

5   In the Save Project As dialog box, navigate to the AECS4_CIB/Lessons/ Lesson11/ Finished_Project folder.

6   Name the project **Lesson11_Finished.aep**, and then click Save.

Creating the composition

The animation you will create in this lesson features a 3D representation of a book about After Effects CS4. First, you'll set up a composition to model the first object.

1   Click the Create A New Composition button (▣) at the bottom of the Project panel.

2   In the Composition Settings dialog box, name the composition **Book**, and choose NTSC DV from the Preset menu.

3 Choose Square Pixels from the Pixel Aspect Ratio menu, because you will be working with graphics that have square pixels.

4 Enter **10:00** for the Duration, and click OK.

Importing assets

You'll use three Photoshop files in this project: images of the front cover, back cover, and spine of the book.

1 Double-click in an empty area of the Project panel.

2 In the Import File dialog box, navigate to the AECS4_CIB/ Lessons/Lesson11/Assets folder.

3 Shift-click to select the AEBack.jpg, AEFront.jpg, and AESpine.jpg files, and then click Open.

Building a 3D object

In order to move the book in 3D space, you'll need to create the 3D object. You'll build it piece by piece. Initially, any layer is flat, with only x (width) and y (height) dimensions. It can be moved only along those axes. But all you have to do to move the layer in three dimensions is to turn on the 3D Layer switch. With that switch on, you can also manipulate the object along its z axis (depth).

Before you build the book, you'll set up the environment to help you with perspective.

Creating the 3D floor

A grid layer, serving as a floor for the 3D space, can help you maintain perspective.

1 Click in the Timeline panel to make it active.

2 Choose Layer > New > Solid.

3 In the Solid Settings dialog box, name the layer **3D Grid**.

4 Enter **800** pixels for the Width and the Height, and then click OK to create the layer.

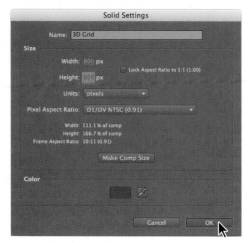

5 With the 3D Grid layer selected in the Timeline panel, choose Effect > Generate > Grid.

The Effect Controls panel displays the Grid effect properties. You can customize the grid if you want to, but the default settings will work for this lesson. The grid is simply to offer perspective as you work.

6 In the Timeline panel, expand the 3D Grid Transform properties. The Position property is at 360, 240, the center of the composition. Whenever you add an element to the Timeline panel, its anchor point will be at this center point.

7 In the Timeline panel, select the 3D Layer switch (⬤) for the 3D Grid layer to make the layer three-dimensional.

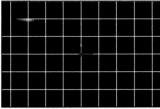

Three 3D Rotation properties appear in the Transform group for the layer, and properties that previously supported only two dimensions now display a third value for the z axis. In addition, a new property group named Material Options appears.

A color-coded 3D axis appears over the layer's anchor point in the Composition window. The red arrow controls the x axis, the green arrow controls the y axis, and the blue arrow controls the z axis. At the moment, the z axis appears at the intersection of the x and y axes. The letters *x*, *y*, and *z* appear when you position the pointer over the corresponding axis. When you move or rotate the layer while the pointer is over a particular axis, the layer's movement is restricted to that axis.

● **Note:** Material Options properties specify how the layer interacts with light. You'll work with the Material Options property group in Lesson 12, "Using 3D Features."

8 In the Timeline panel, change the X Rotation angle to **90** degrees. The grid seems to disappear, but don't worry—it's still there!

Using 3D views

Sometimes the appearance of 3D layers can be deceptive. For example, a layer might appear to be scaling smaller along its x and y axes when it's actually moving along the z axis. You can't always tell from the default view in the Composition panel. The Select View Layout pop-up menu at the bottom of the Composition panel lets you divide the panel into different views of a single frame, so you can see your work from multiple angles. You specify the different views using the 3D View pop-up menu.

1 At the bottom of the Composition panel, click the Select View Layout pop-up menu and choose 2 Views – Horizontal. The left side of the Composition panel displays the Top view of the frame, and the right side displays the Active Camera view, which you've been viewing.

2 Click in the left side of the Composition panel to make the Top view active. Orange corner tabs appear around the active view.

3 Choose Custom View 1 from the 3D View pop-up menu at the bottom of the panel.

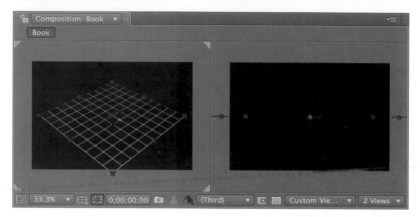

In the Custom View 1 window, you can see that the layer is a grid that can offer true perspective in 3D space.

4 Hide the properties for the 3D Grid layer in the Timeline panel.

5 Choose File > Save to save your work so far.

Creating a guide layer

Guide layers help you position and edit elements in the Composition panel. For example, you can use guide layers for visual reference, audio timing, timecode reference, or even to store comments to yourself. In this project, you want to use the 3D Grid layer to help you place objects, but you don't want to render it in the final artwork. You'll convert it to a guide layer and lock it to ensure it stays in place.

1 Select the 3D Grid layer in the Timeline panel, and choose Layer > Guide Layer. A cyan grid appears next to the layer name in the Timeline panel to indicate that it's a guide layer.

2 Select the Lock switch (🔒) for the 3D Grid layer in the Timeline panel to lock the layer.

Adding the first side of the object

With your grid in place as a guide layer, you're ready to start building the book. What better place to start than the front cover?

1 Click the Project tab to make the panel active, and then drag the AEFront.jpg item into the Timeline panel, placing it at the top of the layer stack, above the 3D Grid layer.

2 Select the 3D Layer switch (⬤) for the AEFront.jpg layer.

The book cover is much larger than the composition, and it intersects the grid. You'll scale the AEFront.jpg layer later, after the entire object is built. But you'll reposition the cover to rest firmly on the floor of the grid now. To do this, you'll reposition the layer's anchor point to the bottom of the book cover.

3 With the AEFront.jpg layer selected in the Timeline, press the **A** key to display the layer's Anchor Point property.

Currently, the anchor point for the AEFront.jpg layer is in the center of the book. You want the anchor point to be at the bottom of the book cover, to match the anchor point at the center of the grid. Because the current y-axis value is at the center, and therefore halfway down the book, you can simply multiply that value by 2 for the new Anchor Point value.

Note: Positive values on the x axis move an element to the right; positive values on the y axis move an element down; and positive values on the z axis move an element away from the active camera.

4 Click the y-axis value (the middle value), and add ***2** to the value, so that it reads **617*2**. Press Enter or Return to accept the calculation. The layer moves to sit on the grid.

Importing 3D images from Adobe Photoshop Extended

Adobe Photoshop Extended can import and manipulate 3D models in several popular formats. You can manipulate these models in Photoshop Extended and then save one or more frames as PSD files for import into After Effects.

Alternatively, you can use the Vanishing Point feature in Photoshop Extended to create 3D images, and then use the Export For After Effects command to save the results as a collection of PNG files—one for each plane—and a .vpe (Vanishing Point Exchange) file that describes the geometry of the scene. When you import the .vpe file, After Effects uses its information to re-create the scene as a composition containing a camera layer and one perspective-corrected 3D layer for each PNG file.

Positioning 3D elements

When you build a 3D object, you need to position the 3D layers in relationship to each other. You'll position the spine of the book by moving its anchor point and then adjusting the front cover as necessary.

1 Drag the AESpine.jpg item from the Project panel into the Timeline panel, placing it at the top of the layer stack.

2 Select the 3D Layer switch (⬡) for the AESpine.jpg layer.

3 Ctrl-click (Windows) or Command-click (Mac OS) the triangle in the Label column for the AESpine.jpg layer to display all of its Transform properties.

4 Click the y-axis value (the middle value) for the Anchor Point property, and then add ***2**, so that its value is **617*2**. Press Enter or Return to accept the calculation.

As with the front cover, moving the anchor point for the spine positions it to sit on the floor of the 3D space. However, the spine is facing the same direction as the front cover. You'll need to rotate it.

5 Change the Y Rotation property for the AESpine.jpg layer to **+90**.

Now the spine is facing the right direction, but it's in the middle of the front cover. To move it into place, you'll use the same simple math trick you used to position the book atop the floor.

6 Select the AEFront.jpg item in the Project panel, and note its width. It's exactly 1000 pixels wide.

The AESpine.jpg layer currently intersects the middle of the AEFront.jpg layer. Therefore, moving the spine 500 pixels to the left will align it appropriately. To move an object to the left on the x axis, subtract pixels.

7 In the Timeline panel, click the x-axis value (the first value) for the Position property, and then append **-500** to the value, so the new value is **360.0-500**. Press Enter or Return.

The spine moves to the end of the book. It's close, but it protrudes from the front of the book. You'll move the AEFront.jpg layer forward to fix that.

8 In the Timeline panel, select the AEFront.jpg layer, and then press **P** to display its Position property.

9 Click the z-axis value (the third value) for the Position property of the AEFront.jpg layer, and change the value to **-56**. A negative value on the z axis moves the layer toward the active camera view (forward).

10 Close all properties for the AESpine.jpg and AEFront.jpg layers to keep the Timeline panel neat.

Replacing a 3D element with another

Instead of repeating all the steps to position the back cover, you'll duplicate the front cover and replace it with the back cover.

1 Select the AEFront.jpg layer in the Timeline panel, and press Ctrl+D (Windows) or Command+D (Mac OS) to duplicate the layer.

2 With the duplicate layer selected, press **P** to display its Position property.

3 Change the z-axis value to **+56** to move the layer away from the active camera view. Because this will be the back cover, you want to position it at the back of the spine, which is 112 pixels wide.

4 In the Composition panel, change the right view to Custom View 3 so you can see both ends of the book.

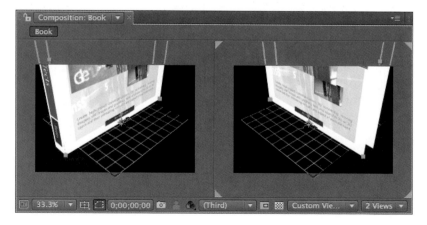

5 With the duplicate layer selected in the Timeline panel, press **R** to display the layer's Rotation properties, and change its Y Rotation value to **180** degrees. The rotation flips the layer.

6 With the duplicate layer selected in the Timeline panel, press Alt (Windows) or Option (Mac OS) as you drag the AEBack.jpg item from the Project panel onto the duplicate layer. After Effects replaces the front cover with the back cover, and changes the layer name to AEBack.jpg.

Adjusting views with the Camera tools

By definition, 3D objects can appear different from different angles. You can adjust the camera view to see the object from other directions so that you can identify gaps, make positioning adjustments, and otherwise evaluate and plan your project.

1 Select the Track Z Camera tool (🕯), hidden behind the Unified Camera tool (📷) in the Tools panel. The Track Z Camera tool lets you zoom in and out of a composition view.

2 Click in the left view (Custom View 1) in the Composition panel to ensure it's active. Then, click and drag to the left or down to zoom out from the scene and see the entire book. You may need to click and drag multiple times.

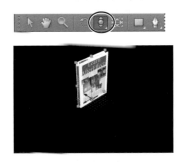

3 Select the Orbit Camera tool (🌐), hidden behind the Track Z Camera tool in the Tools panel. The Orbit Camera tool rotates the current 3D view by moving the camera around the point of interest.

4 Drag the Orbit Camera tool to the left or right in the left view of the Composition window so that you can see the back of the book. Remember, when you're using the Orbit Camera tool, you're rotating the view, not the object itself.

5 Drag the Orbit Camera tool again so that you are viewing the front of the book.

6 Select the Selection tool (⬉) in the Tools panel, and choose File > Save to save your work so far.

Adding solid layers to a 3D object

You've assembled the front cover, back cover, and spine of the book. But it's still lacking a top and right side (opposite the spine). Because these sides don't require specific content, you can create them using solid layers.

1 Press Ctrl+Y (Windows) or Command+Y (Mac OS) to create a new solid layer.

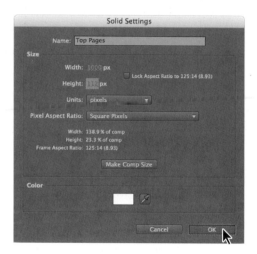

2 In the Solid Settings dialog box, name the layer **Top Pages**, change the width to **1000** pixels (to match the cover width), and the height to **112** pixels (to match the width of the spine).

3 Click the eyedropper and sample a white area of the book cover to match it. Click OK to create the layer.

4 Select the 3D Layer switch (◉) for the Top Pages layer.

5 Press **R** to display the Rotation properties, and change the X Rotation property to **90** degrees.

6 Press **P** to display the Position property. Click the y-axis value, and type **240-1234**. Press Enter or Return to accept the calculation.

Why those numbers? The current position is 240, and you want to move it up the height of the book, which is 1234 pixels.

7 Press Ctrl+Y (Windows) or Command+Y (Mac OS) to create another solid layer for the right side of the book, representing the edges of the pages that are bound by the spine on the left side.

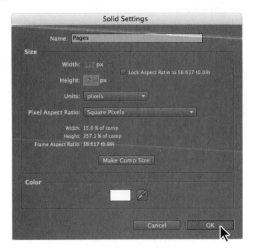

8 In the Solid Settings dialog box, name the layer **Pages**, change the Width to **112** pixels (the width of the spine) and the Height to **1234** pixels (the height of the covers). Make sure the layer is white, and then click OK.

9 Select the 3D Layer switch (⬤) for the Pages layer.

The Pages layer needs to be on the right side of the book. You'll change its Anchor Point, Rotation, and Position properties to get it there.

10 Ctrl-click (Windows) or Command-click (Mac OS) the triangle next to the Label column for the Pages layer to display all its Transform properties.

11 Change the y-axis value for the Anchor Point property to **1234** (placing the layer on the virtual floor); change the Y Rotation amount to **90** to make it face the right direction; and change the x-axis value for the Position property to **360+500** to move the layer to the right side of the book.

● **Note:** For this project, it's unlikely that anyone will see the bottom of the book. But if you want to add a bottom layer, duplicate the top layer and move it into position.

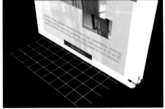

12 With the Timeline panel active, press Ctrl+A (Windows) or Command+A (Mac OS) to select all the layers. Then, press the U key to close all the properties for the layers.

▶ **Tip:** Pressing the U key multiple times cycles through the reveal/hide options.

Working with a null object

A null object is an invisible layer that has all the properties of a visible layer, so that it can be a parent to any layer in the composition. You'll use a null object to scale the layers of the 3D object down to a more manageable size. If you began to scale each of the individual layers, you'd have to reposition each of them again. This way, you can parent all the layers to a single null layer, and then as you scale the null layer, all the other layers follow, maintaining their relationship to each other.

1 With the Timeline panel active, choose Layer > New > Null Object. After Effects names the layer Null 1.

2 Select the 3D Layer switch (⬢) for the Null 1 layer to make it three-dimensional.

The null object moves to the origin point of the composition, at the center of the grid. Though you can see the null object in the Composition panel, remember that there isn't really anything there—it's an invisible layer. The representation of the object is to help you keep track of it as you work with it.

3 In the Timeline panel, select the Pages layer, and then Shift-click the AEFront.jpg layer to select all the layers in between. (Only the 3D Grid and Null 1 layers should not be selected.)

4 Select Null 1 from the Parent pop-up menu for the Pages layer. The same selection is automatically applied to all selected layers.

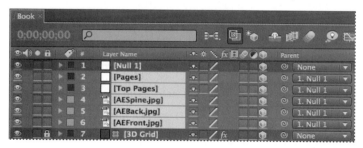

Because the 3D object layers are now parented to the Null 1 layer, any changes to the null object will affect them.

● **Note:** Because the Scale property values are linked, you need only enter the value once to affect all three axes.

5 Select the Null 1 layer in the Timeline panel, and press **S** to reveal its Scale property. Then, change the Scale amount to **20, 20, 20 %**.

The entire book is smaller, and each of the elements retains its relationship with the others.

6   Select the Track Z Camera tool (◈), hidden behind the Orbit Camera tool (◉) in the Tools panel. Then drag to the right in the left view of the Composition panel to zoom into the book so you can see it more clearly.

7   Select the right view in the Composition panel to make it active. Then choose Active Camera from the 3D View pop-up menu at the bottom of the Composition panel.

Working with 3D text

Just as you can create other 3D objects in After Effects, you can create 3D text. Flat text isn't as interesting, so you'll give the text more depth.

Creating the composition

You'll create a new composition for the text, and just as you did before, you'll create a 3D grid to serve as the floor of the space to help you maintain perspective.

1   Click the Create A New Composition button (▣) at the bottom of the Project panel.

2   In the Composition Settings dialog box, name the composition **3D Text**, and choose NTSC DV from the Preset menu. Then, click OK to create the composition.

3   Press Ctrl+Y (Windows) or Command+Y (Mac OS) to create a new solid layer.

4   In the Solid Settings dialog box, name the layer **3D Grid**, set the Width and Height both to **800** pixels, and click OK.

5   With the 3D Grid layer selected in the Timeline panel, choose Effect > Generate > Grid.

6   Select the 3D Layer switch (◉) for the 3D Grid layer.

7 With the 3D Grid layer selected in the Timeline panel, press **R** to reveal its Rotation properties. Then, change the X Rotation value to **90** degrees. Press **R** again to hide the Rotation properties.

▶ **Tip:** If you plan to work with 3D objects in the future, save the composition to use as a basis for later projects so that you'll already have a 3D grid in place.

8 With the 3D Grid layer selected in the Timeline panel, choose Layer > Guide Layer.

You've created a grid to guide you as you work with 3D text, but the layer won't render with your project.

Creating 3D text

With the grid in place, you're ready to create the text. You'll type the words first, and then convert the layer to a 3D layer.

1 Select the Horizontal Type tool (T) in the Tools panel. After Effects opens the Character and Paragraph panels.

2 In the Character panel, do the following:

- Choose Myriad Pro for the font family.
- Choose Bold for the font style.
- Select white for the text color.
- Set the stroke color to none.
- Change the font size to **120** pixels.

3 In the Paragraph panel, select the Center Text alignment option.

4 Click anywhere in the Composition panel, in either view, and type **AECS4**. Then, click in an empty area of the Timeline panel to deactivate the Horizontal Type tool.

5 Select the 3D Layer switch () for the AECS4 layer.

6 With the AECS4 layer selected in the Timeline panel, press **P** to reveal its Position property.

7 Right-click (Windows) or Control-click (Mac OS) the Position property name, and choose Reset from the context menu. The text moves to the center of the grid.

Adding depth to the text with expressions

The text is three-dimensional, but one of those dimensions—the z axis—is only 1 pixel wide. You'll duplicate the layer and offset it by 1 pixel to add depth to the text.

1 Select the AECS4 layer in the Timeline panel, and choose Edit > Duplicate.

2 Double-click the original AECS4 layer in the Timeline panel to select its contents.

3 In the Character panel, change the text color to blue (RGB 19, 125, 245), and click an empty area of the Timeline panel to deactivate the Horizontal Type tool.

4 Press Alt (Windows) or Option (Mac OS) as you click the stopwatch icon next to the Position property for the original AECS4 layer.

After Effects displays the words *transform.position* in the expression field in the time ruler. With expressions, you can create relationships between layer properties and use one property's keyframes to dynamically animate another layer. To learn more about expressions, see the sidebar called "About expressions" in Lesson 6.

5 Type **thisComp.layer(index-1).transform.position+[0,0,1]** to replace *transform.position* in the expression field.

6 Click an empty area of the Timeline panel to accept the expression.

● **Note:** This technique gives you the effect of extrusion in some views, but may not provide good results when you rotate the text at some angles. For true extruded text, use Adobe Photoshop Extended.

● **Note:** The duplicate layer is named AECS5 because After Effects continues the layer numbering from AECS4, but the content of the layer has not been changed.

● **Note:** While you are editing an expression, all previews are suspended; a red bar appears at the bottom of panels until you exit text-editing mode.

The expression you typed instructs After Effects to use the layer immediately above it, changing the Position property by 1 pixel on the z axis. Here's how it breaks down: *thisComp.layer* refers to this composition, *index-1* refers to the layer immediately above the current layer, *transform.position* means to change the Position property, and +*[0,0,1]* means add 1 pixel to the z axis.

You don't have to memorize this expression or learn JavaScript, the language used in expressions. You can adapt simple expressions and modify them to meet your needs. Or you can use a pick whip, as you did in earlier lessons, to create relationships between layer properties.

7 Select the Orbit Camera tool (⚬), and drag across the left view in the Composition window to see the back of the text. The back is blue and the front is white. But it's still only 2 pixels deep.

8 Select the original AECS4 layer in the Timeline panel, and press Ctrl+D (Windows) or Command+D (Mac OS) 19 times to create 19 additional layers.

9 Use the Orbit Camera tool to move around the object. The text object is much deeper now, as you copied the expression along with each of those 19 layers. The front layer is white, but all the other layers are blue. To see the effect more clearly, change the right view to Custom View 3.

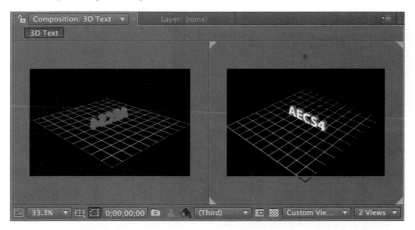

10 Choose File > Save to save your work so far.

Creating a backdrop for 3D animation

The book and text are both ready for animation. But they need to be animated against a backdrop. You'll create a two-dimensional environment for the 3D objects in a new composition.

1 Click the Project tab, and then click the Create A New Composition button (▣) in the Project panel.

2 In the Composition Settings dialog box, name the composition **Final Comp**, and choose NTSC DV from the Preset menu. Then, click OK.

3 In the Composition panel, choose 1 View from the Select View Layout pop-up menu.

4 Choose Custom View 1 from the 3D pop-up menu at the bottom of the Composition panel so you can see the backdrop from a different angle than a flat, forward view.

5 Choose Layer > New > Solid.

6 In the Solid Settings dialog box, name the layer **Backdrop**, set the Width and Height to **1000** pixels, and click OK.

7 With the Backdrop layer selected in the Timeline panel, choose Effect > Generate > Ramp. The layer becomes a gradient.

8 In the Effect Controls panel, change the Start Of Ramp value to **500, 500**. Then, change the Start Color to a dark blue (RGB **36, 77, 254**) and the End Color to black (RGB **0, 0, 0**). Choose Radial Ramp from the Ramp Shape menu.

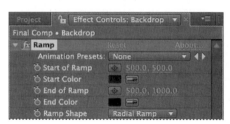

9 Select the Lock switch for the Backdrop layer to prevent accidental changes to it. There's no need to convert this layer to a 3D layer because it will be an infinite distance from the animated 3D objects.

10 Press Ctrl+Y (Windows) or Command+Y (Mac OS) to create a new solid layer.

11 In the Solid Settings dialog box, name the layer **Ground**, and set the Width and Height to **1000** pixels. Then, click OK.

12 With the Ground layer selected in the Timeline panel, choose Effect > Noise & Grain > Fractal Noise.

13 In the Effect Controls panel, choose Dynamic Twist from the Fractal Type menu.

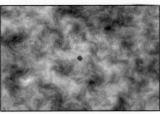

14 In the Timeline panel, select the 3D Layer switch (⬡) for the Ground layer.

15 With the Ground layer selected, press **R** to reveal the Rotation properties, and change the X Rotation value to **90** degrees.

16 Press **S** to reveal the Scale property. Change the Scale values to **1000**, **1000**, **1000**.

17 Click the Toggle Switches/Modes button at the bottom of the Timeline panel to display the Modes column.

18 For the Ground layer, choose Overlay from the Mode menu.

19 Press **S** to close the Scale property, and then lock the Ground layer.

Nesting a 3D composition

You've created the environment for the 3D objects that you created earlier: the book and the text. The Book composition contains all the elements of the book. You'll add that composition to the Final Comp composition, and then select the Collapse Transformations switch so that it behaves as a 3D layer.

1 Click the Project tab to display the panel. Then, drag the Book composition from the Project panel to the Final Comp Timeline panel, placing it at the top of the layer stack.

The Book composition doesn't show up because it's not yet a 3D layer.

2 Click the Toggle Switches/Modes button at the bottom of the Timeline panel to display switches.

3 Select the 3D Layer switch (⬡) for the Book layer to convert it to 3D.

The Book composition appears in the Composition window, but only the front cover appears to be included. When you nest a 3D composition in another composition, you need to select the Collapse Transformations switch for the layer. Otherwise, the composition is rendered as a 2D layer and does not interact with 3D layers.

4 Select the Collapse Transformations switch (✱) for the Book layer.

Now the entire book appears, just as you created it. If you change Rotation property values, the entire object rotates, rather than individual layers. The guide layer is not visible in the nested composition.

Adding a camera

You can view 3D layers from any number of angles and distances using layers called *cameras*. When you set a camera view for your composition, you look at the layers as though you were looking through that camera. You can choose between viewing a composition through the active camera or through a named, custom camera. If you have not created a custom camera, then the active camera is the same as the default composition view.

So far, you have primarily been viewing this composition from the Custom View 1 angle, which doesn't take blending modes or 2D layers into account. Switching to the Active Camera view doesn't let you see your composition from an angle. To see everything you want to see, you'll create a custom camera.

1 Choose Layer > New > Camera.

2 In the Camera Settings dialog box, accept all of the defaults, including the name, Camera 1, and the 50mm preset, and then click OK.

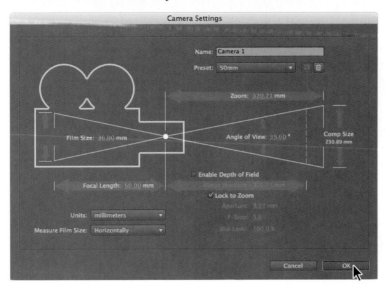

The Camera 1 layer appears at the top of the layer stack in the Timeline panel (with a camera icon next to the layer name), and the Composition panel updates to reflect the new camera layer's perspective. The view doesn't appear to change, however, because the 50mm camera preset uses the same settings as the default Active Camera view.

3 Choose 2 Views – Horizontal from the Select View Layout pop-up menu at the bottom of the Composition panel. Change the left view to Right and the right view to Active Camera.

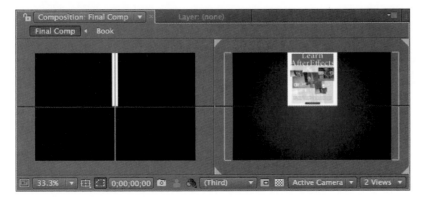

Setting the camera's point of interest

Camera layers have a point of interest that can be used to determine what the camera looks at. By default, the camera's point of interest is the center of the composition. You'll set this camera layer to look at the Book and Ground layers from a very specific angle.

1 Expand the Camera 1 layer's Transform property group in the Timeline panel.

2 While watching the right view (on the left side) in the Composition panel, drag the Point Of Interest property y-axis value to the left in the Timeline panel until the point of interest icon (✧) in the Composition panel is in the middle of the book. The final value should be 123; enter it manually if necessary.

3 In the Timeline panel, change the Point Of Interest x-axis value to **602** and the z-axis value to **157**.

This perspective looks a little more interesting, but the camera is intersecting the Ground layer plane. The Point Of Interest property determines where the camera is looking, but its placement is controlled by its Position property.

4 Change the Position property values for the Camera 1 layer to **27, 132, -640**.

The book in the Active Camera view (on the right) looks a lot better.

5 Close all the properties for the Camera 1 layer, and choose File > Save.

Completing the scene

You're ready to add the 3D Text composition you created earlier. As with the Book composition, you'll need to select the 3D switch and the Collapse Transformations switch for it to behave as a true 3D object.

1   Drag the 3D Text composition from the Project panel to the Timeline panel, placing it directly below the Camera 1 layer.

2   Select the 3D Layer switch (●) and the Collapse Transformations switch for the 3D Text layer.

3   In the Composition panel, choose 1 View from the Select View Layout menu, and choose Active Camera from the 3D View pop-up menu.

4   With the 3D Text layer selected in the Timeline panel, press **R** to reveal the Rotation properties for the layer. Then, change the Y Rotation value to **60** degrees.

5   Press the **P** key to reveal the Position property for the 3D Text layer. Change the Position values to **762, 240, 100**.

6   Close any open properties in the Timeline panel, and choose File > Save.

You've created 3D objects and assembled them in a virtual space. In Lesson 12, "Using 3D Features," you'll continue working on this project. For the final movie, you'll add lights, adjust surface properties, and animate the camera.

About 3D rotation

You can adjust 3D rotation two ways: by changing a layer's Orientation values, or changing its X, Y, and Z Rotation values. You can use the Rotation tool to change any of these values.

When you animate any of a 3D layer's Orientation values, the layer moves along the shortest possible rotational path in 3D space, creating natural and predictable rotations. You can smooth this path by changing the spatial keyframe interpolation to Auto Bezier.

When you animate any of a 3D layer's X, Y, or Z Rotation values, the layer rotates along each individual axis. You can adjust the number of rotations as well as the angle of rotation. You can also add keyframes to the layer's rotation on each axis individually. Animating these properties allows for more alternatives for fine control with keyframes and expressions than animating with the Orientation property, but also may result in motion that is less predictable. The individual Rotation properties are useful for creating rotations with multiple revolutions along a single axis.

Review questions

1   What happens to a layer when you select its 3D Layer switch?

2   Why is it important to look at multiple views of a composition that contains 3D layers?

3   What happens when you move a layer's Anchor Point values in the Timeline panel?

4   What is a camera layer?

Review answers

1   When you select a layer's 3D Layer switch in the Timeline panel, After Effects adds a third axis, the z axis, to the layer. You can then move and rotate the layer in three dimensions. In addition, the layer takes on new properties that are unique to 3D layers, such as the Material Options property group.

2   The appearance of 3D layers can be deceptive, depending on the view in the Composition panel. By enabling 3D views, you can see the true position of a layer relative to other layers in the composition.

3   When you adjust the Anchor Point values for a layer in the Timeline panel, the layer moves in the Composition panel even though its Position values remain the same.

4   You can view After Effects 3D layers from any number of angles and distances using layers called *cameras*. When you set a camera view for your composition, you look at the layers as though you were looking through that camera. You can choose between viewing a composition through the active camera or through a named, custom camera. If you have not created a custom camera, then the active camera is the same as the default composition view.

12 USING 3D FEATURES

Lesson overview

In this lesson, you'll learn how to do the following:

- Animate 3D objects.

- Add reflections to 3D objects.

- Use an adjustment layer to blur multiple layers.

- Animate a camera layer.

- Create and position light layers.

- Add a Linear Wipe effect to reveal objects in the composition.

 This lesson picks up where the previous lesson left off. In Lesson 11, "Building 3D Objects," you created the first half of an animation promoting a book. So far, a 3D representation of the book and 3D text are positioned in 3D space. In this lesson, you will complete the project by adding lights, effects, reflections, and other elements to the composition. In doing so, you'll learn how to use additional 3D features available in Adobe After Effects. This lesson will take approximately 1 hour to complete.

In Lesson 11, you created 3D objects and positioned them in a virtual world. Animation, lights, adjustment layers, and animated cameras complete the composition.

Getting started

This lesson is a continuation of the project you started in Lesson 11. Begin with the Lesson12_Start.aep project file provided with this book, or, if you completed Lesson 11, you can use the project file that you saved at the end of that lesson. The two files should be equivalent.

1 Make sure the following files are in the AECS4_CIB/Lessons/Lesson12 folder on your hard disk, or copy them from the *Adobe After Effects CS4 Classroom in a Book* DVD now:

- In the Assets folder: AEBack.jpg, AEFront.jpg, AESpine.jpg, brush.psd
- In the Sample_Movie folder: Lesson12.mov
- In the Start_Project folder: Lesson12_Start.aep

2 Open and play the Lesson12.mov file to see what you will create in this lesson. When you are done, quit QuickTime Player. You may delete this sample movie from your hard disk if you have limited storage space.

When you begin this lesson, restore the default application settings for After Effects. See "Restoring default preferences" on page 3.

3 Press Ctrl+Alt+Shift (Windows) or Command+Option+Shift (Mac OS) while starting After Effects. When asked whether you want to delete your preferences file, click OK. Click Close to close the Welcome window.

4 Choose File > Open Project.

5 Do one of the following:

- Navigate to the AECS4_CIB/Lessons/Lesson12/Start_Project_File folder, select the Lesson12_Start.aep file, and click Open.
- Navigate to the AECS4_CIB/Lessons/Lesson11/Finished_Project folder, select the Lesson11_Finished.aep file, and click Open.

6 Choose File > Import > File, and then navigate to the AECS4_CIB/Lessons/Lesson12/Assets folder.

7 Select the brush.psd file, and click Open.

8 In the Brush.psd dialog box, select Footage from the Import Kind menu, select Merged Layers, and click OK.

9 Choose File > Save As.

10 Navigate to the AECS4_CIB/Lessons/Lesson12/Finished_Project folder on your hard disk. Name the project **Lesson12_Finished.aep**, and then click Save.

Animating 3D objects

You've animated objects in earlier lessons, but 3D objects can be animated across the x, y, and z axes. You'll animate the 3D Text layer to make the composition more dynamic.

1   Click the Final Comp tab in the Timeline panel if it's not already active.

2   Move the current-time indicator to 0:15.

3   Select the 3D Text layer in the Timeline panel, and press the **P** key to reveal the Position property for the layer.

4   Click the stopwatch icon next to the Position property to set an initial keyframe for the layer.

5   Press the Home key to move the current-time indicator to the beginning of the time ruler.

6   In the Composition panel, click the x-axis control (the red arrow) on the 3D axis, and drag the 3D Text layer to the right until it is completely out of the frame.

When you select only one axis in the Composition panel, you restrict movement of the 3D layer to that axis.

7   Manually move the current-time indicator from 0:00 to 0:15 to see the text come into the frame. It arrives abruptly; you'll ease that transition.

8 Click the Position property name to select all the Position keyframes for the 3D Text layer.

9 Choose Animation > Keyframe Assistant > Easy Ease.

10 Press the **P** key to hide the Position property.

Adding reflections to 3D objects

In the real world, objects cast reflections in certain lighting conditions. Those reflections add depth and interest. After Effects can't cast real reflections on surfaces, but you can add them by duplicating layers and applying a blur effect.

Creating a simple reflection

A reflection is a mirror image of an object, though it's usually a little distorted, depending on the light source. You'll duplicate objects to create a simple reflection.

1 Go to 0:15, if you're not there already, so you can see the text.

2 Select the 3D Text layer in the Timeline panel, and press Ctrl+D (Windows) or Command+D (Mac OS) to duplicate the layer.

3 Select the duplicate layer, press Enter or Return, and rename it **3D Text Reflection**. Press Enter or Return.

4 Move the 3D Text Reflection layer below the Ground layer in the Timeline panel.

The duplicate layer is in the same position as the original 3D Text layer. You'll flip it to create the reflection.

5 With the 3D Text Reflection layer selected in the Timeline panel, choose Layer > Transform > Flip Vertical.

6 Press the **T** key to reveal the Opacity property, and change the Opacity value to **30%**. Then, press the **T** key again to hide the Opacity property.

You've created a reflection for the text. Now, you'll do the same thing for the book.

7 Select the Book layer in the Timeline panel, and press Ctrl+D (Windows) or Command+D (Mac OS) to duplicate the layer.

8 Rename the duplicate layer **Book Reflection**, and move it below the Ground layer in the Timeline panel.

9 With the Book Reflection layer selected, press **S** to reveal the Scale property, click the Constrain Proportions icon to unlink the values, and change the y-axis value to **-100%**.

10 Press the **T** key to reveal the Opacity property, change the Opacity value to **30%**, and press **T** again to hide the Opacity property.

Adding an adjustment layer

A simple reflection is pretty good, but a blur would make it look more realistic. You'll use an adjustment layer to apply a blur effect. Effects applied to an adjustment layer affect all the layers beneath it.

1 Choose Layer > New > Adjustment Layer. After Effects adds a new adjustment layer at the top of the layer stack.

2 Move the Adjustment Layer 1 layer below the Ground layer in the Timeline panel.

Because adjustment layers affect all the layers beneath them, moving the adjustment layer below the Ground layer ensures that its effects will affect only the reflection and Backdrop layers.

3 With the Adjustment Layer 1 layer selected, choose Effect > Blur & Sharpen > Directional Blur.

4 In the Effect Controls panel, change the Blur Length to **20**. Leave the Direction setting at its default, as the reflections are perpendicular to the floor.

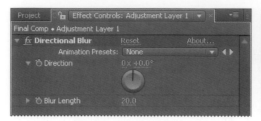 

5 Lock the Adjustment Layer 1 layer to prevent any accidental changes to it.

6 Choose File > Save to save your work so far.

Animating a camera

In Lesson 11, you created a camera layer, Camera 1. So far, that camera has been steady. Now, you'll animate the camera, so that it begins far from the 3D objects and moves closer to them as the movie progresses.

1 Go to 4:00 in the Timeline panel. This is the point where the camera will come to rest, after it's moved closer to the subject.

2 Select the Camera 1 layer in the Timeline panel, and press **P** to reveal its Position property.

3 Press the Shift key as you press **A** to reveal the Point Of Interest property for the Camera 1 layer, as well.

4 Click the stopwatch icons for the Position and Point Of Interest properties to create keyframes for each.

You've set the keyframes for the end of the camera movement. Rather than starting the camera movement at the beginning of the time ruler, you'll begin at 0:10, so that viewers have a moment to orient themselves before the camera begins to zoom in.

5 Go to 0:10 in the Timeline panel.

6 Change the Camera 1 Position values to **-185, 132, -3000**, and the Point Of Interest values to **360, 240, 0**. The camera is much farther from the objects and the book is centered in its view.

7 Shift-click the Point Of Interest and Position property names to select all the keyframes for the layer, and then choose Animation > Keyframe Assistant > Easy Ease.

8 Press the space bar to preview your work so far. Press the space bar again to stop the preview.

9 Hide the Camera 1 layer properties.

Adjusting layer timing

Earlier, you animated the 3D text, so that it arrived at 0:13. But with the book centered at the beginning of the movie, the animated text will be more effective if it arrives much later. You'll move it now.

1 Go to 3:23 in the time ruler. This is just before the camera reaches its resting point, so there will be some overlap in movement as the text comes in.

2 Select the 3D Text layer in the Timeline panel, and then press Ctrl (Windows) or Command (Mac) as you select the 3D Text Reflection layer, as well.

3 Press the [(left bracket) key to move the In point for both layers to the current time.

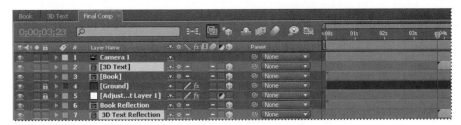

4 Press the Home key to move to the beginning of the time ruler. Then, press the spacebar to preview the animation. When you've finished watching the animation, press the spacebar again to stop the preview.

Using 3D lights

The composition is looking good so far. Adding lighting will give the scene depth and make it more dramatic.

Creating a light layer

In After Effects, a light is a type of layer that shines light on other layers. You can choose from among four different types of lights—Parallel, Spot, Point, and Ambient—and modify them with various settings. Lights, by default, point to a point of interest, just as camera layers do.

1 Press the Home key to make sure the current-time indicator is at the beginning of the time ruler.

2 Choose Layer > New > Light.

3 In the Light Settings dialog box, do the following:

- Name the layer **Spotlight**.

- Choose Spot from the Light Type menu.

- Set Intensity to **100%** and Cone Angle to **90°**.

- Set Cone Feather to **50%**, and set the Color to a light yellow (**255, 255, 230**).

- Select the Casts Shadows option.

- Make sure Shadow Darkness is set to **100%**, and set Shadow Diffusion to **20** pixels.

- Click OK to create the light layer.

The light layer is represented by a light bulb icon (💡) in the Timeline panel, and the point of interest appears in the Composition panel as a cross-hair icon (✛).

Positioning the spotlight

The point of interest for this light is pointed at the center of the scene, which just happens to be where the 3D book is located, so you don't need to adjust it. You only need to change the light position. Simply dragging the axes in the Composition panel would cause the light's point of interest to move, however, so you'll change the light layer's position in the Timeline panel instead.

1   In the Composition panel, choose 2 Views – Horizontal from the Select View Layout pop-up menu. Then, click the left view to make it active, and choose Top from the 3D View pop-up menu. (The right view should be Active Camera.)

2   Go to 5:00 in the Timeline panel.

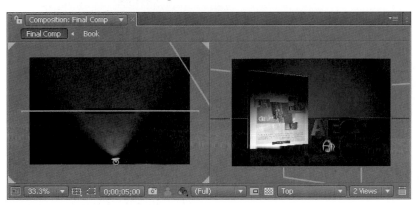

The light will appear throughout the composition, but by working at 5:00, you can see how repositioning the light affects other objects in the scene.

3   Select the Spotlight layer in the Timeline panel and press **P** to display its Position property.

4   While watching the Top and Active Camera views in the Composition panel, drag the Position property y-axis value (the middle value) to the left in the Timeline panel until the light cone is at **-105**, high above the composition.

5 Change the Position property's x-axis value to **-102** and its z-axis value to **-208**. Moving the light to a negative value on the z axis moves the light back in 3D space.

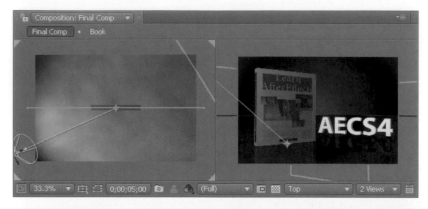

6 Hide the Position property for the Spotlight layer in the Timeline panel.

7 Choose 1 View from the Select View Layout pop-up menu at the bottom of the Composition panel, and make sure Active Camera is selected in the 3D View pop-up menu.

8 Press F2 to deselect all layers in the Timeline panel, press the Home key, and then press the spacebar to preview the lighted animation. Press the spacebar again to end the preview. Then, choose File > Save to save your work.

Adding an ambient light

The shadows are a little harsh, so you'll add ambient light to lighten the scene.

1 Choose Layer > New > Light.

2	In the Light Settings dialog box, do the following:

- Name the light **Ambient Light**.
- Choose Ambient from the Light Type menu.
- Set Intensity to **50%**.
- Change the Color to a light blue (**174, 195, 254**).
- Click OK to create the light layer.

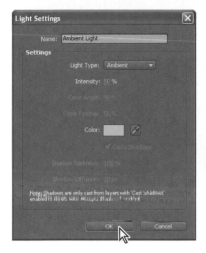 

Animating lights

Light doesn't need to be steady. You'll animate the spotlight so that it flickers on over a second, and fade the ambient light in over 15 frames.

1	Go to 3:15.

2	Select the Ambient Light layer in the Timeline panel, and press the **T** key to display the Light Intensity property for the layer.

3	Click the stopwatch icon next to the Intensity property to set a keyframe.

4	Go to 3:00, and change the Intensity to **0%**.

5	Press **T** to hide the Intensity property.

6	Select the Spotlight layer in the Timeline panel, and press the **T** key to display the Light Intensity property.

7	Go to 3:15, and click the stopwatch icon for the Intensity property to set a keyframe.

8	Go to 3:00, and change the Intensity value to **0%**.

9 Set additional Intensity keyframes for the Spotlight layer as follow:

- At 2:28, **100%**
- At 2:26, **0%**
- At 2:24, **100%**
- At 2:21, **0%**
- At 2:18, **100%**
- At 2:15, **0%**

10 Press **T** to hide the Intensity property.

11 Press the Home key to return to the beginning of the time ruler. Press F2 to deselect all layers. Then press the spacebar to preview the composition.

With the lights off at the beginning of the composition, the book is backlit by the Ramp effect in the Backdrop layer, making for a dramatic opening shot.

Adding effects

After Effects provides many options for special effects that you can use with either 2D or 3D scenes. You'll add a few animated brush strokes to the scene to give it more drama and flair.

Adjusting the Material Options properties

The Material Options properties determine how 3D layers interact with lights and shadows. You'll add a layer that won't be affected by the lights you added earlier.

1 Press the Home key to return to the beginning of the time ruler.

2 Click the Project tab. Then, drag the brush.psd item from the Project panel into the Timeline panel, and place it at the top of the layer stack.

3 Select the 3D Layer switch (⬢) for the brush.psd layer to convert it to a 3D layer.

The layer jumps to the center of the composition, but you can no longer see it. The brush.psd layer is affected by the lights in the scene.

4 Select the brush layer in the Timeline panel, and press **AA** to reveal the Material Options properties for the layer.

5 Click the value for the Accepts Shadows property (currently On) to change it to Off.

6 Click the value for the Accepts Lights property (currently On) to change it to Off.

7 Press the **P** key to display the Position property for the brush.psd layer, and then change the Position value to **-6, 308, -2200**. The layer moves very close to the camera.

Adding a transition effect

Currently, the brush stroke is present throughout the composition. You'll add a transition effect to change the way the brush stroke comes onto the scene.

1 With the brush layer selected, choose Effect > Transition > Linear Wipe.

2 In the Effect Controls panel, change Transition Completion to **100%**, Wipe Angle to **-90** degrees, and Feather to **50**.

3 In the Effect Controls panel, click the stopwatch icon for the Transition Completion property to create an initial keyframe.

4 Go to 0:15.

5 Change the Transition Completion value to **0%**. The brush stroke will be revealed from left to right on the screen.

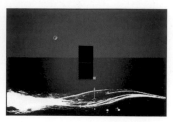

6 In the Timeline panel, hide all the properties for the brush.psd layer.

7 Select the brush.psd layer, and then press Ctrl+D (Windows) or Command+D (Mac OS) to duplicate the layer.

8 With the duplicate layer selected, press **P** to display the Position property, and then enter a new position of **-238, 383, -523**.

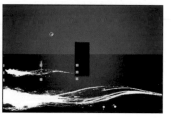

9 Press **P** to hide the Position property.

There are two brush strokes on the screen, one in the foreground and one further back. You'll create two more brush strokes, flipped so that they arrive from the right.

10 Select the lowest brush.psd layer (the original layer) in the Timeline panel, and press Ctrl+D (Windows) or Command+D (Mac OS) to duplicate it.

11 With the middle brush.psd layer selected, press the **S** key to display the Scale property.

12 Click the Constrain Proportions icon (⊕) to unlink the values, and then change the x-axis and y-axis values to **-100%**.

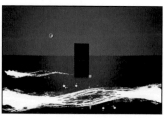

13 Press the **P** key to reveal the Position property for the layer, and change the values to **239, 320, -1680**. Press the **P** key again to hide the Position property.

14 With the middle brush.psd layer selected, press Ctrl+D (Windows) or Command+D (Mac OS) to duplicate it.

15 Move the duplicate layer to the top of the layer stack.

16 With the top layer selected, press the **P** key to reveal the Position layer. Then change the position to **840, 360, -400**.

17 Hide all layer properties, and choose File > Save.

Adjusting the timing of the layers

Currently, the brush strokes all arrive at the same time. You'll shift them so that they enter at different times.

1 Go to 0:10.

2 Select the third brush.psd layer from the top of the layer stack. Press the [(left bracket) key to move the In point for the layer to the current time.

3 Go to 0:20.

4 Select the second brush.psd layer from the top of the layer stack. Press the [(left bracket) key to move the In point for the layer to the current time.

5 Go to 0:30.

6 Select the top brush.psd layer in the layer stack. Press the [(left bracket) key to move the In point for the layer to the current time.

7 Make a RAM preview to see your composition in action. Press the spacebar to stop the preview.

8 Choose File > Save.

Adding motion blur

●Note: Calculating motion blur is processor-intensive. This exercise is optional.

Objects in motion tend to have blur. To make the entire composition more realistic and exciting, you'll add motion blur to all the layers. However, in order to apply motion blur to the 3D compositions, you must apply it to their layers separately.

1 Click the Enable Motion Blur button (●) in the Timeline panel.

2 Select the Motion Blur switch (●) for each layer in the Timeline panel.

When the Collapse Transformations switch is selected, After Effects uses the settings in the original composition to determine whether to apply motion blur. You'll need to open the 3D compositions to apply motion blur to them.

3 Select the Book tab in the Timeline panel to open the Book composition.

4 Select the Motion Blur switch for each of the layers in the Book composition.

5 Click the 3D Text tab in the Timeline panel, and select the Motion Blur switch for each of the layers in the 3D Text composition.

● **Note:** To change a setting for all layers in a composition, press Ctrl+A (Windows) or Command+A (Mac OS) to first select all the layers, and then select the setting for the first layer.

Previewing the entire animation

Congratulations. You've completed the two-part 3D animation for this *Adobe Classroom in a Book*. After all that hard work, you should definitely preview the entire animation.

1 Click the Final Comp tab in the Timeline panel.

2 Press F2 to deselect all layers in the Timeline panel.

3 Press the Home key to go to the beginning of the time ruler.

4 Watch a RAM preview of the entire composition.

5 Choose File > Save to save your project.

If you'd like to render and output the piece, see Lesson 14, "Rendering and Outputting," for instructions.

Review questions

1 How can you animate a 3D layer?

2 How are 3D lights handled in After Effects?

3 What is a point of interest?

Review answers

1 Animating a 3D layer is similar to animating a 2D layer, except that you can move the object on three axes: the x axis, the y axis, and the z axis. You can animate other Transform properties, effects, and other settings just as you would those for a 2D layer.

2 In After Effects, a light is a type of layer that shines light on other layers. You can choose from among four different types of lights—Parallel, Spot, Point, and Ambient—and modify them with various settings.

3 Cameras and lights include a property that specifies the point in the composition at which the camera or light points. By default, this point of interest is set at the center of the composition, and the camera or light's view is automatically oriented toward it. You can change this behavior by choosing Layer > Transform > Auto-Orient. Of course, you can move the point of interest at any time.

13 ADVANCED EDITING TECHNIQUES

Lesson overview

In this lesson, you'll learn how to do the following:

- Use motion stabilization to smooth out a shaky camera shot.

- Use single-point motion tracking to track one object in a shot to another object in a shot.

- Perform multipoint tracking using perspective corner-pinning.

- Use Imagineer Systems mocha for After Effects to track motion.

- Create a particle system.

- Use the Timewarp effect to create slow-motion video.

In previous lessons, you've used many of the essential 2D and 3D tools you need for motion graphics design. But Adobe After Effects CS4 also offers motion stabilization, motion tracking, advanced keying tools, distortion effects, the capability to retime footage using the Timewarp effect, support for high dynamic range (HDR) color images, network rendering, and much more. In this lesson, you will learn how to use the motion-stabilization and motion-tracking features to stabilize a handheld camera shot and to track one object to another in an image so that their motion is synchronized. Then, you will use corner-pinning to track an object with perspective. Finally, you will explore some of the high-end digital effects available in After Effects CS4: a particle system generator and the Timewarp effect. This lesson will take approximately 2 hours to complete.

After Effects CS4 provides advanced motion stabilization, motion tracking, high-end effects, and other features for the most demanding production environments.

Getting started

This lesson includes multiple projects. Take a peek at all of them before beginning.

1 Make sure the following files are in the AECS4_CIB/Lessons/Lesson 13 folder on your hard disk, or copy them from the *Adobe After Effects CS4 Classroom in a Book* DVD now.

   - In the Assets folder: flowers.mov, Group_Approach[DV].mov, majorspoilers. mov, metronome.mov, mocha_tracking.mov, multipoint_tracking.mov

   - In the Sample_Movies folder: Lesson13_Multipoint.mov, Lesson_13_ Particles.mov, Lesson13_Stabilize.mov, Lesson13_Timewarp.mov, Lesson13_ Tracking.mov

2 Open and play the sample movies in the Lesson13/Sample_Movies folder to see the projects you will create in this lesson.

3 When you're done, quit QuickTime Player. You may delete these sample movies from your hard disk if you have limited storage space.

● **Note:** You can view these movies all at once or, if you don't plan to complete these exercises in one session, you can watch each sample movie just before you are ready to complete the associated exercise.

Using motion stabilization

If you shoot footage using a handheld camera, you will probably end up with shaky shots. Unless this look is intentional, you'll want to stabilize your shots to eliminate unwanted motion.

To stabilize footage, After Effects first tracks the motion in the shot. It then shifts the position and rotation of each frame as necessary to remove the motion. When played back, the motion appears smooth because the layer itself moves incrementally to offset the unwanted movement.

Setting up the project

As you start After Effects, restore the default application settings for After Effects. See "Restoring default preferences" on page 3.

1 Press Ctrl+Alt+Shift (Windows) or Command+Option+Shift (Mac OS) while starting After Effects CS4 to restore default preferences. When asked whether you want to delete your preferences file, click OK.

2 Click Close to close the Welcome window.

After Effects opens to display a new, untitled project.

3 Choose File > Save As.

4 In the Save As dialog box, navigate to the AECS4_CIB/Lessons/Lesson13/ Finished_Projects folder.

5 Name the project **Lesson13_Stabilize.aep**, and then click Save.

Importing the footage

You need to import one footage item to start this project.

1 Double-click an empty area of the Project panel to open the Import File dialog box.

2 Navigate to the AECS4_CIB/Lessons/Lesson13/Assets folder. Select the flowers.mov file, and then click Open.

Creating the composition

Now, you will create the composition.

1 Choose Composition > New Composition.

2 In the Composition Settings dialog box, type **Stabilize** for the name.

3 Make sure the Preset pop-up menu is set to NTSC DV. This automatically sets the width, height, pixel aspect ratio, and frame rate for the composition.

4 In the Duration field, type **1000** to specify 10 seconds, which matches the length of the flowers.mov file, then click OK.

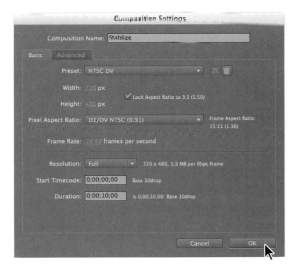

5 Drag the flowers.mov item from the Project panel to the Timeline panel. The flowers image appears in the Composition panel.

6 Drag the current-time indicator across the time ruler to manually preview the footage. This clip was shot with a handheld camera in the late afternoon. A slight breeze rustles the vegetation, and the camera moves unsteadily.

To stabilize this image, your first task is to identify two areas in the shot that are stationary within the context of the frame. These areas are called the *feature regions*. This figure shows two feature regions that will work for this project.

It is important to locate and size feature regions carefully. For the smoothest tracking, try to select areas that:

- Are visible for the entire shot.

- Have a contrasting color from the surrounding area.

- Have a distinct shape (at least within the search region).

- Have a consistent shape and color throughout the shot.

Positioning the track points

After Effects tracks motion by matching pixels from a selected area in a frame to pixels in each succeeding frame. You specify the area to track by using the *track point*. The track point contains the feature region as well as a search region and an attach point. After Effects displays the track point during tracking in the Layer panel.

You'll open the Tracking Controls panel and apply track points to the clip.

● **Note:** The motion tracking will be based on the frame where the current-time indicator is positioned.

1 Press the Home key to make sure the current-time indicator is at the beginning of the time ruler.

2 Choose Window > Tracker to open the Tracker panel. The Tracker panel is where you specify your motion source and motion target layers, the type of tracking you want to use, and other tracking options.

3 Click the Stabilize Motion button in the Tracker panel, and make sure that flowers.mov appears in the Motion Source pop-up menu. This tells After Effects that you want to stabilize the motion in the flowers layer. When you set these options, the Layer panel opens. In the Tracker panel, the Current Track pop-up menu shows Tracker 1 and the Track Type is set to Stabilize.

When you manually previewed the footage, you may have noticed that the camera not only moved left, right, up, and down, but also rotated slightly. So you need to stabilize the shot's rotation as well as its position.

4 Select Position and Rotation in the Tracker panel. You should see two track point indicators in the Layer panel.

5 Notice that Motion Target is the flowers.mov layer. When you stabilize a shot, the resulting data can be applied to the original layer, as specified here, or you can select another layer by clicking the Edit Target button. Leave it set to flowers.mov.

Now, you're ready to set your track points.

6 Using the Selection tool (▶), drag the Track Point 1 indicator (from the center) in the Layer panel to position it over the first feature region, which is the light green, closed flower bud below and to the left of the orange flower in the foreground.

7 Drag the Track Point 2 indicator (from the center) to the second feature region, which is the light green leaf to the right of the orange foreground flower.

Moving and resizing the track points

In setting up motion tracking, it's often necessary to refine your track point by adjusting the feature region, search region, and attach point. You can resize or move these items independently or in groups by dragging with the Selection tool. The pointer icon changes to reflect one of many different activities.

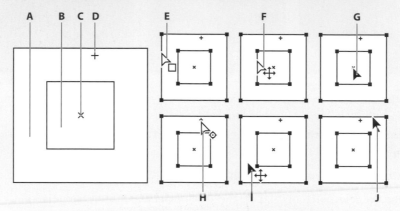

Track point components (left) and Selection tool pointer icons (right):
A. *Search region* ***B.*** *Feature region* ***C.*** *Keyframe marker* ***D.*** *Attach point* ***E.*** *Moves search region* ***F.*** *Moves both regions* ***G.*** *Moves entire track point* ***H.*** *Moves attach point* ***I.*** *Moves entire track point* ***J.*** *Resizes region*

- To turn feature region magnification on or off, choose Magnify Feature When Dragging from the Tracker panel menu. A check mark appears next to the option when it's on.

- To move the feature region, search region, and attach point together, drag with the Selection tool inside the track point area (avoiding the region edges and the attach point); the Move Track Point pointer (▲₊) appears.

- To move just the feature and search regions together, drag the edge of the feature region with the Selection tool; the Move Both Regions pointer (▲₊) appears.

- To move just the feature and search regions together, Alt-drag (Windows) or Option-drag (Mac OS) with the Selection tool inside the feature or search region; the Move Both Regions pointer (▲₊) appears.

- To move only the search region, using the Selection tool, drag the edge of the search region; the Move Search Region pointer (▲▢) appears.

- To move only the attach point, using the Selection tool, drag the attach point; the Move Attach Point pointer (▲₊) appears.

- To resize the feature or search region, drag a corner handle.

For more information about track points, see After Effects Help.

Analyzing and applying stabilization

Now that the two track points are defined, After Effects can analyze the data and then apply the stabilization tracker.

1 Click the Analyze Forward button (▷) in the Tracker panel. After Effects analyzes the motion stabilization for the duration of the clip.

2 When the analysis is complete, click the Apply button.

3 In the Motion Tracker Apply Options dialog box, click OK to apply the stabilization to the x and y dimensions.

The motion-tracking data is added to the flowers layer in the Timeline panel, where you can see the track points, their properties, and their keyframes. You can also see the Anchor Point, Position, and Rotation keyframes that were applied to the layer. Keyframes are created at every frame, so 300 have been created for this 10-second shot. After Effects also opens the flowers image in the Composition panel again.

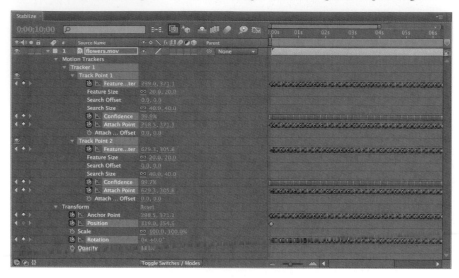

4   Hide the properties for the flowers layer in the Timeline panel.

5   Press the Home key to move the current-time indicator to the beginning of the timeline, and then watch a RAM preview of the stabilized shot. Press the spacebar to stop the playback when you're ready.

Scaling the layer

You've stabilized the footage, but there's still a problem. The tracking was applied to the Anchor Point and Rotation properties of the layer, but the entire layer is moving and rotating. This means you can see the edge of the shot and the empty space around it in some frames. An easy way to fix this is to scale the layer.

1   Press the Home key to go to the beginning of the time ruler.

2   With the flowers layer selected in the Timeline panel, press the **S** key to display its Scale property.

3 Drag the current-time indicator across the time ruler until you find the frame where the layer displacement is the greatest (around 7:16).

4 Increase the Scale values to **110, 110%**. The clip fills the frame completely.

5 Go to 2:16, where you can still see some of the empty area outside of the shot.

Because the tracking data is applied to the anchor point of the layer, you can reposition the entire layer without destabilizing it.

6 With the flowers layer selected in the Timeline panel, press **P** to reveal its Position property. The tracker added an initial Position keyframe to the layer. You don't need it, so click the stopwatch icon (🕲) to delete the keyframe.

7 Change the Position values to **325, 375**.

Note: The greater you scale the layer, the more the image quality will degrade, so keep the scale operation to a minimum.

8 Manually preview the clip once more to check for additional edge slips. You may need to scale the layer another percentage or two. When you're done, go to 0:00.

9 Watch another RAM preview. The shot should now look rock-steady, with the only movement being caused by the wind rustling the flowers.

10 Press the spacebar to stop playback when you're done.

11 Close the properties for the flowers layer in the Timeline panel, press the Home key to go to the beginning of the time ruler, and choose File > Save to save your work.

12 Choose File > Close Project.

As you have discovered, stabilizing a shot is not without its drawbacks. To compensate for the movement or rotation data applied to the layer, you need to adjust the Scale and Position properties, which could ultimately degrade the footage. It is a fine line, but if you really need to use the shot in your production, this may be the best compromise.

Using single-point motion tracking

With the increase in the number of productions that incorporate digital elements into final shots, compositors need an easy way to synchronize computer-generated effects with film or video backgrounds. After Effects lets you do this with the capability to follow, or track, a defined area in the shot and apply that movement to other layers. These layers can contain text, effects, images, or other footage. The resulting visual effect precisely matches the original moving footage.

When you track motion in an After Effects composition that contains multiple layers, the default tracking type is Transform. This type of motion tracking tracks position and/or rotation to apply to another layer. When tracking position, this option creates one track point and generates Position keyframes. When tracking rotation, this option creates two track points and produces Rotation keyframes.

In this exercise, you will track a shape layer to the weighted arm of a metronome. This will be especially challenging because the camera operator chose not to use a tripod.

Setting up the project

If you've just completed the first project, and After Effects is open, skip to step 3. Otherwise, restore the default application settings for After Effects. See "Restoring default preferences" on page 3.

1 Press Ctrl+Alt+Shift (Windows) or Command+Option+Shift (Mac OS) while starting After Effects CS4 to restore default preferences. When asked whether you want to delete your preferences file, click OK.

2 Click Close to close the Welcome window.

After Effects opens to display a new, untitled project.

3 Choose File > Save As.

4 In the Save As dialog box, navigate to the AECS4_CIB/Lessons/Lesson13/ Finished_Projects folder.

5 Name the project **Lesson13_Tracking.aep**, and then click Save.

Importing the footage

You need to import one footage item to start this project.

1 Double-click an empty area of the Project panel to open the Import File dialog box.

2 Navigate to the AECS4_CIB/Lessons/Lesson13/Assets folder. Select the metronome.mov file, and then click Open.

Creating the composition

Now, you will create the composition.

1 Choose Composition > New Composition.

2 In the Composition Settings dialog box, type **Tracking** in the Composition Name field.

3 Make sure the Preset pop-up menu is set to NTSC DV. This automatically sets the width, height, pixel aspect ratio, and frame rate for the composition.

4 In the Duration field, type **800** to specify 8 seconds, which matches the length of the metronome.mov file, and then click OK.

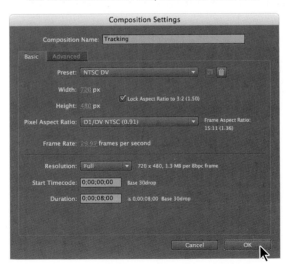

5 Drag the metronome.mov item from the Project panel to the Timeline panel. The metronome image appears in the Composition panel.

6 Drag the current-time indicator across the time ruler to manually preview the footage. You will track the metronome weight (the rhombus at the end of its arm) using the same tracking controls you used with the flowers. However, unlike motion stabilization, you need to place tracking regions around the area that you'll track another layer to.

Creating a shape layer

You're going to apply a star to the end of the metronome. First, you need to create the star. You'll use a shape layer.

1 Press the Home key to make sure the current-time indicator is at the beginning of the time ruler, and then click in an empty area of the Timeline panel to deselect the layer.

2 Select the Star tool (☆), hidden behind the Rectangle tool, in the Tools panel.

3 Click the Fill Color swatch, and select a light yellow such as RGB 220, 250, 90. Click the word *Stroke*, select None in the Stroke Options dialog box, and click OK.

4 In the Composition panel, draw a small star.

5 Use the Selection tool to position the star over the weighted end of the pendulum arm.

6 Make sure the anchor point of the star layer is in the center of the star shape. Use the Pan Behind tool to position the anchor point if necessary.

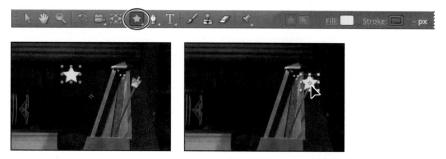

Positioning the track point

With the star shape added to the Tracking composition, you are ready to position the track point.

1 Select the metronome.mov layer in the Timeline panel.

2 Choose Window > Tracker to open the Tracker panel, if it's not already open.

3 Click the Track Motion button in the Tracker panel. The Layer panel opens, with a Track Point 1 indicator in the center of the image.

Notice the settings in the Tracker panel: The Motion Source is set to metronome.mov. The Current Track is Tracker 1, and the <u>Motion Target</u> is Shape Layer 1, because After Effects automatically sets the Motion Target to the layer immediately above the source layer.

Now, you'll position your track point.

4 Using the Selection tool (⬉), move the Track Point 1 indicator (from the center) in the Layer panel over the weight of the metronome.

5 Adjust the feature region (the inner box) within the weight. Because the pendulum moves left and right, enlarge the search region (the outer box) to encompass the area around the pendulum.

● **Note:** In this exercise, you want the star to move atop the metronome weight. However, if you wanted an object to move in relationship to the tracked area but not on top of it, you could reposition the attach point accordingly.

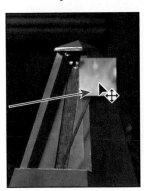

Analyzing and applying tracking

Now that the search and feature regions are defined, you can apply the tracker.

Note: The tracking analaysis may take quite a while. The larger the search and feature regions, the longer After Effects takes to analyze tracking.

1   Click the Analyze Forward button (▶) in the Tracker panel. Watch the analysis to ensure the track point stays with the metronome weight. If it doesn't, stop the analysis and reposition the feature region. (See the sidebar, "Checking for drift.")

2   When the analysis is complete, click the Apply button.

3   In the Motion Tracker Apply Options dialog box, click OK to apply the tracking to the x and y dimensions.

Checking for drift

As an image moves in a shot, the lighting, surrounding objects, and angle of the object can all change, making a once-distinct feature no longer identifiable at the subpixel level. It takes time to develop an eye for choosing a trackable feature. Even with careful planning and practice, you will often find that the feature region drifts away from the desired feature. Readjusting the feature and search regions, changing the tracking options, and trying again are a standard part of digital tracking. When you notice drifting occurring, try the following:

1   Immediately stop the analysis by clicking the Stop button in the Tracker panel.

2   Move the current-time indicator back to the last good tracked point. You can see this in the Layer panel.

3   Reposition and/or resize the feature and search regions, being careful to not accidentally move the attach point. Moving the attach point will cause a noticeable jump in your tracked layer.

4   Click the Analyze Forward button to resume tracking.

The motion-tracking data is added to the Timeline panel, where you can see that the track data is in the metronome layer, but the results are applied to the Position property of the Shape Layer 1 layer. This is another difference between tracking and stabilization: the resulting data is applied to a layer's position, rather than to its anchor point.

4   Watch a RAM preview. The star not only follows the pendulum; it moves with the camera's movement.

5   When you're ready, press the spacebar to stop playback.

6   Hide the properties for both layers in the Timeline panel, choose File > Save, and then choose File > Close Project.

Motion tracking an element onto background footage can be fun. As long as you have a stable feature to track, single-point motion tracking can be quite easy.

Using multipoint tracking

After Effects also offers two more advanced types of tracking that use multiple tracking points: parallel corner pinning and perspective corner-pinning.

When you track using parallel corner-pinning, you simultaneously track three points in the source footage. After Effects calculates the position of a fourth point to keep the lines between the points parallel. When the movement of the points is applied to the target layer, the Corner Pin effect distorts the layer to simulate skew, scale, and rotation, but not perspective. Parallel lines remain parallel, and relative distances are preserved.

When you track using perspective corner-pinning, you simultaneously track four points in the source footage. When applied to the target footage, the Corner Pin effect uses the movement of the four points to distort the layer, simulating changes in perspective.

You'll attach an animation to a computer monitor using perspective corner-pinning. If you haven't already watched the sample movie for this exercise, do so now.

Setting up the project

Start by launching After Effects and creating a new project.

1 If it is not already open, start After Effects. Press Ctrl+Alt+Shift (Windows) or Command+Option+Shift (Mac OS) as you start it to restore default preferences. Click OK when asked whether you want to delete your preferences file, and click Close to close the Welcome window.

After Effects opens to display an empty, untitled project.

2 Choose File > Save As.

3 In the Save As dialog box, navigate to the AECS4_CIB/Lessons/Lesson13/ Finished_Projects folder.

4 Name the project **Lesson13_Multipoint.aep,** and then click Save.

Importing the footage

You need to import two footage items for this exercise.

1 Double-click an empty area of the Project panel to open the Import File dialog box.

2 Navigate to the AECS4_CIB/Lessons /Lesson13/ Assets folder.

3 Ctrl-click (Windows) or Command-click (Mac OS) to select the majorspoilers.mov and multipoint_tracking.mov files, and then click Open.

Creating the composition

Now, you'll create a new composition.

1   Press Ctrl+N (Windows) or Command+N (Mac OS).

2   In the Composition Settings dialog box, type **Multipoint_Tracking** in the Composition Name field.

3   Make sure the Preset pop-up menu is set to NTSC DV. This automatically sets the width, height, pixel aspect ratio, and frame rate for the composition.

4   Set the Duration to **7:05**, which matches the length of the majorspoilers.mov file, and then click OK.

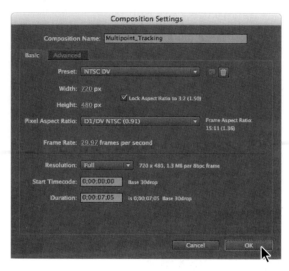

You will now add the footage items to the Timeline panel, one at a time.

5   Drag the multipoint_tracking.mov item from the Project panel to the Timeline panel. It automatically appears in the Composition panel.

6   Manually preview the footage, which is shaky because it was shot with a handheld camera. Because you're positioning the majorspoilers.mov layer on the computer monitor, it will be fairly easy to place tracking markers on the flat plane. By default, the tracker tracks by luminance, so you will use the areas around the screen that have high contrast differences for tracking.

7   Press the Home key to return to the beginning of the time ruler.

8   Drag the majorspoilers.mov footage item from the Project panel to the Timeline panel, placing it at the top of the layer stack.

9 To make it easier to see the underlying movie as you place the tracking points, turn off the Video switch for the majorspoilers.mov layer in the Timeline panel.

Positioning the track points

You're ready to add the track points to the multipoint_tracking.mov layer.

1 Select the multipoint_tracking.mov layer in the Timeline panel.

2 Choose Window > Tracker to open the Tracker panel if it isn't open.

3 In the Tracker panel, choose multipoint_tracking.mov from the Motion Source menu, and then click Track Motion. The desk scene opens in the Layer panel, with a track point indicator in the center of the image. However, you will be tracking four points in order to attach the animated movie to the computer screen.

4 Choose Perspective Corner Pin from the Track Type menu. Three more track point indicators appear in the Layer panel.

5 Drag the track points to four different high-contrast areas of the image. The four corners of the computer screen provide excellent contrast. Use the following image as a guide. (Because the areas of high contrast are also where you want to attach the majorspoilers layer, you do not need to move the attach points.)

▶ **Tip:** Refer to the sidebar, "Moving and resizing the track points," in the first exercise of this lesson, for help moving the track point regions.

▶ **Tip:** It may be helpful to zoom in when placing and adjusting the track points. Zoom out again when you have finished.

Applying the multipoint tracker

You're ready to analyze the data and apply the tracker.

1 Click the Analyze Forward button (▶) in the Tracker panel. Then, when the analysis is complete, click the Apply button to calculate the tracking.

● **Note:** If the composition doesn't appear in the Composition panel, click in the Timeline window to move the current-time indicator and refresh the display.

2 Notice the results in the Timeline panel: you can see the Corner Pin and Position property keyframes for the majorspoilers layer and the track point data for the motion_tracking layer.

3 Make the majorspoilers layer visible again, press the Home key to return to the beginning of the timeline, and watch a RAM preview to see the results of the tracker.

4 When you're done watching the preview, press the spacebar to stop playback.

If you don't like the results, return to the Tracker panel, click the Reset button, and try again. With practice, you will become adept at identifying good feature regions.

5 Press the Home key to go to 0:00, hide the layer properties to keep the Timeline panel neat, and choose File > Save to save your work.

6 Choose File > Close Project.

Mocha for After Effects

In most cases, you will get better and more accurate results using mocha from Imagineer Systems to track points in video. The mocha for After Effects tool is installed in the After Effects CS4 folder on your hard drive.

One advantage of mocha for After Effects is that you don't have to accurately place tracking points to obtain a perfect track. Rather than using tracking points, mocha for After Effects uses a planar tracker, which attempts to track an object's translation, rotation, and scaling data based on the movement of a user-defined plane. Planes provide more detail to the computer than is possible with single-point and multipoint tracking tools.

When you work with mocha for After Effects, you need to identify planes in a clip that coincide with movement you want to track. Planes don't have to be tabletops or walls. For example, if someone is waving goodbye, you can use their upper and lower limbs as two planes.

Mocha for After Effects uses two different spline technologies for tracking: X splines and Bezier splines. X splines may work better for tracking, especially with perspective motion, but Bezier splines work well, too, and are the industry standard.

After you track the planes, you can export the tracking data for use in After Effects.

To learn more about mocha for After Effects, start the application and choose Help > Manual.

We've saved some tracking data for the computer monitor in mocha for After Effects, so that you can apply it in After Effects if you'd like to. To apply the data, follow these steps:

1   Create a new project in After Effects and import the majorspoilers.mov and mocha_tracking.mov files from the Lesson13/Assets folder. Create a new composition from the mocha_tracking.mov file, and then drag the majorspoilers.mov file to the top of the layer stack in the Timeline panel.

2   Open the mocha_data.txt file (in the Lesson 13/Optional_Mocha_Tutorial folder) in a text editor such as WordPad or TextEdit. (Don't use Notepad on Windows. It doesn't retain the mocha formatting, so After Effects doesn't recognize its content on the clipboard.) Choose Edit > Select All, and then Edit > Copy to copy all the data.

3   Select the majorspoilers.mov layer in the Timeline panel, and choose Edit > Paste. All the data is applied to the layer.

4   Watch a RAM preview to see the results.

Creating a particle simulation

After Effects includes several effects that do an excellent job of creating particle simulations. Two of them—CC Particle Systems II and CC Particle World—are based on the same engine. The major difference between the two is that Particle World enables you to move the particles in 3D space, rather than a 2D layer.

In this exercise, you will learn how to use the CC Particle Systems II effect to create a supernova that could be used as the opening of a science program or as a motion background. If you haven't already watched the sample movie for this exercise, do so now before continuing.

Setting up the project

Start by launching After Effects and creating a new project.

1 If it's not already open, start After Effects. Press Ctrl+Alt+Shift (Windows) or Command+Option+Shift (Mac OS) as you start it to restore default preferences. Click OK when asked whether you want to delete your preferences file, and close the Welcome window.

After Effects opens to display an empty, untitled project.

2 Choose File > Save As.

3 In the Save As dialog box, navigate to the AECS4_CIB/Lessons/Lesson13/ Finished_Projects folder.

4 Name the project **Lesson13_Particles.aep**, and then click Save.

Creating the composition

You do not need to import any footage items for this exercise. However, you do need to create the composition.

1 Press Ctrl+N (Windows) or Command+N (Mac OS).

2 In the Composition Settings dialog box, type **Supernova** in the Composition Name field.

3 Choose NTSC D1 from the Preset pop-up menu. This automatically sets the width, height, pixel aspect ratio, and frame rate for the composition.

4 Set the Duration to **10:00**, then click OK.

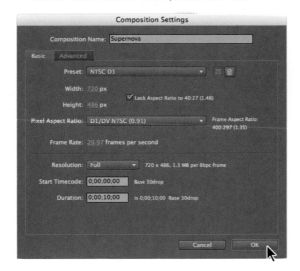

Creating a particle system

You will build the particle system from a solid layer, so you'll create that next.

1 Choose Layer > New > Solid to create a new solid layer.

2 In the Solid Settings dialog box, type **Particles** in the Name box.

3 Click Make Comp Size to make the layer the same size as the composition. Then, click OK.

4 With the Particles layer selected in the Timeline panel, choose Effect > Simulation > CC Particle Systems II.

5 Go to 4:00 to see the particle system.

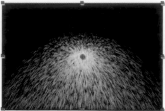

A large stream of yellow particles appears in the Composition panel.

Customizing the particle effect

You will turn this stream of particles into a supernova by customizing the settings in the Effect Controls panel.

1 Expand the Physics property group in the Effect Controls panel. The Explosive Animation setting works fine for this project, but instead of the particles falling down, you want them to flow out in all directions, so change the Gravity value to **0.0**.

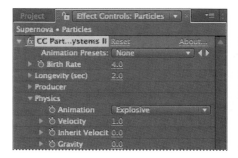
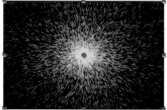

Understanding Particle Systems II properties

Particle systems have a unique vocabulary. Some of the key settings are explained here for your reference. They're listed in the order in which they appear (top to bottom) in the Effect Controls panel.

Birth Rate Controls the number of particles generated per second. This is an arbitrary value and does not reflect the actual number of particles being generated. The higher the number, the more densely packed the particles become.

Longevity Determines how long the particles live.

Producer Position Controls the center point or origin of the particle system. The position is set based on the x, y coordinates. All particles emanate from this single point. You can control the size of the producer by making adjustments to the x and y radius settings. The higher these values, the larger the producer point will be. A high x value and a y value of zero (0) result in a line.

Velocity Controls the speed of particles. The higher the number, the faster the particles move.

Inherent Velocity % Determines how much of the velocity is passed along to the particles when the Producer Position is animated. A negative value causes the particles to move in the opposite direction.

Gravity Determines how fast particles fall. The higher the value, the faster the particles fall. A negative value causes particles to rise.

Resistance Simulates particles interacting with air or water, slowing over time.

Direction Determines which directions the particles flow. Use with the Direction Animation type.

Extra Introduces randomness into the movement of the particles.

Birth/Death Size Determines the size of the particles when they are created and when they expire.

Opacity Map Controls opacity changes for the particle over its lifetime.

Color Map Use with the Birth and Death colors to shade the particles over time.

2 Hide the Physics property group and expand the Particle property group. Then, choose Faded Sphere from the Particle Type menu.

Now the particles look intergalactic. Don't stop there, though.

3 Change the Death Size to **1.50** and increase the Size Variation to **100%**. This allows the particles to change birth size randomly.

4 Reduce the Max Opacity to **55%**. This make the particles semi-transparent.

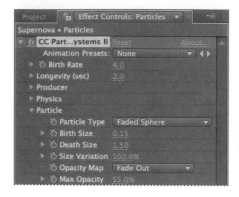 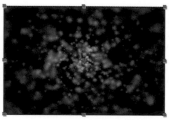

5 Click the Birth Color swatch and change the color to RGB **255, 200, 50** to give the particles a yellow hue on birth, then click OK.

6 Click the Death Color swatch and change the color to RGB **180, 180, 180** to give the particles a light gray hue as they fade out, then click OK.

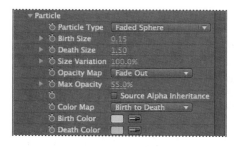 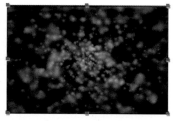

7 To keep the particles from staying onscreen too long, decrease the Longevity value to **0.8** seconds.

● **Note:** Even though they're at the top of the Effect Controls panel, it is often easier to adjust the Longevity and Birth Rate settings after you have set the other particle properties.

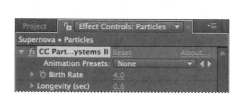 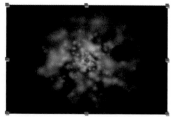

The Faded Sphere particle type softened the look, but the particle shapes are still too sharply defined. You will fix that by blurring the layer to blend the particles with one another.

8 Hide the CC Particle Systems II effect properties.

9 Choose Effect > Blur & Sharpen > Fast Blur.

10 In the Fast Blur area of the Effect Controls panel, increase the Blurriness value to **10**. Then, select Repeat Edge Pixels to keep the particles from being cropped at the edge of the frame.

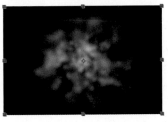

Creating the sun

You will now create a bright halo of light that will go behind the particles.

1 Go to 0:07.

2 Press Ctrl+Y (Windows) or Command+Y (Mac OS) to create a new solid layer.

3 In the Solid Settings dialog box do the following:

- Type **Sun** in the Name box.
- Click Make Comp Size to make the layer the same size as the composition.
- Click the color swatch to make the layer the same yellow as the Birth Color of the particles (**255, 200, 50**).
- Click OK to close the Solid Settings dialog box.

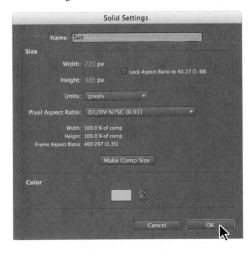

4 Drag the Sun layer below the Particles layer in the Timeline panel.

5 Select the Ellipse tool (⬤) in the Tools panel (behind the Rectangle tool (◼) or the Star tool (★) and Shift-drag in the Composition panel to draw a circle with a radius of roughly 100 pixels, or one-fourth the width of the composition.

6 Using the Selection tool (▸), drag the mask shape to the center of the Composition panel.

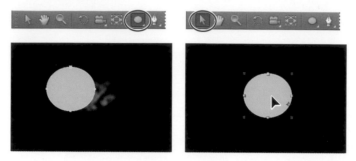

7 With the Sun layer selected in the Timeline panel, press the **F** key to reveal its Mask Feather property. Increase the Mask Feather amount to **100, 100** pixels.

8 Press Alt+[(Window) or Option+[(Mac OS) to set the In point of the layer to the current time.

9 Hide the properties for the Sun layer.

Lighting the darkness

Since the sun is bright, it should illuminate the surrounding darkness.

1 Make sure the current-time indicator is still at 0:07.

2 Press Ctrl+Y (Windows) or Command+Y (Mac OS) to create a new solid layer.

3 In the Solid Settings dialog box, name the layer **Background**, click the Make Comp Size button to make the layer the same size as the composition, and then click OK to create the layer.

4 In the Timeline panel, drag the Background layer to the bottom of the layer stack.

5 With the Background layer selected in the Timeline panel, choose Effect > Generate > Ramp.

The Ramp effect creates a color gradient, blending it with the original image. You can create linear or radial ramps, and vary the position and colors of the ramp over time. Use the Start Of Ramp and End Of Ramp settings to specify the start and end positions. Use the Ramp Scatter setting to disperse the ramp colors and eliminate banding.

6 In the Ramp area of the Effect Controls panel, do the following:

- Change Start Of Ramp to **360, 240** and End Of Ramp to **360, 525**.

- Choose Radial Ramp from the Ramp Shape menu.

- Click the Start Color swatch and set the start color to dark blue (RGB **0, 25, 135**).

- Set the End Color to black (RGB **0, 0, 0**).

 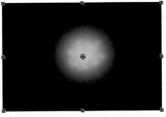

7 Press Alt+[(Windows) or Option+[(Mac OS) to set the In point of the layer to the current time.

Adding a lens flare

To tie all the elements together, add a lens flare to simulate an explosion.

1 Press the Home key to move the current-time indicator to the beginning of the time ruler.

2 Press Ctrl+Y (Windows) or Command+Y (Mac OS) to create a new solid layer.

3 In the Solid Settings dialog box, name the layer **Nova**, click the Make Comp Size button to make the layer the same size as the composition, set the Color to black (RGB **0, 0, 0**), and then click OK. The Nova layer should be at the top of the layer stack in the Timeline panel.

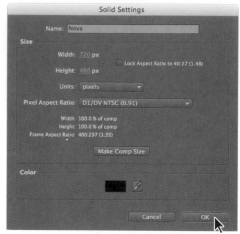

4 With the Nova layer selected in the Timeline panel, choose Effect > Generate > Lens Flare.

 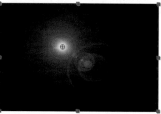

5 In the Lens Flare area of the Effect Controls panel, do the following:

- Change Flare Center to **360, 240**.

- Choose 50–300mm Zoom from the Lens Type menu.

- Decrease Flare Brightness to **0%**, and then click the Flare Brightness stopwatch icon ( ) to create an initial keyframe.

6 Go to 0:10.

7 Increase the Flare Brightness to **240%**.

8 Go to 1:04 and decrease the Flare Brightness to **100%**.

9 With the Nova layer selected in the Timeline panel, press the **U** key to see the animated Lens Flare property.

10 Right-click (Windows) or Control-click (Mac OS) the ending Flare Brightness keyframe and choose Keyframe Assistant > Easy Ease In.

11 Right-click (Windows) or Control-click (Mac OS) the beginning Flare Brightness keyframe and choose Keyframe Assistant > Easy Ease Out.

Finally, you need to make the layers under the Nova layer visible in the composition.

12 Press F2 to deselect all layers, and choose Columns > Modes from the Timeline panel menu. Then choose Screen from the Mode menu for the Nova layer.

13 Watch a RAM preview. When you're done, press the spacebar to stop the preview.

14 Choose File > Save, and then choose File > Close Project.

About high dynamic range (HDR) footage

After Effects CS4 also supports high dynamic range (HDR) color.

The dynamic range (ratio between dark and bright regions) in the physical world far exceeds the range of human vision and of images that are printed or displayed on a monitor. But while human eyes can adapt to very different brightness levels, most cameras and computer monitors can capture and reproduce only a limited dynamic range. Photographers, motion-picture artists, and others working with digital images must be selective about what's important in a scene because they are working with a limited dynamic range.

HDR images open up a world of possibilities because they can represent a very wide dynamic range through the use of 32-bit floating-point numeric values. Floating-point numeric representations allow the same number of bits to describe a much larger range of values than integer (fixed-point) values. HDR values can contain brightness levels, including objects as bright as a candle flame or the sun, that far exceed those in 8-bit-per-channel (bpc) or 16-bpc (non-floating-point) mode. Lower dynamic range 8-bpc and 16-bpc modes can represent RGB levels only from black to white, which represents an extremely small segment of the dynamic range in the real world.

Currently, HDR images are used mostly in motion pictures, special effects, 3D work, and some high-end photography. After Effects CS4 supports HDR images in a variety of ways. For example, you can create 32-bpc projects to work with HDR footage, and you can adjust the exposure, or the amount of light captured in an image, when working with HDR images in After Effects. For more information about support in After Effects for HDR images, see After Effects Help.

Retiming playback using the Timewarp effect

The Timewarp effect in After Effects CS4 gives you precise control over a wide range of parameters when changing the playback speed of a layer, including interpolation methods, motion blur, and source cropping to eliminate unwanted artifacts. The Timewarp effect works independently of the Frame Blend switch in the Timeline panel.

In this exercise, you will use the Timewarp effect to change the speed of a clip for a dramatic slow-motion playback. If you haven't already watched the sample movie for this exercise, do so now.

Setting up the project

Start by launching After Effects and creating a new project.

1 If After Effects isn't open, start it. Press Ctrl+Alt+Shift (Windows) or Command+Option+Shift (Mac OS) as you start it to restore default preferences. Click OK when asked whether you want to delete your preferences file, and close the Welcome window.

After Effects opens to display an empty, untitled project.

2 Choose File > Save As.

3 In the Save As dialog box, navigate to the AECS4_CIB/Lessons/Lesson13/ Finished_Projects folder.

4 Name the project **Lesson13_Timewarp.aep**, and then click Save.

Importing the footage and creating the composition

You need to import one footage item for this exercise.

1 Double-click an empty area of the Project panel to open the Import File dialog box.

2 Navigate to the AECS4_CIB/Lessons/Lesson13/Assets folder on your hard disk, select the Group_Approach[DV].mov, and click Open.

3 Click OK in the Interpret Footage dialog box.

Now, create a new composition based on the footage item's aspect ratio and duration.

4 Drag the Group_Approach[DV].mov file onto the Create A New Composition button ( ) at the bottom of the Project panel. After Effects creates a new composition named for the source file and displays it in the Composition and Timeline panels.

5 Choose File > Save to save your work.

Using Timewarp

In the source footage, a group of young people approaches the camera at a steady pace. At around 2 seconds, the director would like the motion to begin to slow down to 10%, then ramp back up to full speed at 7:00.

1   With the Group_Approach layer selected in the Timeline panel, choose Effect > Time > Timewarp.

2   In the Timewarp area of the Effect Controls panel, choose Pixel Motion from the Method menu. This instructs Timewarp to create new frames by analyzing the pixel movement in nearby frames and creating motion vectors. Also, choose Speed from the Adjust Time By menu to control the time adjustment by percentage, rather than by a specific frame.

3   Go to 2:00.

4   In the Effect Controls panel, set the Speed to **100** and click the stopwatch (🕑) to set a keyframe. This tells Timewarp to keep the speed of the clip at 100% until the 2-second mark.

5   Go to 5:00 and change the Speed to **10**. After Effects adds a keyframe.

6   Go to 7:00 and set the Speed to **100**. After Effects adds a keyframe.

● **Note:** Be patient. The RAM preview might take some time to calculate, but it will provide a more accurate playback than a spacebar preview.

7   Press the Home key to go to the beginning of the time ruler, and then watch a RAM preview of the effect.

You will see that the speed adjustments are rather abrupt, not the smooth, slow-motion curve you would expect to see in a professional effect. This is because the keyframes are linear instead of curved. You'll fix that next.

8   Press the spacebar to stop the playback when you're ready.

9   With the Group_Approach[DV] layer selected in the Timeline panel, press the U key to see the animated Timewarp Speed property.

10 Click the Graph Editor button () in the Timeline panel to see the Graph Editor instead of the layer bars. Then, select the Speed property name for the Group_Approach[DV] layer to see its graph.

11 Click to select the first Speed keyframe (at 2:00), and then click the Easy Ease icon (⤳) at the bottom of the Graph Editor. This adjusts the influence into and out of the keyframe to smooth out sudden changes.

12 Repeat step 11 for the other two Speed keyframes in the motion graph, at 5:00 and 7:00.

▶ **Tip:** Close columns in the Timeline panel to see more icons in the Graph Editor. You can also apply an Easy Ease adjustment by pressing the F9 key.

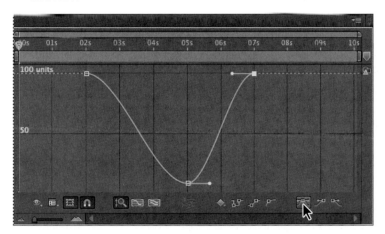

The motion graph is now smoother, but you can tweak it even more by dragging the Bezier handles.

Note: If you need a refresher on using Bezier handles, see Lesson 7, "Working with Masks."

13 Using the Bezier handles for the keyframes at 2:00 and 5:00, adjust the curve so that it resembles the following image.

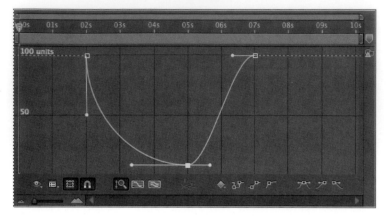

14 Watch another RAM preview. Now, the slow-motion Timewarp effect looks professional.

15 Choose File > Save to save the project, and then choose File > Close Project.

You've now experimented with some of the advanced features in After Effects, including motion stabilization, motion tracking, particle systems, and the Timewarp effect. To render and export any or all of the projects you completed in this lesson, see Lesson 14, "Rendering and Outputting," for instructions.

Review questions

1 What is motion stabilization and when do you need to use it?

2 Why might drifting occur when you're tracking an image?

3 What is the birth rate in a particle effect?

4 What does the Timewarp effect do?

Review answers

1 Shooting footage using a handheld camera typically results in shaky shots. Unless this look is intentional, you will want to stabilize the shots to eliminate unwanted motion. Motion stabilization in After Effects works by analyzing the movement and rotation of the target layer, then applying the opposite values to the anchor point and rotation of that layer. When played back, the motion appears smooth because the layer itself moves incrementally to offset the unwanted motion.

2 Drifting occurs when the feature region loses the feature that's being tracked. As an image moves in a shot, the lighting, surrounding objects, and angle of the object can change, making a once-distinct feature unidentifiable at the subpixel level. Even with careful planning and practice, the feature region often drifts away from the desired feature. Readjusting the feature and search regions, changing the tracking options, and trying again are a standard part of digital tracking.

3 The birth rate in a particle effect determines how often new particles are created.

4 The Timewarp effect in After Effects CS4 gives you precise control over a wide range of parameters to change the playback speed of a layer, including interpolation methods, motion blur, and source cropping to eliminate unwanted artifacts.

14

RENDERING AND OUTPUTTING

Lesson overview

In this lesson, you'll learn how to do the following:

- Create render-settings templates.

- Create output-module templates.

- Process multiple output modules.

- Select the appropriate compressor for your delivery format.

- Use pixel aspect ratio correction.

- Output the final animation for NTSC broadcast video.

- Produce a test version of a composition.

- Render and output a web version of the final animation.

In this lesson, you'll delve deeper into rendering and exporting. In order to produce several versions of the animation for this lesson, you'll explore options available within the Render Queue panel. After creating render-settings and output-module templates, you'll produce both a broadcast version and a web version of the final movie. The total amount of time required to complete this lesson depends in part on the speed of your processor and on the amount of RAM available for rendering. The amount of hands-on time required is less than an hour.

WEB

BROADCAST

The success of any project depends on your ability to deliver it in the format you need, whether it's for the web or broadcast output. Using Adobe After Effects, you can create time-saving templates and then render and export a final composition in a variety of formats and resolutions.

Getting started

This lesson continues from the point at which all preceding lessons end: when you're ready to output the final composition. For this lesson, we provide you with a starting project file that is essentially the final composition from Lesson 5 of this book.

1 Make sure the following files are in the AECS4_CIB/Lessons/Lesson14 folder on your hard disk, or copy them from the *Adobe After Effects CS4 Classroom in a Book* DVD now:

- In the Assets folder: CarRide.psd, GordonsHead.mov, HeadShape.ffx, piano. wav, studer_Comcast.jpg, studer_Map.jpg, studer_music.jpg, studer_Puzzle. jpg, and studer_Real_Guys.jpg

- In the Start_Project_File folder: Lesson14_Start.aep

- In the Sample_Movies folder: Lesson14_MPEG4_Final.mov, Lesson14_ JPEG2000_Final.mov, Lesson14_NTSC_Final.mov

● **Note:** Because the Lesson14_NTSC_Final. mov file is ready for broadcast, it is a large file and may not play back in real time in the QuickTime Player.

2 Open and play the sample movies for Lesson 14, which represent different final versions of the animation that you created in Lesson 5. When you are done viewing the sample movies, quit QuickTime Player. You may delete the sample movies from your hard disk if you have limited storage space.

As always, when you begin the lesson, restore the default application settings for After Effects. See "Restoring default preferences" on page 3.

3 Press Ctrl+Alt+Shift (Windows) or Control+Option+Shift (Mac OS) while starting After Effects. When asked whether you want to delete your preferences file, click OK. Click Close to close the Welcome window.

4 Choose File > Open Project.

5 Navigate to the AECS4_CIB/Lessons/Lesson14/Start_Project_File folder, select the Lesson14_Start.aep file, and click Open.

6 Choose File > Save As.

7 In the Save As dialog box, navigate to the AECS4_CIB/Lessons/Lesson14/ Finished_Project folder.

8 Name the project **Lesson14_Finished.aep**, and then click Save.

9 Choose Window > Render Queue to open the Render Queue panel.

Creating templates for the rendering process

In previous lessons, you selected individual render and output-module settings on those occasions when you output your compositions. In this lesson, you'll create templates for both render settings and output-module settings. These templates are presets that you can use to streamline the setup process when you render items for the same type of delivery format. After you define these templates, they appear in the Render Queue panel on the appropriate pop-up menu (Render Settings or Output Module). Then, when you're ready to process a job, you can simply select the template that is appropriate for the delivery format that your job requires, and the template applies all the settings.

Creating a render-settings template for full resolution

The first template you'll create is for full-resolution output.

1   Choose Edit > Templates > Render Settings to open the Render Settings Templates dialog box.

2   In the Settings area, click New to open the Render Settings dialog box.

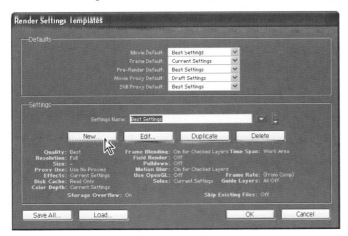

3   In the Render Settings area, confirm that Best is selected for Quality and Full for Resolution.

4 In the Time Sampling area, do the following:

- For Frame Blending, make sure On For Checked Layers is selected.

- For Motion Blur, make sure On For Checked Layers is selected.

- For Time Span, choose Length Of Comp.

- In the Frame Rate area, make sure Use Comp's Frame Rate is selected.

5 Click OK to return to the Render Settings Templates dialog box. All the settings you selected appear in the lower half of the dialog box. If you need to make any changes, click Edit and then adjust your settings.

6 For Settings Name, type **Final Render_Fullres** (for *full resolution*).

7 At the top of the dialog box, in the Defaults area, choose Final Render_Fullres for Movie Default. Then click OK to close the dialog box.

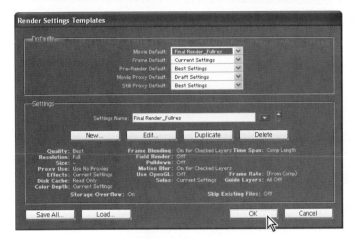

► **Tip:** If you want to save a render-settings template for use on another system, click Save All in the Render Settings Templates dialog box before you close it in step 7. Save the file with an .ars extension and copy it to the other system. There, choose Edit > Templates > Render Settings, click Load, and select the .ars file to load the settings you saved.

Final Render_Fullres is now the default Render Settings option and will appear (instead of Current Settings) when you add a composition to the Render Queue panel to make a movie, which you'll do later in this lesson.

Creating a render-settings template for test renderings

Next, you'll create a second render-settings template, selecting settings appropriate for rendering a test version of your final movie. A test version is smaller—and therefore renders faster—than a full-resolution movie. When you work with complex compositions that take relatively long times to render, it is a good practice to render a small test version first. This helps you find any final tweaks or blunders that you want to adjust before you take the time to render the final movie.

1 Choose Edit > Templates > Render Settings. The Render Settings Templates dialog box appears.

2 In the Settings area, click New to create a new template.

3 In the Render Settings area of the Render Settings dialog box, do the following:

- Leave Quality at Best.

- For Resolution, choose Third, which reduces the linear dimension of the composition to one-third.

4 In the Time Sampling area, do the following:

- For Frame Blending, choose Current Settings.
- For Motion Blur, choose Current Settings.
- For Time Span, choose Length Of Comp.

5 In the Frame Rate area, select Use This Frame Rate, and type **12** (fps). Then click OK to return to the Render Settings Templates dialog box.

6 For Settings Name, type **Test_lowres** (for *low resolution*).

7 Examine your settings, which now appear in the lower half of the dialog box. If you need to make any changes, click Edit to adjust the settings. Then click OK.

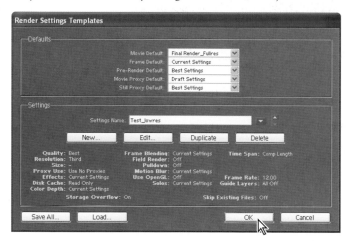

The Test_lowres option will now be available on the Render Settings pop-up menu in the Render Queue panel.

You have now created two render-settings templates. One is for a full-resolution final version, and one is for a low-resolution test version of your final composite.

Creating templates for output modules

Using processes similar to those in the previous section, you'll now create templates to use for output-module settings. Each will include unique combinations of settings that are appropriate for a specific type of output.

Creating an output-module template for broadcast renderings

The first template you'll create for output-module settings is appropriate for an NTSC broadcast-resolution version of your final movie.

1 Choose Edit > Templates > Output Module.

2 In the Settings area, click New to open the Output Module Settings dialog box.

3 In the Output Module area, do the following:

- For Format, choose QuickTime Movie. In Windows, if the Compression Settings dialog box appears, click OK to close it for the moment.

- For Post-Render Action, choose Import.

4 In the Video Output area, click Format Options.

5 In the Compression Settings dialog box, choose Animation from the Compression Type menu. In the Compressor area, choose Millions Of Colors from the Depth menu. Click OK to close the dialog box.

6 Review the settings in the Output Module Settings dialog box to make sure that the Channels pop-up menu is set to RGB and Depth is set to Millions Of Colors.

7 Select the Audio Output option, and make sure that the pop-up menus are set (from left to right) to 44.100 kHz, 16 Bit, Stereo.

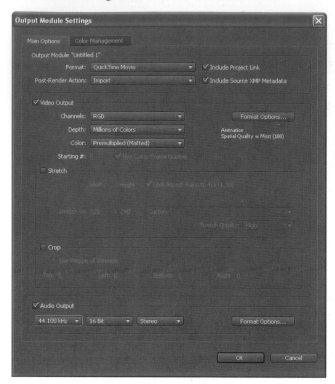

8 Click OK to return to the Output Module Templates dialog box. Review the settings in the lower half of the dialog box; click Edit if you need to adjust your settings.

9 For Settings Name, type **Final Render_QT_audio** (to remind you that this template for QuickTime includes audio).

10 In the Defaults area, choose Final Render_QT_audio from the Movie Default menu. Then click OK.

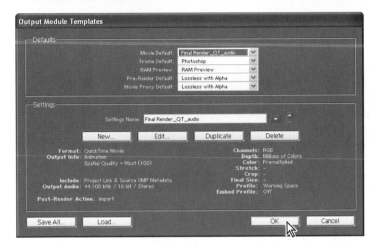

The Final Render_ QT_audio template is now the default selection for the Output Module pop-up menu and will appear (instead of Lossless) each time you add a composition to the Render Queue panel.

The Final Render_ QT_audio template is now the default selection for the Output Module pop-up menu and will appear (instead of Lossless) each time you add a composition to the Render Queue panel.

▶ **Tip:** As with the render-settings templates, you can save output-module templates for use on other systems. Click Save All in the Output Module Templates dialog box. Save the file with an .aom extension, and copy it to another system. There, choose Edit > Templates > Output Module, click Load, and select the .aom file to load the settings.

Creating a low-resolution output-module template

Next, you'll create a second output-module template with settings appropriate for producing a low-resolution test version of the movie. In this case, the settings that you'll select are also appropriate for a web version of the movie.

1 Choose Edit > Templates > Output Module to open the Output Module Templates dialog box.

2 In the Settings area, click New to create a new template.

3 In the Output Module Settings dialog box, for Format, choose QuickTime Movie. Close the Compression Settings dialog box if it opens in Windows.

4 For Post-Render Action, choose Import.

5 In the Video Output area, click Format Options, and then select the following settings in the Compression Settings dialog box:

- For Compression Type, choose MPEG-4 Video. This compressor automatically determines the color depth.

- Set the Quality slider to High.

- In the Motion area, select Key Frame Every, and then type **30** (frames).

- Select Limit Data Rate To, and type **150** (KBytes/sec).

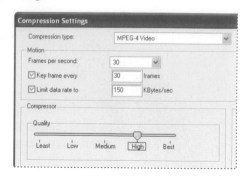

6 Click OK to close the Compression Settings dialog box and return to the Output Module Settings dialog box.

7 Select Audio Output, and then click Format Options to open the Sound Settings dialog box and select the following:

- For Compressor, choose IMA 4:1.

- For Rate, choose 22.050.

- For Size, select 16 Bit.

- For Use, select Stereo, and then click OK to close the Sound Settings dialog box.

Your sound settings now appear in the Audio Output area in the Output Module Settings dialog box.

8 Click OK to close the Output Module Settings dialog box.

9 In the lower half of the Output Module Templates dialog box, examine your settings, and click Edit if you need to make any changes.

10 For Settings Name, type **Test_MPEG4**, and then click OK. Now this output template will be available on the Output Module pop-up menu in the Render Queue panel.

● **Note:** The IMA 4:1 compressor is commonly used when compressing audio for web or desktop playback.

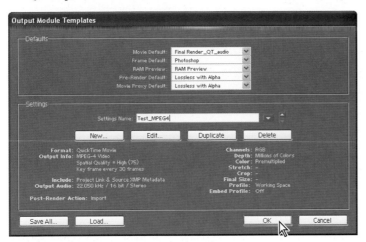

As you might expect, greater compression and lower audio sample rates create smaller file sizes, but they also reduce the quality of the output. However, this low-resolution template is fine for creating test movies or movies for the web.

To render with OpenGL

OpenGL is a set of standards for high-performance processing of 2D and 3D graphics. For After Effects users, OpenGL provides fast, high-quality rendering for previews and final output by moving rendering from the CPU to the OpenGL hardware (GPU).

To use OpenGL in After Effects, you'll need an OpenGL card that supports OpenGL 2.0 and has Shader support and support for NPOT (Non Power Of Two) textures. You can view information about your OpenGL card by choosing Edit > Preferences > Previews (Windows) or After Effects > Preferences > Previews (Mac OS) and clicking the OpenGL Info button.

Note that only features supported by OpenGL and your graphics card will be rendered into the final movie. If your card doesn't support advanced OpenGL features, don't use OpenGL to render. For a list of features supported by OpenGL, see After Effects Help.

To render using OpenGL support, add a composition to the Render Queue panel, and then click the underlined text next to Render Settings and select Use OpenGL Renderer.

Exporting to different output media

Now that you have created templates for your render settings and output modules, you can use them to export different versions of the movie.

Preparing to output a test movie

First, you'll produce the test version, selecting the Test_lowres render-settings template and the Test_MPEG4 output-module template that you created.

About compression

Compression is essential to reduce the size of movies so that they can be stored, transmitted, and played back effectively. When exporting or rendering a movie file for playback on a specific type of device at a certain bandwidth, you choose a compressor/decompressor (also known as an encoder/decoder), or *codec*, to compress the information and generate a file that is readable by that type of device at that bandwidth.

A wide range of codecs is available; no single codec is the best for all situations. For example, the best codec for compressing cartoon animation is generally not efficient for compressing live-action video. When compressing a movie file, you can fine-tune it for the best-quality playback on a computer, video playback device, the web, or from a DVD player. Depending on which encoder you use, you may be able to reduce the size of compressed files by removing artifacts that interfere with compression, such as random camera motion and excessive film grain.

The codec you use must be available to your entire audience. For instance, if you use a hardware codec on a capture card, your audience must have the same capture card installed, or a software codec that emulates it.

For more about compression and codecs, see After Effects Help.

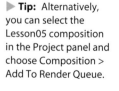
Tip: Alternatively, you can select the Lesson05 composition in the Project panel and choose Composition > Add To Render Queue.

1 Drag the Lesson05 composition from the Project panel to the Render Queue panel.

In the Render Queue panel, note the default settings in the Render Settings and Output Module pop-up menus. You'll change those settings to your low-resolution templates.

2 Choose Test_lowres from the Render Settings menu.

3 Choose Test_MPEG4 from the Output Module menu.

4 Click the orange, underlined words next to Output To.

5 In the Output Movie To dialog box, locate the AECS4_CIB/Lessons/Lesson14 folder, and create a new folder called **Final_Movies**:

- In Windows, click the Create New Folder icon, and then type a name for the folder.

- In Mac OS, click the New Folder button, name the folder, and click Create.

6 Open the Final_Movies folder.

7 Name the file **Final MPEG4.mov**, and then click Save to return to the Render Queue panel.

8 Choose File > Save to save your work.

You'll do a few more things before you render the movie. Leave the Render Queue panel open for the next exercise.

Working with multiple output modules

Next, you'll add another output module to this render queue item so that you can compare the results of two compressors. You'll set this one for JPEG 2000 compression.

Note: You do not
need to render a movie
multiple times to export
it to multiple formats
with the same render
settings. You can export
multiple versions of the
same rendered movie
by adding output
modules to a render
item in the Render
Queue panel.

1   With the Lesson05 composition still selected in the Render Queue panel, choose Composition > Add Output Module. A second set of Output Module and Output To options appears directly beneath the first.

2   From the lower Output Module pop-up menu, choose Test_MPEG4.

3   Click the orange, underlined words *Test_MPEG4* to open the Output Module Settings dialog box, and then click Format Options in the Video Output area.

4   In the Compression Settings dialog box, choose JPEG 2000 from the Compression Type menu. Select Millions Of Colors from the Depth menu.

The other settings should remain the same from the Test_MPEG4 template, as shown in the following image.

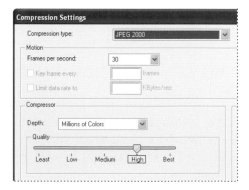

5 Click OK to close the Compression Settings dialog box.

6 Click OK again to close the Output Module Settings dialog box.

7 Next to Output To, click the orange, underlined words *Lesson05.mov* to open the Output Movie To dialog box.

8 Name the movie **Final_JPEG2000.mov** and save it in the AECS4_CIB/Lessons/ Lesson14/Final_Movies folder.

9 Choose File > Save to save the project, and then click the Render button in the Render Queue panel. After Effects renders the movie and processes both of these formats simultaneously.

When the processing is complete, both the Final_MPEG4 and Final_JPEG2000 movies appear in the Project panel.

You can double-click each movie to preview it in the Project panel and compare the results. Then, in Explorer or the Finder, select the movie that looks better to you, and rename it **Final_Web.mov** (do not rename it within After Effects). This version is ready for Gordon Studer's prospective clients to view on the web.

● **Note:** You may find it helpful to further reduce the size of the movie before posting it to a website. You may want to create streaming video, or simply reduce the size based on the majority of the audience's available bandwidth. You can do this with a media-compression or media-cleaner application specifically designed for this purpose.

If you need to make any final changes to the animation, reopen the composition and make those adjustments now. Remember to save your work when you finish, and then output the test movie again using the appropriate settings. After examining the test movie and making any necessary changes, you'll proceed with outputting the movie for full-resolution broadcast.

Exporting to SWF

You can also use After Effects to export compositions as SWF files for playback within a web-browser application. However, certain types of artwork are more suitable than others for export to SWF. Rasterized images and some effects cannot be represented by vectors, and therefore are not efficiently saved to SWF format. You can export them, but the files will be larger in size.

Also, it is helpful when exporting items to SWF to place all your layers within a single composition rather than using precompositions or nested compositions. Using a single composition also tends to reduce the size of the exported file.

To learn how to export a composition to SWF format, see Lesson 2, "Creating a Basic Animation Using Effects and Presets."

Preparing the composition for full-resolution output

Next, you'll prepare to render and output the final composition at full resolution. This animation is intended primarily for NTSC video output. You'll begin by creating a new composition at the appropriate size for your final delivery format.

1 Choose Composition > New Composition.

2 In the Composition Settings dialog box, do the following:

- For Name, type **Final Comp NTSC**.

- For Preset, choose NTSC D1. This automatically sets the dimensions (720 x 486), pixel aspect ratio (D1/DV NTSC), and frame rate (29.97).

- For Resolution, choose Full (or lower if necessary for your system).

- For Duration, type **2000** to specify 20 seconds, and then click OK.

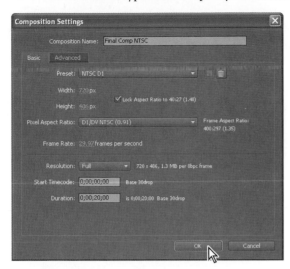

The new, empty composition opens in the Composition and Timeline panels.

3 In the Project panel, drag the Lesson05 composition onto the Final Comp NTSC composition icon.

Using pixel aspect ratio correction

As you preview the animation, you may notice that the items in the Composition panel now appear a bit wider than before. That's because this D1 NTSC composition has a nonsquare pixel aspect ratio. However, your computer monitor displays images using square pixels. Therefore, the images that you see in the Composition panel appear stretched unless you enable a feature called *pixel aspect ratio correction*. Pixel aspect ratio correction squeezes the view of the composition slightly to display the image as it will appear on a video monitor. By default, this feature is turned off, but you can easily turn it on.

1   Go to 3:00, where there are a few elements, including Gordon Studer's masked head, in the Composition panel.

2   Choose View Options from the Composition panel menu.

3   In the View Options dialog box, select Pixel Aspect Ratio Correction (in the Window area). Then, click OK to close the dialog box.

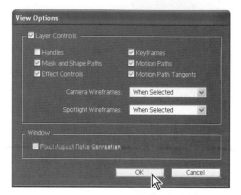

The image in the Composition panel is squeezed, appearing (at a modified pixel aspect ratio) as it will when this item is rendered, laid off to tape, and viewed on a video monitor. The layers in the Composition panel may appear a bit jagged while you have this view turned on. You'll want to turn it off to see your images with full anti-aliasing. This view does not affect rendering or output.

4 Turn pixel aspect ratio correction off and on a couple of times by clicking the Toggle Pixel Aspect Ratio Correction button (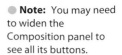) at the bottom of the Composition panel.

● **Note:** You may need to widen the Composition panel to see all its buttons.

Using pixel aspect ratio correction, you can work in a composition with a non-square pixel aspect ratio but still view your images as they would appear on a video monitor.

Preparing movies for mobile devices

You can create movies in After Effects for playback on mobile devices, such as the Apple iPod and mobile phones. To render your movie, use format options presets in the Output Module menu in the Render Queue panel. For example, use the H.264 preset to render movies for iPod playback.

Adobe Device Central, which comes with After Effects CS4, lets you preview movies for specific devices. You used Device Central to prepare compositions for mobile phones and Flash Lite in Lesson 9, and you can learn more about Device Central in Device Central Help.

For the best results, consider the limitations of mobile devices as you shoot footage and work with After Effects. For a small screen size, pay careful attention to lighting, and use a lower frame rate. See After Effects Help for more tips.

Rendering the final movie for broadcast

Now, you'll render and output the NTSC broadcast version of your final animation. This may take half an hour or more, depending on your system.

1   Click the Render Queue panel tab to bring the panel forward, and then drag the Final Comp NTSC composition from the Project panel to the Render Queue panel below the Lesson05 composition.

2   Next to Output To, click the orange, underlined words *Final Comp NTSC.mov* to open the Output Movie To dialog box.

3   Name the movie **Final_NTSC.mov** (indicating that this item will be rendered at NTSC D1 resolution) and specify the AECS4_CIB/Lessons/Lesson 14/Final_ Movies folder. Then click Save to return to the Render Queue panel.

The Final Render_Fullres setting is selected in the Render Settings menu and the Final Render_QT_audio setting is selected in the Output Module menu because you set these as the default settings when you created the templates.

The composition is now ready to render.

4 Save the project one more time, and then click the Render button.

5 When After Effects has finished rendering and outputting the file, close the Render Queue panel.

6 In the Project panel, double-click the Final_NTSC.mov file to open it in the Footage panel. Or, you can play the movie from the Explorer or Finder.

As you play the movie, compare your final rendered output to the NTSC sample movie you watched at the beginning of this lesson. If necessary, reopen the composition and make changes. Then save the project and render the movie again.

You now have both a web version and a broadcast version of the final animation.

Congratulations! You have now completed all the lessons in *Adobe After Effects CS4 Classroom in a Book*. To continue learning about After Effects, visit the Adobe website.

● **Note:** Because this movie is so large, it may not play back at real time in QuickTime Player. If you have a video playback card installed on your system, output the movie choosing the appropriate compressor and frame size for that card in the Compression Settings dialog box. Import the movie into your editing software and play it back using your hardware for real-time playback.

Review questions

1 Name two types of templates and explain when and why to use them.

2 What is compression, and what are some issues associated with it?

Review answers

1 In After Effects, you can create templates for both render settings and output-module settings. These templates are presets that you can use to streamline the setup process when you render items for the same type of delivery format. After you define these templates, they appear in the Render Queue panel on the appropriate pop-up menu (Render Settings or Output Module). Then, when you're ready to render a job, you can simply select the template that is appropriate for the delivery format that your job requires, and the template applies all the settings.

2 Compression is essential to reduce the size of movies so that they can be stored, transmitted, and played back effectively. When exporting or rendering a movie file for playback on a specific type of device at a certain bandwidth, you choose a compressor/decompressor (also known as an encoder/decoder), or codec, to compress the information and generate a file readable by that type of device at that bandwidth. A wide range of codecs is available; no single codec is the best for all situations. For example, the best codec for compressing cartoon animation is generally not efficient for compressing live-action video. When compressing a movie file, you can fine-tune it for the best-quality playback on a computer, video playback device, the web, or from a DVD player. Depending on which encoder you use, you may be able to reduce the size of compressed files by removing artifacts that interfere with compression, such as random camera motion and excessive film grain.

Appendix: Color Management in After Effects CS4

About color management

Without color management, the color you see at one stage of design and production may not match what you see at another. In other words, color is device-dependent: the color you see depends on the device producing it. A color management system is designed to reconcile the different color capabilities of the various components in your workflow—cameras, scanners, monitors, televisions—to ensure consistent color throughout the production process, and to help you see accurately the colors you specify in a project.

A color management system maps colors from the color gamut of one device, such as a digital camera, to a device with a different color gamut, such as a monitor. ICC color profiles, which describe the colors available to each device or color model, are used by a color management system (CMS) to map colors into device-independent gamuts, and then back to different devices.

In After Effects CS4, color management makes it possible for you to do the following:

- View accurate color and tone when using linear light (gamma 1.0) for compositing.
- Repurpose material for different output conditions.
- Work on projects using different computers.
- Manage footage from multiple sources.
- View color consistently in other applications.
- Simulate different output conditions without altering the color values in your project.

Using color management in After Effects CS4

To turn color management on, choose File > Project Settings, and then select a working space color profile from the Working Space menu.

To assign a color profile to footage, select the footage item, and choose File > Interpret Footage > Main. Then, click the Color Management tab, and select an ICC profile.

To color-manage a file you're rendering, click the Color Management tab in the Output Module Settings dialog box, and choose the appropriate ICC color profile.

To simulate output, choose View > Simulate Output > [film or print stock]

For more information about color management in After Effects CS4, specific ICC color profiles, and specific color management workflows, see After Effects Help.

INDEX

Contributors

Mark Christiansen—is the author of Adobe After Effects 6.5 Studio Techniques (Adobe Press). He has created visual effects and animations for feature films, network television, computer games, and an array of high-technology companies. Recent clients include Adobe Systems, Inc., The Orphanage (for Dimension Films), Telling Pictures (for The History Channel), and the Couturie Company (for HBO), as well as Seagate, Sun, Intel, and Medtronic. Feature credits include The Day After Tomorrow and films by Robert Rodriguez.

Takeshi Hiraoka—Plucked out of paradise, Hiraoka moved to chilly San Francisco from Honolulu, Hawaii, one cold winter in 2002. In San Francisco, he attended the Academy of Art University, graduating in May 2004. This is where Hiraoka met Sheldon Callahan, with whom he directed and produced the feature-length, DV film Origin. In addition to being a DV producer, Takeshi is also a 2D and 3D animator.

Stephen Schleicher—has travelled from Kansas to Georgia to California working as an editor, graphic designer, videographer, director, and producer on a variety of small and large video productions. Currently, Stephen teaches media and web development at Fort Hays State University. He also works on video and independent projects for state and local agencies and organizations, as well as his own works. Stephen is a regular contributor to Digital Media Net (www.digitalmedianet.com).

Anna Ullrich—is a pale but fine digital artist based in Seattle, Washington, although her heart resides in Minnesota, where her spry and brilliant Democratic grandmother lives. Anna earned a BFA from the University of Washington in Seattle and an MFA from the University of Notre Dame in Indiana (both in photography).